International Study Guide

African Theology on the Way

Current Conversations

Edited by
Diane B. Stinton

D1253331

AFRICAN THEOLOGY ON THE WAY

Fortress Press Edition © 2015

Cover design: Laurie Ingram

Library of Congress Cataloging-in-Publication Data
Print ISBN: 978-1-4514-9964-3
eBook ISBN: 978-1-5064-0030-3

The paper used in this publication meets the minimum requirements of American National Standard for Information Sciences — Permanence of Paper for Printed Library Materials, ANSI Z329.48-1984.

Manufactured in the U.S.

To
the Revd Professor Kwame Bediako (1945–2008)
and
the Revd Professor John Mary Waliggo (1942–2008)
men of God, mentors

Contents

Contributors   vii
The International Study Guides   xiii
Acknowledgements   xiv
Introduction by Diane B. Stinton   xv

Part 1 Methodological issues in African theology

1 Contextual theological methodologies   3
   Agbonkhianmeghe E. Orobator, SJ

2 Biblical exegesis in Africa: the significance of the
   translated Scriptures   12
   Kwame Bediako

3 Biblical hermeneutics in Africa   21
   Gerald West

Part 2 Contemporary issues in African theology

4 'The Synod of Hope' at a time of crisis in Africa   35
   John Mary Waliggo

5 Contributions and challenges of the African Instituted
   Churches in developing African theology   46
   Thomas Oduro

6 Pentecostalism in Africa   56
   J. Kwabena Asamoah-Gyadu

7 African Christian spirituality   68
   Laurenti Magesa

8 Distinctives of African ethics   79
   Bénézet Bujo

9 African women's theologies   90
   Isabel Apawo Phiri and Sarojini Nadar

10 The challenges of ecumenism in African Christianity today 101
   Hamilton Mvumelwano Dandala

Part 3 The Church in the world

11 Interfaith relations in Africa   109
   Johnson A. Mbillah

12 The problem of evil and suffering: theological
reflections from an African perspective   118
   Isaiah M. Dau

13 Christian identity and ethnicity in Africa: reflections on the
gospel of reconciliation   128
   Philomena Njeri Mwaura

14 Theology of reconstruction   139
   Jesse N. K. Mugambi

15 A postcolonial South African Church: problems
and promises   150
   Tinyiko Sam Maluleke

16 African Christianity in diaspora   161
   Afe Adogame

Copyright acknowledgements   172
References and further reading   174
Index   183

Contributors

Afe Adogame holds a Ph.D. in history of religions from Bayreuth University, Germany. He is Associate Professor and teaches world Christianity and religious studies at the University of Edinburgh. His fields of expertise include African religions in diaspora; indigenous religions; and African Christianity – particularly African Instituted Churches and Pentecostal/charismatic churches. He is the author of *Celestial Church of Christ: The Politics of Cultural Identity in a West African Prophetic-Charismatic Movement* (1999). He has also co-edited *European Traditions in the Study of Religion in Africa* (2004); *Religion in the Context of African Migration* (2005); *Christianity in Africa and the African Diaspora: The Appropriation of a Scattered Heritage* (2008); and *Unpacking the New: Critical Perspectives on Cultural Syncretization in Africa and Beyond* (2008). He is General Secretary of the African Association for the Study of Religion, and International Advisory Board Member of the *Journal of Religion in Africa and African Diaspora* (Brill) and *Studies in World Christianity* (Edinburgh University Press).

J. Kwabena Asamoah-Gyadu, an ordained minister of the Methodist Church Ghana, is Associate Professor of Contemporary African Christianity and Vice-President at the Trinity Theological Seminary, Legon, Ghana. In 2004 he was Senior Visiting Scholar at the Center for the Study of World Religions at Harvard University, Massachusetts, USA, and in 2007, he was Visiting Professor at Luther Seminary, Minnesota, USA. He has published widely on Pentecostal/charismatic Christianity, including his book, *African Charismatics* (2005).

Kwame Bediako (1945–2008) was Fellow of the Ghana Academy of Arts and Sciences and an ordained minister of the Presbyterian Church of Ghana. He earned doctorate degrees in French literature from the University of Bordeaux, and in divinity from the University of Aberdeen.

From 1987 until his death in June 2008, he was Executive Director of the Akrofi-Christaller Memorial Centre for Mission Research and Applied Theology (now Akrofi-Christaller Institute of Theology, Mission and Culture) in Akropong-Akuapem, Ghana. For a term each year over several years, he was a visiting lecturer in African theology in the University of Edinburgh, Scotland. He was also a member of the Board of the Oxford Centre for Mission Studies (OCMS), Oxford, England. In 1998 he was made an honorary professor in the School of Theology, University of Natal, Pietermaritzburg,

South Africa. Throughout his career, he lectured in many theological institutions in Europe, the USA and Africa.

Bediako has written extensively in the fields of gospel, culture and Christian identity, and contributed significantly to the development of new contextual theologies in Africa. Key publications include *Theology and Identity: The Impact of Culture upon Christian Thought in the Second Century and Modern Africa* (1992, reprinted 1999); *Christianity in Africa: The Renewal of a Non-Western Religion* (1995; reprinted 1997); and *Jesus and the Gospel in Africa: History and Experience* (2004).

Bénézet Bujo is a priest of the Diocese of Bunia, in the northeast of the Democratic Republic of Congo. After studying philosophy and theology in the Congo, he earned his doctorate in Germany. Since 1989, Professor Bujo has held the chair of moral theology and social ethics at the University of Friborg, Switzerland. He is also a visiting lecturer at the Catholic University of Eastern Africa, Nairobi. Besides collaborating on many ecclesial commissions, Bujo has been a member of the Swiss National Commission of Justice and Peace, as well as a member and vice-president of the Theological Commission of the Episcopal Conference of Switzerland. Bujo has authored many books and articles on intercultural morality and African theology, including the following key publications in English: *African Christian Morality at the Age of Inculturation* (1990, 1998); *African Theology in Its Social Context* (1992); *The Ethical Dimension of Community* (1997); *Foundations of an African Ethic* (2001); and *Plea for Change of Models for Marriage* (2009). He also co-edits a series entitled *African Theology: The Contribution of the Pioneers*, Vols. 1 (2003) and 2 (2006).

Hamilton Mvumelwano Dandala is President of the Congress of the People political party in South Africa. Until 2008 he was General Secretary of the All Africa Conference of Churches (AACC) and between 1997 and 2003 Presiding Bishop of the Methodist Church in Southern Africa and President of the South African Council of Churches. Dandala is a peacemaker and advocate for social justice. He holds a diploma in theology from John Wesley College in South Africa and a BA and MA from the University of Cambridge. He has honorary doctoral degrees from the University of Transkei and the Faculty of Protestant Theology in Cameroon.

Isaiah M. Dau is a Sudanese theologian whose experience of the civil war in Sudan has significantly shaped his theological formation and ministry. He completed his doctorate in theology (D.Th.) at the University of Stellenbosch, South Africa. He is currently Principal of Nairobi Pentecostal Bible College, a senior pastor of the Sudan Pentecostal Church, and Chief Executive Director of the Ayual Community Development Association. Dau is actively engaged in Kenya and the Sudan as a theological educator and community leader dealing with leadership training, health care, and capacity-building. He has written extensively on the theology of suffering, including *Suffering and God: A Theological Reflection on the War in Sudan* (2002).

Laurenti Magesa is a Catholic priest who has done pastoral ministry for many years in his home diocese of Musoma in Tanzania. He is currently a senior lecturer at Hekima College Jesuit School of Theology and at the Maryknoll Institute of African Studies in Nairobi, Kenya. He also teaches occasionally at other institutions in Nairobi, in Kenya and worldwide. He has published widely on African religion and theology. His books include *African Religion* (1997); *African Christian Ethics* (2002); *Anatomy of Inculturation* (2004); *Rethinking Mission* (2006); and *African Religion in the Dialogue Debate* (2010).

Tinyiko Sam Maluleke earned his doctorate in theology from the University of South Africa (UNISA), where he is currently Professor of African theology. He has published dozens of articles and book chapters in mission studies, Black theology and African theology. He was former General Secretary of the South African Missiological Society. He is currently Executive Director for Research at UNISA and also President of the South African Council of Churches. Maluleke has lectured internationally in Africa, Europe and the USA, and he is widely respected as a public intellectual and social commentator in South Africa.

Johnson A. Mbillah is an ordained minister of the Presbyterian Church of Ghana. Born in Zottirkuom, a small village in north-eastern Ghana, Dr Mbillah studied at Trinity Theological College in Legon, Accra (1982) and later completed a postgraduate certificate in mission studies at Selly Oak College, Birmingham (UK) in 1987. He obtained a postgraduate diploma in Islam in 1988, an M.Phil. also in Islam in 1990, and a Ph.D. in Islam and Christian–Muslim relations in 1999, all three degrees from the University of Birmingham (UK).

Dr Mbillah began his ministry as an evangelist and later became a hospital chaplain. After obtaining his academic degrees, he lectured in various Bible and theological colleges in Ghana and Kenya where he currently resides. He has served as Interfaith Director of the Presbyterian Church of Ghana, Area (Ghana) Adviser of the Programme for Christian–Muslim Relations in Africa (PROCMURA), and Regional Coordinator for Anglophone West Africa for PROCMURA. He is currently General Adviser of PROCMURA, which has its central office in Nairobi. Dr Mbillah has also published extensively on issues of Christian–Muslim relations in Africa.

Jesse N. K. Mugambi is Professor of Philosophy and Religious Studies at the University of Nairobi and Professor Extraordinarius at the University of South Africa, Pretoria. He served as Visiting Mellon Distinguished Professor at Rice

University in 1990–1, and as Guest Professor at several universities in Europe, North America and Africa. He is on the editorial board of the *Cambridge Dictionary of Christianity*. His books include *Contextual Theology across Cultures*, co-author (2009); *Responsible Leadership: Global and Contextual Ethical Perspectives*, co-ed. (2008); *Christian Theology and Social Reconstruction* (2003); *The Church and the Future in Africa*, ed. (1997); *Democracy and Development in Africa*, ed. (1997); *The Church and Reconstruction of Africa*, ed. (1997); *Religion and Social Construction of Reality* (1996); *From Liberation to Reconstruction* (1995); *Critiques of Christianity in African Literature* (1992); *A Comparative Study of Religions*, ed. (1990); *African Christian Theology: An Introduction* (1989); *The Biblical Basis for Evangelization* (1989); *African Heritage and Contemporary Christianity* (1989); *Christian Mission and Social Transformation*, ed. (1989); *Philosophy of Religion* (1988); *God, Humanity and Nature* (1987); *Ecumenical Initiatives in Eastern Africa*, co-author (1982); and *The African Religious Heritage*, co-author (1976). He has also co-edited several books and published many scholarly articles. He is an ecumenist, ecologist and educationist. His ecclesial identity is Anglican, and his nationality is Kenyan.

Philomena Njeri Mwaura earned her Ph.D. at Kenyatta University, Nairobi, Kenya, where she is a senior lecturer in the Department of Philosophy and Religious Studies. She is a former President of the International Association for Mission Studies and a current co-coordinator of the Theology Commission of the Ecumenical Association of Third World Theologians, Africa Region. Dr Mwaura is also a member of the Circle of Concerned African Women Theologians and the Ecumenical Symposium of Eastern Africa Theologians. Besides teaching at Kenyatta University, Dr Mwaura has been an adjunct lecturer at the Akrofi-Christaller Memorial Centre for Mission Research and Applied Theology, Ghana, and at Daystar University, Hekima College Jesuit School of Theology and the Catholic University of Eastern Africa, in Nairobi, Kenya. She has also been a consultant for various churches and non-government organizations (local and international) on education, development, monitoring and evaluation of programmes. She has published widely in the areas of African Christianity, new religious movements, and gender and theology.

Sarojini Nadar earned her Ph.D. from the University of Natal. She is a senior lecturer in the School of Religion and Theology, University of KwaZulu-Natal, and Director of its Gender and Religion Programme. She is also International Coordinator of the International Network of Advanced Theological Education, and a member of the Circle of Concerned African Women Theologians. In addition to several co-edited volumes, she has written widely in the areas of gender and theology, biblical studies and hermeneutics.

Thomas Oduro earned an MA in systematic theology (1994) and a Ph.D. (distinction) in the history of Christianity (2004) at Luther Seminary, St Paul, MN, USA. He has written many articles and presented many papers on the history and ministries of African Instituted Churches (AICs). His most recent publications are: *Catechism for Today: 130 Questions and Answers on What Christians Believe* and *Christ Holy Church International: The Story of an African Independent Church.* He is presently Principal of the Good News Theological College and Seminary, Accra, Ghana, an ordained minister and an executive member of the Organization of African Instituted Churches, a continental organization for AICs. He lectures in Christian history and doctrines, new religious movements, and African Christian theology.

Agbonkhianmeghe E. Orobator, SJ, received his Ph.D. from the University of Leeds and is currently Provincial Superior of the Eastern Africa Province of the Society of Jesus, as well as a lecturer in the theology at Hekima College Jesuit School of Theology. He is a specialist in ecclesiology and ethics, and his recent publications include *From Crisis to Kairos: A Critical Theology of the Mission of the Church in the Time of HIV/AIDS, Refugees and Poverty* (2005); *Faith Doing Justice: A Manual for Social Analysis, Catholic Social Teachings, and Social Justice*, with Elias O. Opongo (2007); *Theology Brewed in an African Pot* (2008); and 'Church, State, and Catholic Ethics: The Kenyan Dilemma', *Theological Studies*, vol. 70, no. 1 (2009). He is preparing to edit a volume on the Second African Synod.

Isabel Apawo Phiri earned her Ph.D. from the University of Cape Town. She is Professor of African Theology and Gender and Theology, and the former Head of the School of Religion and Theology, at the University of KwaZulu-Natal. She is also Director of the Centre for Constructive Theology, based in Durban, and Moderator of the World Council of Churches Commission on Education and Ecumenical Formation. Professor Phiri is the former General Coordinator of the Continental Circle of Concerned African Theologians, in which she remains a member. She is also a member of several professional associations including the Executive Committee of the World Conference of Associations of Theological Institutions, the Ecumenical Association of Third World Theologians, and the International Association of Mission Studies. Her extensive publications include *Women, Presbyterianism, and Patriarchy* (1997) and, as joint editor with Sarojini Nadar, *Her-Stories: Hidden Histories of Women of Faith in Africa* (2002); *On Being Church: African Women's Voices and Visions* (2005); and *African Women, Religion and Health: Essays in Honour of Mercy Amba Oduyoye* (2006).

Diane B. Stinton is a Canadian who was born in Angola and has spent most of her adult life as a theological educator in Kenya. She is currently an associate professor of theology at the Africa International University/Nairobi Evangelical Graduate School of Theology in Karen, Nairobi, where she lectures in the Master of Theology in World Christianity programme. Previously, she was Coordinator of the Master of Theology in African Christianity programme at Daystar University, Nairobi. She is Secretary and a general editor of the Ecumenical Symposium of Eastern Africa Theologians, and a member of the International Association for Mission Studies. Her publications include *Jesus of Africa: Voices of Contemporary African Christology* (2004), and numerous articles on African Christianity in books and refereed journals.

John Mary Waliggo (1942–2008) was a Ugandan priest with the Catholic Church. He obtained a BA and MA in theology from Urbanian University, Rome, as well as a BA, MA, and Ph.D. in history from Cambridge University, UK. He lectured at Katigondo Seminary and at the Protestant Theological College of Mukono. He then became a pioneer lecturer and head of the History Department at the Catholic University of Eastern Africa in Nairobi, and later a professor of history at Uganda Martyrs University. Waliggo was among the architects of the 1995 Constitution, having served as Commissioner and Secretary of the Uganda Constitutional Commission. He was also one of the founding commissioners of the Uganda Human Rights Commission, and he served as Executive Secretary of Uganda's Catholic Justice and Peace Commission. Waliggo wrote extensively on topics such as the history of Uganda, the history of Christianity in Africa, human rights, constitution-making and the 1995 Constitution Development, justice and peace, African theology, ecumenism in Africa, women's emancipation and equality, methodology for research, political and economic systems in Africa, and democracy in Africa.

Gerald West is Professor of Old Testament and Biblical Hermeneutics at the School of Religion and Theology at the University of KwaZulu-Natal, Pietermaritzburg, South Africa. He is also Director of the Ujamaa Centre for Community Development and Research, which provides an interface between academic biblical scholarship and Bible reading in local churches and communities. He has published a number of books and articles, among which is the volume he edited with Musa Dube on *The Bible in Africa: Transactions, Trajectories and Trends* (2000); *The Academy of the Poor: Towards a Dialogical Reading of the Bible* (2003); a commentary on the book of Genesis, *Genesis: The People's Bible Commentary* (2006); and an edited volume on *Reading Other-Wise: Socially Engaged Biblical Scholars Reading with Their Local Communities* (2007).

The International Study Guides

The global nature of Christianity has become perhaps its most defining feature in the last century. The need for resources that reflect this nature not only in topic but in approach and authorship has never been greater. To meet this need Fortress Press is proud to present a curated selection of volumes from the International Study Guides series. The product of a decades-long commitment on the part of the Society for Promoting Christian Knowledge (SPCK), the International Study Guides present projects in Bible, theology, and Christian history from a decidedly global vantage point.

Acknowledgements

An Amharic proverb from Ethiopia says 'When spider webs unite, they can tie up a lion.' Certainly this project has taken on 'lion-like' proportions at times, given the number of authors involved and the complex demands of their respective lives and ministries. During the process of preparing the manuscript, we have celebrated the lives and mourned the home call of two contributors to the volume: Revd Professor Kwame Bediako and Revd Professor John Mary Waliggo. We have witnessed some contributors suffer the loss of immediate family members, illness and other hardships, and we have rejoiced with others who have been blessed with life's deep joys. All these circumstances form part of the journey in which the present conversations in African theology have taken place. Therefore I am deeply grateful to each author for his or her time and effort in contributing a 'web' of thought that connects us together, and in solidarity with others across Africa who seek the presence and transforming power of God in Christ in our midst today.

I am especially thankful to the Editorial Board at SPCK for all they have done to help 'tie up this lion', from their initial invitation to me to edit this volume, to their oversight of the manuscript production. In particular, Emma Wild-Wood, Commissioning Editor, has extended generous grace, valuable insight and tangible support throughout the entire process. Special thanks as well to Rima Devereaux, Project Editor, Lauren Chiosso, Editorial Assistant, and to Malcolm Day and Trisha Dale, the copy editors, for their vital contributions to the completion of this work.

I also thank the following institutions for providing ministry contexts in which to complete this work: Daystar University, Nairobi, where I was coordinating the M.Th. in African Christianity programme when this project began; the Overseas Ministries Study Center, New Haven, CT, USA, and Regent College, Vancouver, Canada, where I was a visiting scholar during my academic sabbatical; and the Africa International University/Nairobi Evangelical Graduate School of Theology, where I have joined the faculty in the new M.Th. in World Christianity programme.

Finally, deep gratitude to my daughter Zawadi for the indescribable gift you are to me in this ongoing adventure of life with God.

Introduction

Diane B. Stinton

Conversations 'on the way'

Imagine their shock! With hearts of lead, they trudged the dusty way home-
wards to Emmaus. The only way to ease their pain was to share it in conversation together as they walked. After a while, a stranger drew near and
walked with them, listening in to their gloomy despair. Yet they were not
able to recognize him. The stranger asked, 'What's this you're discussing so
intently as you walk along?' (Luke 24.17, *The Message*). They just stood there,
dejected, seemingly unable to speak. Then one of them, named Cleopas,
replied, 'Are you the only one in Jerusalem who hasn't heard what's happened during the last few days?'

'What has happened?' he asked. In a torrent of grief, Cleopas and his
companion poured out their profound sense of loss, hopelessness and bitter
disillusionment: that Jesus of Nazareth was a prophet, mighty in word and
deed before God and all the people, that the chief priests and leaders had
him condemned to death and crucified, and that they had so hoped Jesus
was the one who was going to deliver Israel from all her oppressors. Yet it
was now the third day since his devastating death.

Then grief turned to perplexity as they recounted the strange events of
that day. Some of the women disciples of Jesus had astounded them, saying
they had gone to his tomb at dawn, only to find the stone rolled back and
his body not there. Instead, the women spoke of angels announcing that he
was alive! They rushed back to tell the other disciples, some of whom hur-
ried back to the tomb and found it empty, just as the women had said. Yet
they did not see Jesus.

At this point in Cleopas and his friend's account, the stranger interjected:
'So thick-headed! So slow-hearted! Why can't you simply believe all that the
prophets said? Don't you see that these things had to happen, that the Messiah
had to suffer and only then enter into his glory?' He then started with the
books of Moses and went on through the Prophets, pointing out and explaining all the references to himself in the Scriptures.

As they neared the village of Emmaus, the stranger appeared to be going
further. But Cleopas and his friend urged him to stay with them, so he did.
When they sat down together at the table, he took the bread, blessed and
broke it, and gave it to them. Then their eyes were opened! They recognized

him as Jesus, just as he vanished from their sight. And they exclaimed to each other, 'Didn't we feel on fire as he conversed with us on the road, as he opened up the Scriptures for us?'

Without any delay, they were back on the road again – this time the seven miles to Jerusalem vanishing behind them in their renewed vigour to tell the other disciples. As they burst into the room where their friends were gathered, their own news was delayed in the telling by their friends' exuberant cry, 'It's really happened! The Master has been raised up – Simon saw him!' Then in the flurry of excitement, Cleopas and his companion recounted everything that had happened to them 'on the way', and how they had come to recognize Jesus in their midst when he blessed and broke the bread.

The story continues with even greater suspense and exhilaration, as the Risen Christ suddenly appears among them all again to converse with them further, to convince them of the reality of his resurrection, and to commission them as his witnesses to all nations. Yet let's pause at this point in the Emmaus disciples' experience to consider: what do you think they talked about on their way back to Jerusalem? What questions might they have asked when they joined with their friends again? And what new insights or reflections emerged in that initial discussion when, completely overwhelmed with shock and delight, they grappled to make sense of the reality of the Risen Lord Jesus in their midst?

Conversations today

Imagine another scenario: almost two thousand years later, another group of Jesus' disciples dialogue together in Africa. Like the Emmaus disciples long ago, their hearts are leaden with disappointment, bordering on disillusionment. Their continent is bleeding from too many wars, their peoples divided along too many lines of nationality and ethnicity, of language and ideology, of economic class and religious creed, of age and gender. All too often, their wealthy rape the continent of its resources, with impunity, while their poor languish in poverty and preventable disease, without adequate regard. And yet, the Risen Christ appears powerfully in their midst, calling them to renewed hope on the basis of his own death and resurrection. How can they make sense of it – the exhilarating, life-transforming presence of Jesus alive, and the devastating conditions in which he appears?

As the conversations spread across Africa today, theologians call for 'Christian palaver'. The term 'palaver' comes from the Portuguese word *palavra*, meaning 'speech' or 'word', stemming from the Latin *parabola* ('parable', 'speech'). While the English term 'palaver' often carries the sense of prolonged, tiresome talk or idle chatter, the concept and practice of 'palaver' in Africa is very different. The fundamental notion of 'word' remains at the heart of African palaver, where the word, whether spoken or unspoken, carries great power for it can either create or destroy the community. The word may be danced or dramatized or symbolized in art, or manifested in action or behaviour within the community.

Importantly, in Africa the concept of community is three-dimensional, encompassing the living, the dead and those not yet born. So, as Laurenti Magesa explains, 'The sole purpose of the African palaver aims at creating, strengthening or restoring relationships for the sake of "the fullness" of life of the community through fellowship among all three dimensions of the community' (Magesa, 2004: 161). In addition, the community exists only in relation to the Transcendent and the entire cosmos.

Bénézet Bujo adds that 'the art of the palaver consists in setting out on a journey of exploration' (Bujo, 2001: 76). Every member of the community has the right to participate, whether in speech or symbolic action. Hence African palaver guarantees equality in terms of accessing speech. In addition, the community reaches decisions not by compromise or voting according to the majority view, but only by establishing a solid consensus among all members. Thus the fundamental experience is based on communion, as participants engage together in 'receiving', 'chewing' and 'digesting' those words that bring life to the community. As Bujo explains,

> In the palaver each person who speaks is a *ruminant* who, like certain animals, rechews the word eaten and drunk for a long time. In this way each person who speaks puts their word to the test so that the community can confirm or invalidate the vivifying effectiveness of what comes out of the mouth.
> (Bujo, 1995: 21–2)

In the context of Christian palaver, the creative, life-giving Word of God has now become flesh in the person of Jesus Christ. Just as the Emmaus disciples came to perceive the Risen Jesus in the opening of Scripture and the breaking of bread, with overtones of the eucharistic celebration, so African believers come to perceive Christ's presence today through reflecting on Scripture and engaging in Christian worship and ministry. African palaver thus provides one image for understanding African theology, in terms of a serious conversation among believers who meditatively chew on the word of God in their respective contexts and offer an interpretation of its meaning and implications for communal consideration.

Certainly the process of constructing theology along these lines is not new to Africa. Indeed, early Christianity in Africa had an enormous impact in shaping the exegetical methods, doctrinal content and conciliar processes that have shaped Christian theology worldwide. Likewise, more recent conversations by African Christians in the past century have resonated around the globe, particularly with the shift of world Christianity from the global North to the global South. A few notable examples include the following: francophone Catholic priests met for a symposium in Paris, published as *Des prêtres noirs s'interrogent* (Abble *et al.*, 1956), to contend for an African theology that takes into account the African heritage. Similarly, Protestant theologians held a consultation in Accra in 1955, published as *Christianity and African Culture.*

Even more influential in the development of African theology was the Ibadan Conference, organized by the All Africa Conference of Churches (AACC) and published as *Biblical Revelation and African Beliefs* (1969). Then in 1976, Africa hosted the First Ecumenical Dialogue of Third World Theologians in Dar es Salaam, which resulted in the founding of the Ecumenical Association of Third World Theologians. The corresponding foundation of the Ecumenical Association of African Theologians followed in 1977 in Accra. Significantly, the 1989 inauguration of the Circle of Concerned African Women Theologians has greatly enhanced the contribution of women's perspectives into the ongoing theological conversations. Since then, these and other theological associations, plus a growing number of African theologians and theological journals, have stimulated the burgeoning literature on African theology.

As these conversations in theology have continued across the continent of Africa and beyond, the SPCK International Study Guide Series has made a valuable contribution to the process. In 1987, John Parratt edited *A Reader in African Christian Theology*, which drew together selected writings from African theologians representing various church traditions, plus geographical and linguistic regions. The aim was to introduce readers around the world, particularly in theological seminaries, to the wealth of emergent African theologies and to the major theological questions they raised. The volume was structured in three sections: Part 1 dealt with introductory issues such as defining African theology, tracing its development and outlining its sources and methodologies. Part 2 examined specific issues of doctrine, such as the doctrine of God, Christology, the cross, and salvation, from African perspectives. Part 3 addressed practical issues of the Church's ministry in the world, including healing and the role of the Church in society. The overall purpose was not only to introduce the ideas of leading African theologians, but also to stimulate original thought as Parratt encouraged readers to address themselves to the issues raised in the volume.

A decade later, in 1997, Parratt produced a second edition of *A Reader in African Theology*, in view of important developments in Africa that influenced the shape of African theology. He identified the most spectacular development as the achievement of majority rule in South Africa. With the end of apartheid and the consequent need for Black theology to be rethought, Parratt wondered what 'theology after Mandela' would look like. He also noted developments in the Church in Africa, including the 'third wave' of the newer Pentecostal movements and their impact in Africa, the noticeable rise in conservative evangelicals' engagement in debates about African theology, and the commendable increase in the contributions from women theologians plus the translations available from francophone theologians. On the basis of these developments, Parratt added further chapters to make the volume more current and more representative of the growing range of theological perspectives.

Now, another decade and more has passed, and there is need again to update the SPCK reader in view of further developments that shape African theology. This present volume reflects both continuity with the previous editions and further innovation in theological expression in Africa. While there is little if any need today to justify the discipline of African theology, there is certainly ongoing need to consider methodological issues in its development. Therefore Part 1 addresses enduring methodological issues such as contextual methodological approaches, biblical exegesis and biblical hermeneutics.

Part 2 focuses on selected issues in contemporary African theology, including assessments of developments in the Catholic Church in Africa, the African Instituted Churches (AICs), and Pentecostalism in Africa. African contributions to Christian spirituality and ethics are also highlighted, as well as those of African women theologians. Then, in view of all the divisions that riddle Christianity across the continent, this section closes with a passionate plea for African Christian ecumenism.

Finally, Part 3 attends to issues arising in relation to the ministry of the Church in the wider world. If the end of apartheid in 1994 marked the most momentous event of the 1990s in Africa, undoubtedly the events of September 11, 2001, with the terrorist attacks in the USA and the subsequent, so-called war on terrorism, have most transformed the geopolitical world since then. Ramifications in Africa include the heightened need to responsibly address interfaith relations, as outlined in Chapter 11. Ongoing political and ethnic conflicts in Africa prompt the next two chapters: theological reflections on evil and suffering, from the context of prolonged civil war in the Sudan, and on Christian identity and ethnicity, illustrated from the contexts of Rwanda and Kenya. Chapter 14 advocates the theology of reconstruction, relevant to many contexts in Africa, and Chapter 15 assesses the state of the Church in postcolonial South Africa. The final chapter then directs our attention to what is perhaps the most striking of all developments in African Christianity: namely, its proliferation in diaspora, and its consequent significance to the present face of world Christianity.

Like any conversation, the current one has its constraints. It is necessarily limited in the number of participants involved and the theological issues addressed. The current selection follows previous editions in seeking representative men and women from various church traditions, geographical regions and linguistic zones. Unfortunately, it does not achieve the balance of anglophone, francophone, lusophone and especially African mother-tongue theologies that would ideally reflect such a conversation in African theology. Nor are the topics of discussion exhaustive, as further theological reflection is required on issues regarding globalization, environmental crises, good governance, constitutional reform, health care, human rights, sexuality and many other factors that hinder Africans from experiencing God's comprehensive *shalom* ('peace', 'well-being'), or the fullness of life Christ offers (John 10.10) through the power of the Holy Spirit (John 14.15–27).

So as you enter into this conversation, do what you would naturally do in any human conversation: first, listen carefully to what each speaker says.

Even before listening for the content of their ideas, get a feel for who the speaker is through the bio-data provided and through any additional research you can do. A person's theology almost certainly reflects his or her life experience, so try to discern what has shaped the person's views. Second, take note of how the various contributors reflect on Scripture and church tradition, how they engage with their own context, and how they draw these together in their current thinking. And third, take time to think carefully through the theological issues discussed. The questions at the end of each chapter are designed to assist you in reflecting personally on the readings, both to summarize key aspects of the theology expressed and to respond to the discussion yourself. To what extent do the theological issues arise in your own context? What insights do you gain from the African authors? What would you contribute to the conversation, either in agreement or disagreement, or by way of additional input from your own understanding and experience? And how might you act upon these discoveries in your own context of ministry?

Finally, keep in mind that this current conversation is truly 'on the way', in the double sense of the term. Just as the Emmaus disciples shared their hopes and fears, their certainties and their doubts, their grief and their joy 'on the way' of discovering the Risen Jesus with them, so African believers continue to grapple with recognizing and appropriating the Risen Christ in our midst today. So this current volume is simply one conversation along the way. In this sense, African theology, like any theology, is necessarily context-bound and provisional. However, the author of Luke–Acts uses the term 'way' literally, in terms of 'way, road', or as an action, 'way, journey', as in the account of the Emmaus disciples. Yet Luke also uses the term figuratively for 'way of God' (Luke 20.21), and Acts uses 'the Way' to designate the Christian community in its preaching and its praxis, or particular way of life (e.g. Acts 9.2; 19.9, 23; 22.4; 24.14, 22). In this sense, the present volume also represents African theology on the way, the way of Christ. Therefore, though these particular expressions of theology are admittedly contextual and provisional, they offer enduring insights on the way, as the Risen Christ meets with his people here in Africa today.

Part 1

Methodological issues in African theology

1

Contextual theological methodologies

Agbonkhianmeghe E. Orobator, SJ

Abstract

This chapter prioritizes context as the primary factor of theological reflection in African Christianity and presents theology as a discipline grounded in the ordinary experience of Christians and their faith communities. It argues that contextual theological methodologies draw on the incarnation as the key biblical foundation. Just as God enters completely into human reality, theology touches the depth of human experience in order to make sense of it. An example of this approach is inculturation, understood as a dynamic meeting of faith and culture that generates fresh and transforming syntheses of faith and its implication for everyday life. In light of this, theology becomes an ongoing effort to discover the faith dimension of the totality of human experience. This task involves specific methodological steps: personal immersion, openness to various fields of study, awareness of the historical development of faith and dialogue with the deeply rooted religious sensibilities of African Christians.

Introduction

St Anselm of Canterbury (1033–1109) once defined theology in very simple terms as 'faith seeking understanding'. This definition, though simple, raises the further question of identifying how in fact this quest of faith functions in everyday life. The position that will be set forth in this chapter holds that 'context' is the key word that answers this question. As a discipline that strives to articulate in an explicit manner the various dimensions of an individual's or a community's faith in God, theology does not operate outside the boundaries of our ordinary human experience. The 'raw material' for theological reflection is our faith, that is, how God reveals God's self to us, how we respond to this revelation, and what implications it has for daily living. In other words, our faith is grounded on the reality of our human experience.

Yet the understanding of our experience (of God, self and the world) varies from one particular situation to another. This awareness allows us to affirm that we cannot neglect the role of human experience in the theological enterprise. In the sixteenth century, the leader of the Protestant Reformation, Martin Luther (1483–1546), stated among other things that *experientia sola facit theologum* ('experience alone makes a theologian'). Taking experience into account in our theological reflection places us squarely in the domain of context.

The overall intention of this chapter is to demonstrate that paying attention to human experience and situation constitutes the foundation of contextual theological methodologies. The experience or situation may vary, but a contextual theological methodology neither circumvents nor ignores its importance in elaborating an appropriate theology – one that makes sense not only to the theologian, but also especially to his or her community.

The basic premise of this chapter can be formulated in the following terms: as faith seeking understanding, theology does not operate in a vacuum; every attempt to understand faith is grounded on our experience. The questions we raise about our relationship with God, others and the universe come from our everyday experience in life. You can hardly place a limit on the variety and extent of this experience: joy and sorrow, life and death, freedom and bondage, success and failure, comfort and deprivation, etc. Making sense of this experience in the light of faith is what makes theology contextual. Understood this way, what we call theology differs considerably from the exact sciences. Researchers engaged in the latter always strive to isolate their experience so that they can examine the data objectively, that is, without allowing their emotions, feelings and personal experience to influence the result of the experimentation. Theologians do not enjoy this luxury of bracketing or isolating their experience. Human experience appears as the primary data for the quest to understand, live and articulate faith.

Another way of putting this is to say that theology is about life. In more recent decades many theologians have creatively examined the reality called faith based on their experience of gender (feminist theology), racial discrimination (Black theology), or oppression and marginalization (liberation theology). This short list is only an example of the dynamic development of contextual theological methodologies in recent times. The important point to bear in mind is that the days are over when theology was simply exported wholesale from one context to another, without paying attention to the specificity of the host culture. Divorced from the local context in which we are situated, theology makes little or no sense at all. It is not an exaggeration to say that contemporary theological methodologies are all contextual. We can trace this imperative of contextual theological methodologies through the history of Christianity, especially in the Scriptures.

Many aspects of Christianity retain significant imprints of particular cultures where the religion grew. If we take the Scriptures, for example, we see how context affects the development of faith and belief. Elements like the treatment of women in Jewish cultures, the laws of inheritance, the institution of slavery, the experience of captivity, occupation and exile all feature as basic elements for developing the people's understanding of God. How the people conceived the nature of God drew more on their experience than on their capacity for abstract thinking.

In light of the above considerations, we can identify some of the key elements of contextual theological methodologies.

Contextual theological methodology is incarnational

In the New Testament nothing describes the necessity of contextual theological methodology better than the notion of incarnation: 'the Word became flesh and lived among us' (John 1.14). Several attempts have been made to explain the meaning of this expression. However we understand it, we cannot avoid the basic fact that it presents to us a clear recognition of the importance of context in understanding the Christian faith. We can compare this faith to a seed: just as a seed cannot take root and grow without falling on a soil, faith cannot develop, let alone be understood, without situating it in context. Context is to faith what soil is to a seed. This analogy is mirrored in the notion of the incarnation: the word became flesh and pitched tent in our midst. Christian faith is based on the 'stubborn' fact that God fully became human without ceasing to be God. This process is so radical it defies belief.

To say that the incarnation is a radical fact of Christian faith forms part of the broader claim that it leaves no aspect of human experience untouched. It is neither superficial nor partial. In other words, because of the incarnation, no aspect of humanity is alien to God. The consequences for theological methodology are twofold. It means that for theology to be authentic, no aspect of our humanity may be excluded from the focus of its reflection. Methodologically speaking, it also implies that reality as we encounter it is already imbued with meaning; in fact, reality serves as a means for a privileged encounter with God. The Scriptures show a variety of ways by which people encounter God: natural phenomena, victory and defeat, sickness, dying and death, etc. Today human experience remains a valid space for ongoing divine self-revelation. Disclosing and understanding this meaning as it unfolds represents one of the principal tasks of theological reflection that prioritizes a contextual methodology.

Another implication of the incarnational dimension of contextual theological methodology concerns the nature of faith as an encounter: Word becomes flesh. What Christians embrace is not first and foremost a set of ideas. Faith is a personal encounter: a response by a human person to a loving invitation from a loving God. To say that faith is an encounter is to insist that any attempt to understand it must take seriously those elements that determine, condition, or influence this encounter. Here again we are in the realm of context. Whether an African Christian encounters God as the God who frees the people from the bondage of oppression and marginalization will be influenced by his or her actual experience of bondage and lack of freedom. Theology cannot simply affirm liberation as integral to God's nature without at the same time seeking to understand and explore the mechanisms of oppression in human societies.

✳ Contextual theological methodology in African theology

When we talk about African theology, we understand this to mean the ongoing attempt to make sense of the African reality in the light of Christian faith and revelation. As thousands of Africans daily embrace the Christian faith, they come with their joys and sorrow, their hopes and despair, seeking to make sense of them in the light of faith. Theology neither ignores nor undermines this 'faith expectation'. It addresses it, aiming to point out the relevance of the Christian message to the experience of African Christians. Such a theology will necessarily be contextual. It does not float above human reality; rather, it is rooted firmly in it. This is the only way that theology can make sense as faith seeking understanding.

In African theology the best-known model of contextual theological methodology remains inculturation. Many definitions have been proposed for this model of contextual methodology and much has been written about it. It can be defined in simple terms as a way of doing theology that takes into account the religious sensibility and disposition of the people. Inculturation does not presuppose a kind of tabula rasa, a blank slate merely waiting to be filled by a foreign religious element. When Christianity meets a new culture, several elements come into play. This meeting is dynamic rather than static or passive. The first task of contextual theology is to recognize the validity of the host culture's way of understanding God, its religious world view and its moral codes and principles, all of which have a long history. Rather than sweeping these aside, the methodology of inculturation enters into dialogue with them. This kind of dialogue is based on a set of clear presuppositions.

In the first place, the host culture already has a valid experience of revelation. It knows who God is, what faith in God means and what it demands. According to one African proverb, 'No one teaches a child who God is.' Some agents of missionary Christianity assumed that Africa was a dark, savage and soulless continent. As a result of this view, they inflicted considerable violence on Africans. Their approach forms the direct antithesis, or opposite, of the approach of inculturation, or dialogue between Christianity and the religious traditions of the host culture. Another presupposition concerns the values inherent in the host culture's religious traditions. If revelation has already taken place in the host culture, it means not only that it has values that demand respect, but also that these values can become valid sources of an appropriate understanding of the Christian message.

The final presupposition appears more radical. As in any meeting of cultures, the possibility exists for change and transformation. The understanding of Christianity and the host culture do not emerge unchanged from the dialogue. This final presupposition points to a significant advantage of this methodology of theological reflection. It sets up the very real possibility of creating something new in terms of how Christian faith is understood and lived. This outcome is not a hybrid religion; what is of value in both is retained and transformed into an understanding of faith and culture that is uniquely Christian and African. This Christianity will have the flavour and the characteristics of the local context, without necessarily appearing alien or strange in comparison to other expressions of Christian faith that have emerged from other contexts. It will be recognizable both as local and universal.

The methodology of inculturation has been criticized for remaining too much at the superficial level of folkloric expressions. There is some validity to this criticism, although it represents an earlier phase in the development of the methodology of inculturation. The focus was to use songs, colours and liturgical gestures drawn from the host cultures. However, the awareness that the Christian message permeates all of culture has opened up the possibility of a deeper understanding and practice of the methodology of inculturation. What this methodology needed to take into account was the many different facets of life in the host culture – not just culture conceived of in narrow terms, but as the totality of the ways people experience life in society. In this sense, to quote a very famous text from Vatican II (1962–5),

> The joys and hopes, the grief and anguish of the people of our time, especially of those who are poor or afflicted, are the joys and hopes, the grief and anguish of the followers of Christ as well. Nothing that is genuinely human fails to find an echo in their hearts.
> ('The Church in the modern world', *Gaudium et spes*, 7 December 2007, no. 1)

A method of theological methodology that proceeds according to this affirmation goes beyond merely translating the Christian message into local idioms. It also goes beyond a selective application of this message using an equally selective list of items from the local culture.

In light of the foregoing, a very important dimension of inculturation methodology concerns its comprehensiveness. Taking a cue from Latin American liberation theology, theologians in Africa are taking issues of politics and economics as valid loci, or situations, of theological activity. If theology is to become relevant to the African context, the issues that 'disturb' human life in Africa also need to be integrated into the scope of this theological reflection. The range of issues is as wide as they are pertinent: war, violence, peace, forced migration, ecology, gender, development, poverty, disease, social instability, etc. Recent theological scholarship in Africa bears ample witness to this shift, both in the focus and the methodology of African theologians. The underlying concern relates to the fact that these issues raise substantial matters for theological examination and analysis. Viewed from the perspective of contextual theological methodology, theology or an understanding of faith has a word on these issues, just as these issues in turn shape the understanding of faith and revelation.

 # Contextual theological methodology is correlative

The concluding statement of the preceding paragraph indicates yet another dimension of this contextual methodology of theological activity. It is of nature correlative, in the sense that it seeks to reveal more explicitly the faith dimension of socio-economic and political issues. This recalls the earlier assertion that human reality is of its nature revelatory. It bears the imprint of God not only in the original activity of creation, but also in the ongoing process of grace and redemption. God does not leave the world to its fate; the world continues to be a ground of discovering what God is doing in our time and age. Therefore, enquiring into the meaning of human experience in the world creates the possibility of discovering not only God's activity in this reality, but also the message of that activity for our time. This idea of discovery has at least two implications for how we understand theology as a discipline and the theologian who engages in this discipline.

First, theological reflection constitutes an ongoing creative activity. The idea that there is a universal theology valid for all times and all places finds very little support within this methodological approach. Reality evolves, and so does the attempt to correlate it with the message of Christianity. Christian revelation may be closed, in the sense that Christ's revelation is valid for all times. Yet the way it is understood and appropriated reflects the evolving patterns of human life within a clearly defined context.

Second, a theologian is a person who engages actively in the quest for the understanding of faith in everyday life. The situations that theology deals with are neither imaginary nor merely speculative, just as the incarnation was neither imaginary nor speculative. The theologian is a member of a faith community, who strives to understand its 'joys and hopes, grief and anguish' in the light of God's self-revelation. As a general principle we may assert that a theologian is necessarily a contextual theologian.

Some practical elements of contextual theological methodology

In the light of the foregoing reflection, it may be useful at this point to briefly identify some particular features of contextual theological methodologies.

Insertion

I have made the point above that a contextual theological methodology requires an active engagement in real-life situations, that is, situations that challenge and shape our understanding and practice of faith. For this to happen, it is important that in the process of theological reflection the theologian be able to experience for himself or herself the realities of life.

We can take the example of the challenge of HIV & AIDS for the Christian community. A theological reflection that seeks to address this issue stands to gain much by actual engagement with the lives and situations of people infected and affected by AIDS. Only by doing this will the outcome of such theological reflection be relevant to their conditions. Insertion comes in various forms. One form could be dialogue with people directly affected by HIV & AIDS. Essentially this will prioritize listening to their stories as essential data for theological reflection. In this context, the outcome of such an exercise will rarely be merely speculative or disincarnate.

Inter-disciplinarity

One notable characteristic of contemporary theological issues is their complexity. These issues are multifaceted; they occur at so many different levels of human existence. To remain with the same example of HIV & AIDS, our current knowledge clearly shows that to treat it simply as a matter of medical care is an oversimplification. The last 25 years of the growth of the pandemic have revealed the intertwining of many dimensions, which include social, economic, political, religious and cultural aspects. From the point of view of methodology, this implies that dealing with its challenges involves dialoguing with different disciplines at the same time. The disease has religious implications in terms of the ethical responsibilities of compassionate care for people living with HIV & AIDS. But these cannot be dealt with in isolation. It becomes imperative for the theologian to engage other disciplines in view of proposing and articulating a sound theological reflection and position on the issue of HIV & AIDS.

The nature of this interdisciplinary engagement varies. In one instance, this may involve adopting and adapting methodologies of other disciplines. This would be the case, for example, when a theologian integrates social analysis into his or her research or carries out an ethnographic survey in order to gain a better understanding of a particular situation. Such a theologian might use survey questionnaires and interviews. In another instance, the findings of other disciplines (data and statistical analysis) can become the basis for a theological reflection on a particular issue. It is important to bear in mind that this approach of inter-disciplinarity does not diminish the theological value of the outcome of this methodology. Even here, theology retains its proper identity as faith seeking understanding, or a reflection on human condition in the light of Christian faith.

Historical development

For many reasons the place of history in contextual theological methodologies appears to be crucial. First, theological issues or questions develop over time. A contextualized approach requires a very keen sense of the historical development of the issues under consideration. This need for historical awareness also affects the nature of faith itself. The way Christians over the centuries have understood or responded to particular issues in the light of their faith develops over time. The ability to situate theological questions within their respective historical contexts is an important dimension of contextual theological methodologies.

To take one example that would be familiar to Catholic Christians, Vatican II defines a significant moment in the history of the Roman Catholic Church. With this council many elements of Christian faith and belief were reconsidered and redefined. Contextual theological methodologies need to be able to account for these changes in order to understand in what particular ways our understanding and practice of faith have been shaped by history.

Another interesting aspect of the need for historical awareness derives from the fact that not all the issues have been covered in the Scriptures and Christian traditions. There are contemporary issues that pose new questions and new challenges to our understanding of the Christian faith. Rather than ignoring them, the method of contextual theology addresses them to the extent that they affect or shape the life of a believing Christian community. For example, how to conceive Christian sexual ethics in the time of HIV & AIDS represents one of the historically developing issues of faith. We could also point out the issue of economic, social and cultural globalization, the increasing demand for gay rights in church and society, and the challenges these issues pose to the Christian faith. A contextualized theological methodology takes these issues seriously to the extent that they affect the life of the believing community. Avoiding these challenging and often difficult issues represents a convenient option only for a theological reflection that remains at the level of brilliant intellectual speculation, but one which misses the real context where faith is lived, tested, understood and celebrated by the Christian community. To pay genuine attention to new and emerging theological questions is to open up the real and exciting possibility for discovery, transformation and newness.

Indigenous religion

In the context of Africa, one very important element of a contextualized theology concerns the relationship between Christian faith and African religion. This relationship has been dealt with in many different ways. One of the approaches presents them in mutually exclusive and antagonistic terms. This is characteristic of many forms of missionary Christianity, whose objective was to discredit and eliminate African religion in order to impose Christianity, however kindly. The effect of this model of evangelization has been well documented.

The preferred approach in contextual theology follows the path of dialogue, as indicated above. The recognition of the role of African religion in shaping the religious consciousness, beliefs and practices of African Christians constitutes an important requirement for genuine theological activity. African Christians are a product of two traditions. Maintaining a proper balance and determining the specific nature of these respective traditions arguably represents the most important source of contextualized theology in Africa. The corresponding theological methodology recognizes that in Africa, Christian beliefs and practices thrive both on the enduring foundations of indigenous African religious traditions and the foundations of Christian faith and revelation. The combination of both defines the dynamism and uniqueness of African Christianity and contemporary African contextual theological methodologies.

This brief reflection on contextual theological methodologies addresses the subject in general terms. Our immediate purpose, however, also allows us to relate it to the particular question of method in African theology. In the view advanced here, the necessity of a contextual theological methodology emerges as a function of the nature of Christian faith and belief, neither of which appears alien to human situations nor ignores the social concerns of the believing community. The quest for a critical understanding of Christian faith in such concrete contexts represents the primary goal of contextual theological methodologies.

 ## STUDY QUESTIONS

1 As a Christian, how do you understand the incarnation in your everyday life?

2 What particular contributions does your culture or traditional religion make to your understanding of the Christian faith?

3 What are some of the contemporary issues that challenge or make you question your faith? How might you respond to the challenges they pose?

2

Biblical exegesis in Africa: the significance of the translated Scriptures

Kwame Bediako

 ## Abstract

This chapter explores the significance of the translated Scriptures for biblical exegesis and for Christian mission, both in Africa and throughout the world. Beginning with the Septuagint, the Greek translation of the Hebrew Scriptures, the author outlines the importance of this translation in shaping the nature and thought of the Christian Scriptures. From this example, he explains the principle of translatability: since the eternal Word became flesh, going beyond human words to take on human form, the incarnation is itself a form of translation. Therefore the incarnation renders all translations of the word of God into whatever vernacular, or mother tongue, essentially equal in validity. The remainder of the chapter builds on this premise, demonstrating the contributions of African translations of Scripture, particularly in the Twi language of Ghana, to biblical exegesis.

Scripture as vernacular, or mother tongue translation

Clement of Alexandria (*c.*150–215 CE) was an evangelist and apologist for the Christian faith. He was especially concerned to gain a hearing from, and win the confidence of, educated Greek-speaking people with whom he shared a common intellectual culture. Clement was convinced not only that God had inspired the Hebrew Scriptures, but also that God had produced the Greek translation of it known as the Septuagint. For Clement, therefore, the Septuagint had acquired the authoritative character of 'Greek prophecy': that is, it was no less prophecy, or God's word, for being in Greek. Rather, the God who gave the Scriptures in Hebrew must be understood to have intended also to communicate in Greek. Indeed, the existence of the Septuagint was the sign that God did, in fact, communicate in Greek! Before Plato came along, Moses did, as it were, speak Attic Greek.

What Clement was affirming is, in fact, the principle of translatability, and how this relates to the nature of Scripture itself. In our time, the central role of Scripture translation for Christian mission has been rightly recognized as being among the most important developments in recent Christian history. Therefore Clement contributes a very important insight to our present circumstance: namely, the process of mission by translation. This process was at play in the initial encounter of the Christian faith with the Hellenistic world outside of the birthplace of the faith in Palestine.

The significance of that first encounter for us lies in the fact that it was that process of mission by translation that produced the Scriptures of the Christian Church. It is a curious fact that the earliest languages of Christianity were Greek and Aramaic. Although Christianity emerged out of Judaism, the Jewish Scriptures, which became the Church's Scriptures, were at first read and studied primarily in Greek translation. As a result, this Greek translation, the Septuagint, became essentially the shaper of the theology of the Church. Andrew Walls points out that the effect of the Septuagint, as the first pre-Christian translation, was crucial for the development of an indigenous Hellenistic Christianity. Likewise it was exemplary for the subsequent history of Gentile Christianity in providing direction for many peoples in their encounter with the Christian faith. Therefore, we must consider how Scripture translation continues to affect the development of Christianity in the world.

For our present purpose, we note that one way the Septuagint influenced Christian thought is in contributing to the shape of the Scriptures themselves. For example, the authors of the New Testament made extensive use of the Old Testament in their writings. Since these New Testament writers often used the Greek translation of the Hebrew Scripture, the Septuagint influenced the literary form and expression of the New Testament. It also influenced the theology, to some extent. For example, Matthew 1.23 quotes Isaiah 7.14. While the Hebrew text of Isaiah uses the word *almah*, meaning 'a young woman', Matthew uses the word from the Septuagint: *parthenos*, meaning 'a virgin'. Did Matthew use the 'wrong' text? Or did he inherit a Greek translation that now, in the light of the birth of Jesus, has gained a new theological significance? This, in turn, illuminates in a fresh way the relevant Old Testament passage and, indeed, the whole Old Testament, a significance confirmed by the Vulgate's (the Latin translation of the Bible) use of *virgo* for this passage.

Another example is found in Acts 15, where James sums up the apostles' and elders' decision at the Council of Jerusalem. In Acts 15.16–18 James quotes Amos 9.11–12, and he evidently follows the text of the Septuagint more closely than the Hebrew Masoretic text. The Masoretic text states that God will restore the undivided kingdom of Israel 'so that they may possess the remnant of Edom and all the nations that bear my name' (Amos 9.12,

13

NIV). In other words, God would expand the kingdom of Israel to its limits under David's reign. However, Acts 15.17 follows the Septuagint text in stating that God will restore Israel so that 'the remnant of men [adam, man, i.e. humanity, rather than *Edom*] may seek the Lord, and all the Gentiles who bear my name' (NIV). While there is debate over the textual evidence for these passages, it is fair to observe that the early Christian Church inherited a Greek translation that enabled it to understand the significance of its own historical moment. In the light of modern politics of land in the Middle East, we may even be grateful for the direction that the Septuagint indicates in its rendering of Amos' prophecy. Is God concerned with the expansion of the kingdom to its Davidic (territorial) limits? Or is he not concerned about people, 'the nations [Gentiles] who bear my name'?

There are many debates regarding discrepancies between the Hebrew text and the wording of the Greek translation. Yet clearly, it was the Septuagint that proved decisive in shaping the mind of the Church in relation to its own self-understanding, its faith in Jesus of Nazareth as the Saviour of the world, and its call to mission in the world. Lamin Sanneh's central thesis in *Translating the Message* is therefore fitting. Sanneh argues that from its origins, Christianity recognized its need to translate out of Aramaic and Hebrew. It therefore exerted a dual force throughout its historical development: one was to relativize its Judaic roots and the other was to break down the stigma of Gentile culture and to adopt it for the expansion of the new religion. These two forces, relativizing Jewish roots and destigmatizing Gentile culture, were complementary, so that the Judaic and the Gentile became closely intertwined in the formation of Christianity.

It is this dual action of relativizing and destigmatizing that lies behind the argument of scriptural translatability. For translatability is another way of saying universality, or being applicable to all. The ultimate basis for translatability lies in the central affirmation of the Christian faith itself, namely, that 'the Word became flesh and lived among us' (John 1.14). For the incarnation, in which the fullest divine communication reached beyond human words to take on the human form itself, is also translation. This therefore renders all translations of the word of God into whatever language essentially and substantially equal. In every instance of Scripture translation into any language, the eternal Word of God becomes flesh to dwell among a people. In this way, they are enabled to perceive that the Living God, who has never been far from them, is now heard to speak their language, calling them to turn to Christ all that they are and have been (Acts 14.15–17; 17.24–31).

The Church's Scriptures, as we have them in all their numerous linguistic forms in the world Church today, are the fruit of translation. This means that it is helpful to think of Scripture as essentially vernacular, or mother tongue.

Translatability and the Scriptures as context

The prevalent view regarding translation is that it is impossible to make a 'true' translation from one language into another. Something is always lost in translation, so it is essential to study a text in its original language. However, does not the principle of translation allow us to think of the Scriptures as more than merely text? Indeed, it is possible to think of the Scriptures also as context, a context that the reader (or hearer) may enter and so actually participate in their world of meaning and experience. This forms the basis for the Scriptures to make sense to modern Christians, who are so many centuries removed from their initial composition. The Scriptures are not only a text that modern Christians may appropriate through the required skills and techniques of exegesis and hermeneutics. They are also a context in which modern Christians can share as illuminating of their own human experience. This lies behind the apostle Paul's recalling of Psalm 116.10, relating the psalmist's words to himself in 2 Corinthians 4.13: 'But just as we have the same spirit of faith that is in accordance with scripture – "I believed, and so I spoke" – we also believe, and so we speak.'

It seems that this must form part of what is meant in the Christian affirmation of belief in the Holy Spirit and in the communion of saints. Kenneth Cragg suggests that these beliefs could equally mean a 'participation in holy things' (1968: 71). This participation adds new dimensions to biblical exegesis and interpretation. For biblical narrative comes to function sacramentally, so to speak, enabling the reader or hearer to gain access to the world of experience intended for all those to whom the Scriptures are addressed. All Christians worship the God of Israel, all believers in Christ being 'descendants of Abraham' (Galatians 3.7). In this sense, the Scriptures can be said to reflect and interpret the spiritual experience of all Christian believers.

But translatability and the impact of the translated Scriptures also ensure that the 'world of experience' can be expanded in the other direction. This may occasionally lead to new and startling ways of participating in the Scriptures that are shaped by the cultural world of experience of the reader or hearer. For example, according to the testimony of William Wade Harris, the twentieth-century West African Christian prophet, during his ministry he experienced trance-visitations in which he saw Moses, Elijah, the Angel Gabriel and Jesus, and he alone would speak with them. In other words, Harris, who evidently underwent a deep Christian conversion experience, appeared also able to function in a spiritual universe that seemed similar to his African world of ancestors, the living dead. In *Christianity in Africa: The Renewal of a Non-Western Religion*, I treat Harris as a paradigm, or a typical example, of what I term 'the primal imagination'. By this I mean that Harris seemed to operate on the assumption that the spiritual universe of the African primal world offered valid perspectives for participating in the world of the Scriptures.

For our present purposes, it is how this outlook affected Harris's relation to the Bible that is important. Significantly, David Shank, a non-African, studied Harris's career and came to identify the concept of participation – generally associated with Africa's primal religious traditions – as the most adequate explanation for Harris's understanding of his direct involvement with Moses, Elijah, the Angel Gabriel and Jesus Christ. Shank (1980: 466–7) describes how Harris appropriated the truth of the Bible not as patterns of 'belief in' the truth, but more in line with the African pattern of 'participation in' the truth. It was not so much a question of establishing what Moses or Elijah or Jesus said or did, but of involvement with these biblical figures as with the ancestors, the living dead.

Thus the Scriptures may also be viewed as context, so that persons of varied cultural backgrounds can enter and participate in them, bringing their own cultural worlds of meaning with them. If this be the case, then the exegesis of biblical texts may not be taken as completed when one has established meanings in Hebrew, Aramaic and Greek. Instead, the process needs to continue into all possible languages in which biblical faith is received, mediated and expressed. This makes the task infinitely more difficult than any one person or group of persons can achieve, and it shows all the more how tentative, provisional and contextual all theological efforts are.

New dimensions of biblical exegesis in mother tongues

'Nsɛm nyinaa ne Nyame' is a well-known and well-used proverbial saying among the Akan people of Ghana, whose main dialect is Twi. Perhaps a simple translation is: 'All wisdom is from God.' There are two important words here: Nsɛm and Nyame. Nsɛm is the plural of what has become in the Akan biblical account the common rendering for logos ('word') in Greek, or its equivalent in Hebrew, dabar. But Asɛm, the singular form, is also open to a range of meanings, from an item of speech to a matter for public discussion or even disputation. It can also refer to reality as experienced or observed, and therefore can be used to mean a self-evident truth that is recognized as such within the community. Indeed, proverbs are formulated in the first place to affirm and reinforce such self-evident truths.

John 1.1 reads in Twi as follows: 'Mfiase no na Asɛm no wɔ hɔ, na Asɛm no ne Nyankopɔn na ɛwɔ hɔ, na Asɛm no yɛ Onyankopɔn'. To the Akan mind that is exposed to Christ, Christ appears to signify precisely this kind of self-evident truth or reality as Asɛm. Therefore, Akan Christian thought has moved the discussion on, taking a direction almost like that in the development in Hellenistic Christian thought when it moved back and forth between logos ('word') and sophia ('wisdom'). What comes to mind here especially is the theology of the Cappadocians in the fourth century.

But there is a second important word in our Akan proverb, namely, *Nyame*. As noted earlier, *'Nsɛm nyinaa ne Nyame'* cannot be claimed as the fruit of Christian missionary proclamation among the Akan. In other words, the insight predates Christian preaching among the Akan. Yet, is it not significant that the God whose name has been revered in pre-Christian religious tradition, borne along by the indigenous language, has now turned out to be the God of the Bible? The Akan case is in no sense exceptional. In virtually every Christian community in Africa, the Christian name for God is usually a divine name for the Supreme God inherited from the pre-Christian tradition. African Christians do not seem to recognize how remarkable this fact is. Nor did the early Western missionaries in Africa, who, because of their prior outlook and formation, were not inclined to find God in Africa. Instead, they were more concerned to teach Africans about God.

What is more, this process of identifying the biblical God with the African God has taken place in a way that none of the old European gods – whether Zeus, Jupiter or Odin – could be. The biblical God had to be distinguished from these European gods, and so European Christian tradition drew upon the generic term *gott*, or God, for the Divine. Yet if the Scriptures are in fact the revelation of *Olorun, Chineke, Ngai, Muungu, Nkosi, Unkulunkulu, Nyame* (or *Nyankopɔn*, a more intense form of *Nyame*), then what does this signify for the nature of the biblical account itself from an African perspective?

The question has significance, for almost all the early missionary encounters with African pre-Christian religious practice gave the impression of a widespread African polytheism. As a consequence, in relation to the Akan world, the early missionaries felt bound to devise a plural form, *anyame* (gods), of *Onyame*, the Akan personal name for God.

Once again, attention to mother tongue sheds light on the issue. Johannes Gottlieb Christaller (1827–95), one of the leading linguists of the nineteenth century, was a German missionary to the Gold Coast. He conducted serious study and translation of the Twi language, one of the major dialects of the Akan people. In an illuminating observation on how the Akan divine name, *Onyame*, came to acquire a plural form, *anyame*, Christaller noted that missionaries 'merely introduced' the term in order to describe the religious outlook of people who were presumed to be polytheists! However, on the basis of his own deep entry into the Twi language, he affirmed that the Africans were monotheists, to a great extent, for they applied the term for God only to one Supreme Being.

Furthermore, in an article published over twenty years ago in the *Journal of Religion in Africa*, Patrick Ryan argued that the Akan and the Yoruba of West Africa are better equipped linguistically to express the absolute uniqueness of God than the Semites, Greeks, Romans and their European successors. Ryan drew his conclusion from a study of 'the problem of God and the gods', in other words, the problem of 'the One and the many' in the religious view of the Akan and the Yoruba. Ryan's study confirmed that, in Africa, God is understood to be a hospitable deity who is approached

17

through the mediation of lesser deities. However, Africans generally knew who was God and could distinguish him from the various beings that the academic literature called 'lesser deities, divinities, gods', that were not God.

Yet the question remains: can the African sense of divine hospitality reflect an adequate and authentic participation in the biblical account? Or does such a sense of God represent an unjustified deviation from the biblical tradition? There is no need to make a tally of the large number of scriptural passages, particularly in the Old Testament, where the language of 'God and the gods' occurs. Very often God, Yahweh, is said or called upon to rise against the 'gods', or against 'other gods'. In addition, it is rather extraordinary how few references there are in the New Testament to other 'gods'. When the apostle Paul expresses his concern for the Galatian Christians, for fear that they entertain rivals to the Living God, the reference is to 'beings that by nature are not gods' (Galatians 4.8). If, for some, there are many so-called 'gods and . . . lords', for us, there is only one God (1 Corinthians 8.5, 6). This is a theological insight that, interestingly, will be confirmed when the biblical account is expressed in African languages.

So, might the African sense of divine hospitality allow God to be hospitable and yet have no rivals? For, if it is indeed the case that the Yoruba and the Akan are better equipped linguistically to express the absolute uniqueness of God than the Semites, Greeks, Romans and their descendants, then might African languages permit a fresh participation in the Scriptures? If so, by bringing to light these subtle differences in interpretation, African languages might point to new dimensions of biblical exegesis.

The Akan world of transcendent power is basically made up of the following, in descending order of supremacy: *Onyame* (*Nyame*) or *Onyankopɔn* (God), *nananom nsamanfo* (ancestors or spirit fathers), *abosom* (divinities or 'lesser deities'), and *asuman* (material stores of impersonal power). There are no 'gods' beside God, for *abosom* are not gods. Here are indigenous religious categories that can have far-reaching consequences for theological understanding of the biblical account. Yet their full implications have not been realized. Nor has biblical exegesis adequately recognized the significance of assimilating *Onyame* (*Onyankopɔn*) into Yahweh of the Old Testament and the God and Father of our Lord Jesus Christ of the New Testament. For example, Exodus 15.11 has been translated as follows:

Hena na ɔte sɛ wo, Awurade, wo anyame mu?
Hena na ɔte sɛ wo, kronkron yɛ mu onunyamfo,
Nea ne ho yɛ hu ayeyi mu, awonwadeyɛfo.
                          (Twi, Akuapem, UBS, 1964)

Who is like you, O LORD, *among the gods?*
Who is like you, majestic in holiness,
awesome in splendour, doing wonders?

Likewise Psalm 86.8 is rendered:

> *Obiara nte sɛ wo, anyame mu, Awurade;*
> *Na biribiara nte sɛ wo nnwuma.* (Twi)

> *There is none like you among the gods, O Lord,*
> *nor are there any works like yours.*

When one reads these verses in Twi, the word *anyame* sticks in the throat. Akan do not know *anyame*, for only *Nyame* is *Nyame*, *Onyankopɔn* alone is *Onyankopɔn*, just as Yahweh alone is Yahweh.

How then may the Akan mind respond to the first commandment of Exodus 20.1–3?

> *Na Onyankopɔn kaa nsɛm yi nyinaa sɛ: Mene Awurade wo Nyankopɔn a miyii*
> *wo Misraim asase so nkoafi mu no. Nnya anyame foforo nka me ho.* (Twi)

> *Then God spoke all these words: I am the LORD your God, who brought you out*
> *of the land of Egypt, out of the house of slavery; you shall have no other gods*
> *before [or besides] me.*

Since Akan do not have, strictly, *anyame* alongside *Onyame* (*nka me ho*), the use of *anyame* obscures the meaning. Yet if one were to use authentic Akan religious categories, replacing *anyame* with *abosom*, the way would be open for recognizing, through exegesis of the Akan biblical text, that the dire warning implied in the first commandment has to do with the inward disposition of the worshipper, much more than with any external or material objects of rival worship. For this latter concern is adequately addressed in the second commandment.

If these Akan religious categories had been understood, there would have been no need to introduce a plural of *Onyame*, *anyame* – a semantic non-sense – on the grounds that Akan converts, presumed to be originally polytheists, had to be taught to have 'no other gods beside God'. For even before Muslims and Christians arrived in West Africa, the Yoruba and Akan spoke of the supremacy of the One Transcendent Being.

Conclusion: 'God speaks in our own languages'

We must conclude, therefore, that biblical exegesis in the African context cannot be considered adequate if it bypasses the factor and impact of the translated Scriptures in the actual languages in which the majority of Christians in Africa read, hear and experience the word of God. Such an extension of the range of biblical exegesis can have two effects. First, by encouraging a meeting of the Scriptures in various translations produced by the same Spirit, it can achieve a fuller sense and understanding of the

Scriptures. Since different languages have different capacities, this result is possible only if biblical exegetes from different cultural and linguistic backgrounds are open to learning from one another.

Second, and perhaps more important, such an enhanced appreciation of the exegetical significance of the translated Scriptures will be an effective response to what appears to be a sort of 'Bible deism'. This term represents the view of those who suggest that after God spoke in Hebrew, Aramaic and Greek, he ceased to speak to humanity in any other language. Yet this presumption is firmly contradicted by the Scriptures, which show themselves to be continuously communicative. Therefore, recognizing the place of the translated Scriptures and integrating them into biblical exegesis becomes a theological affirmation that God has 'not left himself without a witness' anywhere (Acts 14.17). Likewise, it affirms that:

> *The heavens are telling the glory of God;*
> *and the firmament proclaims his handiwork.*
> *Day to day pours forth speech,*
> *and night to night declares knowledge.*
> *There is no speech, nor are there words;*
> *their voice is not heard;*
> *yet their voice goes out through all the earth,*
> *and their words to the end of the world.*
>   (Psalm 19.1–4; cf. Romans 10.18)

 STUDY QUESTIONS

1 Why was the Septuagint significant for early Christianity? What relevance does this have for Christian mission today?

2 Explain in your own words the 'principle of translatability' in relation to the Christian Scriptures. What implications does this have for the language(s) in which you read the Scriptures?

3 What does the author mean in suggesting that the Scriptures are 'more than merely text', but also 'context, a context that the reader (or hearer) may enter and so actually participate in their world of meaning and experience'? Do you agree? Why or why not?

4 In what ways, if any, do the examples cited from the Twi translation enhance our understanding of the Scriptures?

3
Biblical hermeneutics in Africa

Gerald West

Abstract

The three key elements of African biblical interpretation are the biblical text, the African context, and the act of appropriation through which they are linked. The biblical text and the African context do not, on their own, participate in a conversation. For dialogue to take place between text and context, a real, flesh-and-blood African reader is required! This reader moves constantly back and forth between the biblical and African contexts, bringing them together in an ongoing conversation that we call appropriation. How readers move between text and context is determined by a range of factors, including their ideo-theological orientation, their ecclesio-theological missionary heritage, their engagement with ordinary readers of the Bible in the church and community, and the important issues that require attention in the African context. This essay explores each of these elements in African biblical hermeneutics.

Introduction

Biblical interpretation in Africa typically consists of three poles: the pole of the biblical text, the pole of the African context, and the pole of appropriation. Jonathan Draper has referred to this as a 'tri-polar' approach (Draper, 2001). What is helpful about Draper's analysis is that it brings to the fore the often hidden third pole of 'appropriation'.

Most characterizations of African biblical hermeneutics tend to portray a bi-polar approach, referring for example to 'the comparative method' (Ukpong, 2000: 12; Holter, 2002: 88–9), in which African context and biblical text interpret each other. Knut Holter articulates this clearly when he says comparative studies can be characterized 'as studies whose major approach is a comparative methodology that facilitates a parallel interpretation' of certain biblical texts or motifs and supposed African parallels, 'letting the two illuminate one another'. 'Traditional exegetical methodology' is of course, he goes on to say, part of the interpretive process. However, in African biblical hermeneutics the biblical text 'is approached from a perspective where African comparative material is the major dialogue partner and traditional exegetical methodology is subordinated to this perspective' (Holter, 2002: 88).

But implicit in these bipolar-like formulations are aspects of the third pole – the reader's appropriation. While the real reader who brings the biblical text and African context into dialogue tends to remain 'hidden' in Holter's explanation of the comparative method, it is always a reader who enables the text and context to come into conversation. So when Holter refers to the ways in which biblical text and African context 'illuminate one another', we must remember that they are only able to illuminate one another through the active participation of the reader.

Justin Ukpong, a key commentator on the comparative method, takes us a step further in his own comments on the comparative approach. He says that the goal of comparative interpretation is 'the actualization of the theological meaning of the text in today's context so as to forge integration between faith and life, and engender commitment to personal and societal transformation' (Ukpong, 2000: 24). What connects text and context, then, is a reader who activates a form of dialogical appropriation that has a theological and a praxiological (i.e. committed action) dimension. What we can term an 'ideo-theological orientation' in the reader is what characterizes the third pole of appropriation. This ideo-theological orientation can take various forms, resulting in at least four different emphases in African biblical interpretation: inculturation, liberation, feminist and postcolonial hermeneutics. But before we discuss each of these, we must reflect more fully on the third pole – appropriation.

Appropriation

The third pole offers an important starting point in understanding the different emphases in African biblical hermeneutics. The other two poles, the biblical text and the African context, are no less important, but an examination of the third pole clarifies how these two fundamental poles are brought into dialogue.

That there is engagement between biblical text and African context is fundamental to African biblical scholarship. While Western forms of biblical interpretation have been reluctant, until recently, to acknowledge that text and context are always, at least implicitly, in conversation, the dialogical dimension of biblical interpretation has always been an explicit feature of African biblical hermeneutics. This is readily apparent from even a cursory survey of the published work of African biblical scholarship. Interpreting the biblical text is never, in African biblical hermeneutics, an end in itself. Biblical interpretation is always about changing the African context. This is what links ordinary African biblical interpretation and African biblical scholarship, a common commitment to 'read' the Bible for personal and societal transformation. The focus of this essay is African biblical scholarship, but its close alliance with ordinary African interpretation – indeed, its partial constitution by ordinary African interpretation – should not be forgotten.

The kind of contextual change and transformation envisaged in particular African contexts shapes how biblical text and African context are brought into dialogue. The two most established forms of appropriation in African biblical scholarship have been inculturation and liberation hermeneutics. In the last decade, however, another form of appropriation has emerged, known as postcolonial hermeneutics. In the next four sub-sections I will discuss each of these in turn, showing how each in its own way is a form of ideo-theological appropriation that brings the African context and the biblical text into conversation (or, perhaps, contestation).

Each of these forms of appropriation has what I refer to as an 'ideo-theological' orientation. Because the act of appropriation involves a dynamic, back-and-forth movement and engagement, both the Bible and the context contribute to and constitute the ideo-theological orientation of any particular interpreter. But other aspects of the interpreter's experience and life interests also impart their imprint on his or her ideo-theological orientation. This is why the interpreter's ideo-theological orientation is often not foregrounded in the interpretive act – it seems to the interpreter to be a self-evident product of the biblical text, the context and the interpreter's reality. But one of the tasks of academic biblical scholarship is to analyse what appears self-evident.

 ## Inculturation hermeneutics

The most common African form of ideo-theological orientation is inculturation hermeneutics. Like other forms of African biblical interpretation, inculturation hermeneutics takes its cue from life outside the academy. The general experience of African Christians was that African social and cultural concerns were not reflected in missionary and Western academic forms of biblical interpretation. Inculturation hermeneutics arose as a response, 'paying attention to the African socio-cultural context and the questions that arise therefrom' (Ukpong, 1995: 4). Inculturation hermeneutics 'designates an approach to biblical interpretation which seeks to make the African . . . context the *subject* of interpretation'; which means that every dimension of the interpretive process is '*consciously* informed by the world-view of, and the life experience within that culture' (Ukpong, 1995: 5). While the Nigerian biblical scholar Justin Ukpong includes the historical, social, economic, political, and religious as elements of inculturation hermeneutics (Ukpong, 1995: 6), the tendency of most African inculturation hermeneutics is to concentrate on the cultural and religious elements. These elements, then, make a substantial contribution to the ideo-theological orientation of inculturation hermeneutics.

Another element in the constitution of inculturation hermeneutics is the recognition that African biblical interpretation is always in some sense 'over against', or in opposition to, the forms of biblical interpretation imposed by and inherited from missionary Christianity and Western academic biblical studies. The missionary–colonial axis is always a factor in inculturation hermeneutics, providing it with a particular ideo-theological orientation.

Alongside this oppositional element is another element, somewhat in tension with it. As Ukpong says, 'The focus of [African] interpretation is on the theological meaning of the text within a contemporary context' (Ukpong, 1995: 6). This formulation recognizes that the Bible is a significant sacred text with a message for African socio-cultural contexts. As Ukpong goes on to say, 'This involves interactive engagement between the biblical text and a particular contemporary socio-cultural issue such that the gospel message serves as a critique of the culture, and/or the cultural perspective enlarges and enriches the understanding of the text' (Ukpong, 1995: 6). Here he captures succinctly the two-way engagement between text and context. What he also captures here is the predominant attitude of trust towards the Bible within inculturation hermeneutics. Though the Bible has come to Africa as part of the missionary–colonial imperialistic package, the Bible itself has 'good news' for Africa, and/or Africa is able to illuminate the biblical message in a way that Western biblical scholarship has not been able to do. So an attitude of trust towards the Bible itself is a feature of inculturation hermeneutics, alongside its oppositional stance towards colonialism.

Liberation hermeneutics

Almost all of the above elements are also constitutive of liberation hermeneutics, though the mix is somewhat different. Like inculturation hermeneutics, African liberation hermeneutics has its starting point with the experience of the masses. In the words of the South African biblical scholar Itumeleng Mosala, the hermeneutical starting point of liberation hermeneutics is the 'social and material life' of 'the black struggle for liberation' (Mosala, 1989: 67).

However, while African liberation hermeneutics acknowledges the importance of both the spiritual and the material, like inculturation hermeneutics, the emphasis in liberation hermeneutics is on the economic and political dimensions of African life. Religion and culture are important but peripheral, and economic and political analysis is central. Race and class, not religion and culture, are the critical categories of liberation hermeneutics. And while inculturation hermeneutics is quite eclectic in the kinds of sociological conceptual frameworks it draws on, liberation hermeneutics is more specific, drawing heavily on Marxist conceptual frameworks (Mosala, 1989).

African liberation hermeneutics also clearly shares the oppositional stance of inculturation hermeneutics to the missionary–colonial project, though its categories of contestation are different, as indicated. However, liberation hermeneutics raises questions about the Bible itself, with a clarity not found in inculturation hermeneutics. The Bible is a resource for liberation, but it is also a source of oppression and domination, and not just in the way it has been used by the missionary–colonial project; the Bible is in part intrinsically oppressive (Mosala, 1989: 41). The ideological ambiguity of the Bible is a significant feature of liberation hermeneutics, resulting in an intertwining of suspicion and trust in the ideo-theological orientation of liberation hermeneutics.

The ambiguous attitude to the Bible in liberation hermeneutics has also had methodological consequences for some. The predominant interpretive methodologies for engaging with both the African context and the biblical text in inculturation hermeneutics have been historical and sociological forms of analysis. With respect to the biblical text, historical-critical and an eclectic range of sociological methods are used (Ukpong, 1995). With respect to the African context, an eclectic range of religio-cultural forms of analysis within African theology and anthropology are used (Ukpong, 1995). African liberation hermeneutics inherits but then rejects this eclectic assortment of socio-historical analytical resources (Mosala, 1989: 43–66), arguing instead for a more structured and systemic analysis of both the biblical text (within its sites of production) and the African context, using historical-materialist categories of analysis. According to Mosala, the biblical text and African context should not only be brought into dialogue in terms of content; they should also be brought into dialogue in terms of methodology. Both the Bible and the Black experience and struggle must be analysed structurally using historical-materialist categories. In other words, African interpreters must recognize that the biblical texts are rooted in the struggles of their material sites of production, just as the life of ordinary Black South Africans is rooted in particular socio-historical modes of production (Mosala, 1989: 31–2).

To sum up so far, it is apparent that though African inculturation hermeneutics and African liberation hermeneutics share a number of significant features, there are also a number of distinctive features in their ideo-theological orientations. What they have in common is a commitment to relate their biblical scholarship to the realities of ordinary Africans, an oppositional stance towards the missionary–colonial enterprise which brought the Bible to Africa, a recognition that the Bible is an important text in the African context which must be engaged with by critical scholarship, and a preference for socio-historical modes of analysis for both the biblical text and the African context. What is different are the dimensions of African social reality that they emphasize (religion and culture versus economics and politics), their attitude to the Bible (trust versus suspicion), and their advocacy of specific methodological models and analytical tools (eclectic sociological analysis versus historical-materialist analysis). All of these similarities and differences constitute how they connect text and context – how appropriation takes place.

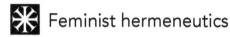 Feminist hermeneutics

African feminist hermeneutics – and the designation 'feminist' is problematic, with some preferring to borrow the African American term 'womanist' (Nadar, 2001), some adopting an African indigenous designation, such as *bosadi* (Masenya, 2001), and others using the general phrase 'African women's hermeneutics' – emerges from within African inculturation and African liberation hermeneutics, and so shares features with both.

African feminist hermeneutics has been in dialogue with both the religio-cultural emphasis of inculturation hermeneutics and the racial-economic-political emphasis of liberation hermeneutics, though the former is predominant. Because of the predominance of a religio-cultural emphasis in African feminist hermeneutics, it could be argued that much of this work is really a form of inculturation hermeneutics. However, African feminist hermeneutics usually shares the attitude of suspicion towards the biblical text of African liberation hermeneutics. Most importantly, African feminist hermeneutics, like African liberation hermeneutics, insists on a related structured and systematic analysis of both the African context and the biblical text. Its distinctive feature is the focus on gender and the systemic nature of patriarchy (Okure, 1993).

A methodological innovation in some African feminist hermeneutics has been its use of literary exegetical modes of analysis of the biblical text. The predominant exegetical modes of analysis of both African inculturation and liberation hermeneutics have been socio-historical, with only a few voices advocating and using literary modes of exegesis (West, 1995). In contrast, African feminist hermeneutics has been quite receptive to literary modes of interpretation (Nadar, 2001).

In sum, African feminist hermeneutics shares elements with both inculturation and liberation hermeneutics. African feminist hermeneutics straddles both, sharing all the common features, but tending towards inculturation hermeneutics in its focus on religion and culture and its eclectic array of sociological analytical tools, and tending towards liberation hermeneutics in its suspicion of the (patriarchal) ideology of the text.

Postcolonial hermeneutics

African biblical hermeneutics, whether tending towards inculturation or liberation or feminist trajectories in its ideo-theological orientation, has always been resolutely situated over against missionary–colonial imperialism

(West, 2005). So it is strange that African biblical scholarship has been slow to engage explicitly with emergent forms of postcolonial hermeneutics (see Sugirtharajah, 1998). However, as with all forms of academic African biblical hermeneutics, the wider world of biblical scholarship has offered African biblical scholarship potentially useful resources that it can refashion to fit to African contexts.

It is from within African feminist hermeneutics that the most sustained engagement with postcolonial hermeneutics has come (Dube, 2000; Nzimande, 2008). Like other forms of African biblical hermeneutics, postcolonial biblical hermeneutics has its starting point in the realities of ordinary Africans. For these people the Bible has become an African book, but an African book 'that will always be linked to and remembered for its role in facilitating European imperialism' (Dube, 2000: 3). The complicity of the Bible with European imperialism is explicit and central to the ideo-theological orientation of African postcolonial biblical hermeneutics. What the other forms of African biblical hermeneutics do not address in sufficient detail is the question of 'why the biblical text, its readers, and its institutions are instruments of imperialism' (Dube, 2000: 6). This is the first part of the task of postcolonial hermeneutics.

Together with African liberation and feminist hermeneutics, postcolonial hermeneutics is deeply suspicious of the Bible's own imperial charter (Dube, 2000: 10). In other words, the kinds of imperial attitudes and practices performed by missionaries and colonial forces are related to the imperial tendencies of the biblical texts themselves (Dube, 2000: 15). The next crucial question, therefore, is how postcolonial African subjects should read the texts that have been instrumental to the establishment of colonialism in their contexts (Dube, 2000: 16). So the second part of postcolonial hermeneutics is to read the Bible for decolonization.

Musa Dube argues that reading for decolonization must follow the logic of imperialism, understanding its grammar and then reading against it. This includes reading against the geography of biblical and Western imperial expansionism, reading against the racializing potential of the biblical text (expressed in ethnic terms) and the racial politics of Western imperial ideology, reading against the sanctioning of unequal power relations in biblical texts and colonial projects, reading against the universalizing tendencies of both the Bible and Western imperialism, and reading against the suppression of the female presence in the Bible and imperial project (Dube, 2000: 16–21).

While the Bible can and must be read for decolonization, it is not the only resource. Among the resources for reading for decolonization are the very languages and literatures (including the oral) that were denigrated and supplanted by the Bible and Western imperialism (Dube, 2000: 49). However, African postcolonial hermeneutics recognizes that the vast literature 'born from the encounter with imperialist forces' is itself 'partly shaped by the textual forms of their imperial counterparts' (Dube, 2000: 50-1). African resources, particularly those forged in resistance to imperialism, partake in a form of hybridity (Dube, 2000: 122), in which something new and vital is constructed from the encounter with colonialism. One of the most significant contributions of African postcolonial hermeneutics is this recognition that African postcolonial interpretation (like African postcolonial identity) is itself partially constituted by colonialism. Instead of denying this by claiming an authentically African interpretation, postcolonial interpretation embraces the multiplicity of identities and differences that constitute the postcolonial African context, but always with a view to harnessing these hybrid resources for decolonization.

While all forms of African biblical hermeneutics, whether inculturation, liberation, feminist, or postcolonial, are committed to identifying and recovering African interpretive resources, they also engage critically with the pre-colonial African heritage. African postcolonial hermeneutics is no exception, recovering but also questioning, for example, the power of pre-colonial African queens (Nzimande, 2008).

In sum, in its present form, African postcolonial hermeneutics shares much in common with the ideo-theological orientations of liberation and feminist hermeneutics, but also shares elements of the ideo-theological orientation of inculturation hermeneutics.

Before concluding this discussion of the appropriation pole, three other elements which cross-cut and contribute to the ideo-theological orientations of academic African biblical interpretation deserve our attention. These are the ecclesio-theological heritage of the missionaries, the role of ordinary non-academic African interpreters of the Bible, and the specific contextual struggles and issues of African life.

Ecclesio-theological missionary heritage

In his detailed study of the role of religion in the making of the Yoruba people of West Africa, J. D. Y. Peel reminds us of the enduring contribution of the world religions (specifically Christianity and Islam) in any postcolonial context. These are 'great vehicles of trans-historical memory' which are 'ceaselessly re-activated in the consciousness of their adherents' (Peel, 2000: 9). Peel cautions that while we must of course ground African Christianity and Islam in African history, we must not neglect the specific ways in which they also belong to Christian or Muslim stories (Peel, 2000: 9). The Christian narrative, Peel reminds us, has its own power. However, while there are cases in which African postcolonial Christianity has had almost no influence from Western missionary Christianity, most African Christianities have strong and enduring missionary ecclesio-theological memories. In other words, besides the Bible there are almost always residual, at least, missionary ecclesio-theological influences in all four forms of African biblical hermeneutics.

Each of the many missionary movements that brought the Bible, Christianity and colonialism to Africa had its own ecclesio-theological emphasis.

The grand narrative of missionary Christianity – 'the religious project which brought the missionaries in the first place' (Peel, 2000: 4) – has an enduring impact in African biblical interpretation. The clearest cases are found in the Catholic and the evangelical missionary ecclesio-theological legacies and the more recent impact of Pentecostal and charismatic Christianities.

Each of the four primary forms of African biblical hermeneutics is impacted by elements of the missionary ecclesio-theological legacy. However, there are correlations between particular ecclesio-theological traditions and particular forms of biblical hermeneutics. Those biblical scholars from evangelical ecclesio-theological traditions, for example, tend to work mainly within inculturation hermeneutics because of its attitude of trust towards the Bible. Yet this is not without its tensions for those who want to recover aspects of their culture denigrated and denied by missionary Christianity. In sum, the ecclesio-theological heritage of missionary Christianities influences and contributes to the ideo-theological orientations of African biblical hermeneutics.

Non-academic African interpreters

Being rooted in African realities, African biblical hermeneutics is accountable to ordinary African interpreters of the Bible. This includes allowing ordinary African interpreters partially to constitute the kind of discipline African biblical scholarship is (Okure, 1993: 77). They do this in a variety of ways. For example, ordinary African interpreters are, in part, the implied readers of African biblical scholarship. They constantly call on African biblical scholars to share their resources with them in order to address their contextual needs. They also share their local and indigenous interpretive resources with biblical scholarship, thereby participating with African biblical scholarship in the interpretation of biblical texts.

The African biblical scholar is never allowed to settle in the academy alone; there is a constant call from ordinary African interpreters for African biblical scholars to engage with them and their realities. In sum, alongside the contribution of the text and the context (as engaged by the biblical scholar), the presence of ordinary African interpreters and their concerns shapes the ideo-theological orientation of African biblical hermeneutics.

African issues

While a great diversity of African issues are brought to bear on African biblical hermeneutics, there are moments when particular issues dominate the landscape, forcing African biblical scholars to engage with these realities alongside the other contextual features they may want to engage with. One example is the emergence of African feminist hermeneutics in response to gender issues and the grip of patriarchy on the African continent. More recently, the continental crisis of HIV & AIDS has summoned all four major forms of African biblical hermeneutics to respond (see for example Dube and Kanyoro, 2004; West and Zengele, 2004). Whether the advent of HIV & AIDS will give rise to a new form of African biblical hermeneutics remains to be seen; for the present, the forms we have are both responding to and being shaped by the epidemic. HIV & AIDS pose pertinent challenges to the ideo-theological orientation of each, demanding responses from both text and context.

All of the above contribute to and constitute the third pole of African biblical interpretation – appropriation. I have focused on this pole precisely because it is so often assumed to be self-evident and because this pole plays a pivotal part in how the dialogue between text and context is mediated. Traditionally, most of the attention in describing and analysing African biblical interpretation goes to the other two poles – the text and the context. However, because African biblical interpretation almost always brings these two poles into conversation, the question of how this is done is paramount. Having interrogated 'the how', we can now turn to the other more familiar poles of African biblical interpretation.

❋ The text

Most attention in African biblical interpretation focuses on the biblical text and the methodologies used to exegete it. African biblical scholarship, like Western biblical scholarship, insists on distantiation. The Bible is a collection of ancient texts, each produced in particular socio-historical contexts, and the task of biblical scholarship is 'to hear' the distinctive, ancient voice of the text within its own socio-historical context. Before the text can be brought into dialogue with the context, it must be given its own voice. Biblical interpreters therefore seek to locate the text historically, using historical-critical tools, and then situate the historical text sociologically, within a particular social context, using sociological tools. While Mosala, as we have seen, insists on particular sociological tools (historical-materialist sociology), most African biblical scholars are more eclectic, using a whole range of sociological tools.

Some African scholars, though a minority, have used literary tools instead of historical-critical and sociological tools. They prefer to locate the text within its linguistic, literary or canonical contexts. The purpose, however, is the same – an exegesis of the biblical text, allowing it to speak with its own voice.

However, the ideo-theological orientation of the biblical interpreter influences what it is in the text that is the focal point of historical-critical, sociological and/or literary analysis. Inculturation hermeneutics concentrates on the religio-cultural dimensions of the biblical text, liberation hermeneutics on the socio-economic dimensions, feminist hermeneutics on the gender dimensions, and postcolonial on the imperial dimensions.

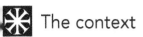 # The context

While Western forms of biblical interpretation have tended to hide or omit the contemporary context of the biblical interpreter, African biblical interpretation is overt about the context from which and for which the biblical text is interpreted. African biblical scholarship tries to be as thorough in its analysis of the details of African contexts as it has been about the details of the biblical text, using a whole array of historical and sociological tools.

However, here too the ideo-theological orientation of the biblical interpreter influences what it is in the context that is the focal point of analysis. Inculturation hermeneutics concentrates on the religio-cultural dimensions of the context, liberation hermeneutics on the socio-economic dimensions, feminist hermeneutics on the gender dimensions, and postcolonial on the colonial and neocolonial dimensions.

 # Conclusion

Clearly African biblical hermeneutics is a complex process involving three poles: text, context and appropriation. Though each can be analysed separately, they continually reconstitute each other. The ideo-theological orientation of appropriation is itself partially constituted by the contextual features of a particular African context, just as it is by the regular reading of the Scriptures. And the ideo-theological orientation influences both what becomes the focus of analysis within the biblical text and the African context and how they are brought into dialogue.

 # STUDY QUESTIONS

1 What are the three key elements of African biblical hermeneutics?

2 What are some of the main differences between Western biblical hermeneutics and African biblical hermeneutics?

3 What are the four main types of ideo-theological orientation in African biblical hermeneutics? Summarize the key characteristics of each type.

4 In what ways does one's ecclesio-theological missionary heritage shape African biblical interpretation?

5 What form of ideo-theological orientation do you prefer? Why?

Part 2

Contemporary issues in African theology

4

'The Synod of Hope' at a time of crisis in Africa

John Mary Waliggo

 Abstract

With candour and insight, John Mary Waliggo critiques the African Synod held in Rome in 1994. Drawing upon a phrase from the synod fathers' concluding message, 'the Synod of Hope', Waliggo reviews the process and the content of the synod to assess whether or not this title is apt. His criticism focuses largely on the preparation, composition and methodology of the synod. He then concentrates on the concluding message, summarizing its achievements and outlining ten indications of hope. In the process, Waliggo offers a perceptive portrait of the contemporary Catholic Church in Africa, its progress and its pointed challenges in implementing the synod.

 Introduction

The Special Assembly for Africa of the Synod of Bishops met in Rome from 10 April to 8 May 1994. In their concluding message, the synod fathers referred to their encounter as 'the Synod of Hope'. Were they too optimistic of what they had achieved or were they being realistic? In using the word 'hope', were they referring to the Church in Africa, to the African continent as a whole, or to both? And what exactly did they mean by that?

The present chapter is somewhat dated for two reasons. First, John Mary Walig̶ had agreed to write a chapter for this volume, 'African theologies of liberation justice', but unfortunately he died before he was able to do so. Second, for th₣ years of his life, Waliggo was so engaged in matters of national governance did not publish as much academically that could be drawn on for republicat⸱ Although the Second African Synod took place in October 2009, addres⸱ of the issues raised in this chapter, Waliggo's reflections remain valual⸱ incisive analysis of the challenges and contributions of the Catholic Ch₣ during the period described.

In the opinion of some participants and observers, the synod process had shortcomings. I want to touch on these areas of disappointment in order to show that what was achieved by the synod can be transformed into liberative action only if these shortcomings are overcome. My evaluation touches on the preparation of the synod, its composition, methodology, and its concluding message, including its achievements and indications of hope.

✳ Preparation

It must be emphasized that the preparation of the synod was inadequate, primarily because it failed to actively involve the very people who make up the Church in Africa – the laity. Yet the impact of the synod depends on their participation. The people of God includes all the baptized and all men and women in society. If the family is the most basic unit of the Church (indeed, the domestic Church), the entire process should have begun there and moved upwards to the diocesan, national, regional and continental levels.

The Catholic Church takes pride, and legitimately so, in the fact that it has an outstanding organizational structure. But we fail miserably when we try to utilize it fully for a process like the synod. The African Synod praised thousands of catechists for their commitment, yet left them out. It also ignored numerous apostolic movements of the laity and the many Catholic intellectuals and professionals. Women, in their various movements and associations, were not listened to. Youth, millions of children, workers, rural farmers, the urban poor, refugees, the sick, the old – none were helped to voice their real concerns in their own words and sentiments. Neither were the priests, as individuals or through their associations, nor the many indigenous religious congregations empowered to speak their deep-felt sentiments and views.

The Church exists in society. The best way to discover its true image is to involve society in its self-evaluation and self-criticism. Christians of other denominations, Muslims, members of other religious bodies and the traditionalists have much to offer in evaluating the Church's presence in Africa. Nowhere were any of these actively involved in the process. Even political leaders and politicians, economic leaders and business people, cultural leaders and grass-roots communities would have had a lot to offer on the theme of evangelization chosen by the pope. But they were not asked.

Ultimately, at its heart the failure was ecclesiological. Deep down, many of us still continue to define the Church in terms of the clergy. The bishop and the clergy become the local church, especially in terms of decision-making. This may be why many dioceses in Africa have so far resisted holding fully representative diocesan synods. These stumbling blocks must be removed as African Catholics begin to implement the synod. We must change from a clerical notion of Church to an understanding of Church as a communion, a people of God in which every member has both rights and duties and is entitled to full respect and involvement in what goes on in the Church. Indeed, there is genuine need to develop an ecclesiology of communion in the true African sense. We need to focus on democratization, consultation and deliberations within the Church to strengthen its structures and institutions.

 ## Composition of the synod

In both Church and society today, there is general support for strategies which include rather than exclude any section of community, and which aspire to empower those marginalized to speak for themselves rather than always be spoken for. Unfortunately, the synod did not make use of such strategies. Indeed, this was a bishops' synod. That is accepted. But even a bishops' synod can make ample room for including other sections. As we know, the synod was composed of bishop delegates from the national Episcopal conferences of Africa and Madagascar, some theologians, the heads of the Roman Curia as well as some of its members, some representatives from continental and regional conferences outside Africa, several superiors general of missionary congregations working in Africa, a few lay African Christian observers, and at least five representatives of the All Africa Conference of Churches.

Having excluded the largest majority of the African laity from participating in the preparatory stage, the synod should have been more sensitive to their representation within its deliberations, even as mere observers. The few lay observers who were invited went to the synod in their private and individual capacity. You wonder what their presence added to the synod and what message they took back to their fellows in the African laity. Certainly, with a meaningful, effective representation, African catechists, lay men and women, youth, intellectuals and professionals, indigenous congregations of women and men, and so forth, could have contributed significantly to the synod's understanding of the Church-as-family. Again, the theology of communion, of Church as people of God, and of Church-as-family must be visible in all that the Church does and plans. This is a major challenge for us.

 ## The methodology

The methodology for any major endeavour, such as the African Synod, is as important as the content itself. The methodology greatly affects the content and the outcome. As an observer from outside the synod, I need only indicate a few aspects of the methodology that I found lacking.

First, a crucial aspect that was neglected in the preparation of the African Synod was a serious and scientific social analysis of the African Church and African society. This was needed in order to evaluate critically the pastoral methods used and the areas of success and failure in evangelization. Such an analysis would have examined the social and cultural milieu in which evangelization has been taking place, the process of conversion, the interaction, the response, the spirituality and the maturity of African Christians. Such a study should have yielded relevant and significant themes for the synod.

A similar study of African society could have revealed the main areas for deeper evangelization and the nature of dialogue and relationship demanded today of the Church in Africa. Such studies would have provided a rich historical and contextual background for the synod. Even if this process of social analysis was lacking in the preparation, it is not too late to undertake it in order to confront the real issues of Church and society during the implementation phase.

Second, on a practical note: most bishop delegates came with prepared, written interventions. Yet these were not available before the synod. Therefore the first two weeks were spent listening to these interventions, which were often unnecessarily repetitive. Thus the time could have been spent more productively with better logistical planning.

Third, the identification of only five sub-themes under that all-embracing theme of evangelization tended to stifle free discussion in other areas that are equally important and relevant. Evangelization certainly includes the five sub-themes outlined: proclamation (*kerygma*), service (*diakonia*), witness (*marturia*), worship (*leiturgia*), and building community and solidarity (*koinonia*). But evangelization should be considered in relation to all human dimensions: religious and spiritual, moral and ethical, cultural and educational, political and economic, physical and environmental. Evangelization extends from each individual person to the family, community, nation and the global human family. Evangelization includes the message, the pastoral methods, the animating theologies, the interaction, the special situations and the vision for the future. Evangelization means concrete plans and strategies to share the good news with children, youth, adults, men and women, the old, the sick, workers and unemployed, leaders and public servants, refugees and displaced people, the poor, prisoners, rural farmers, and the handicapped and disabled. In a word, evangelization is all-encompassing. To reduce it to five sub-themes without first allowing a free and general discussion of the general theme certainly affected the content and conclusions of the synod itself.

Fourth, the one-month schedule was restrictive for such a unique meeting of such importance. Since this was the first synod in two thousand years of evangelization to deal with the Church in Africa, it would have been more prudent to allow more time for wider discussion and, above all, to develop an adequate theology to support the rich pastoral sharing.

Finally, a synod of this nature and at this time did not need to be as secretive and closed in as it was. One of the sub-themes was the means of social communication. Having realized the importance of media in our present world, the synod should have been more sensitive to the media. It also should have been more open and hospitable, in keeping with African cultural values, to the groups of Africans and Africanists who were not part of the synodal assembly, yet who gathered in Rome to support this important event. The process and theology of inculturation that was unanimously called for by the synod fathers includes promoting positive societal values, which include support groups, in all activities carried out by church leaders. It is only when we become a secretive, closed-in church that we fear the contributions of well-intended supportive groups. As we embark on implementing the synod, it is necessary to develop attitudes that appreciate pluralism and the unique contribution of every group.

 # The concluding message of the synod: indications of hope

Having talked to several synod fathers and studied their concluding message, it is my view that it is both correct and appropriate to call this encounter 'the Synod of Hope'. I shall identify ten topics that clearly show that the African Church is moving forward. Hope and optimism are realistic if the African Church plans carefully for the implementation of the synod, if we develop theologically what has been provided and then translate it into liberative pastoral action.

The first achievement of the synod, which was shared by almost every delegate, was the atmosphere of friendliness and freedom of expression that dominated the synod. Bishops got to know one another. They shared ideas and experiences, and gradually came to discover they had a lot in common. Geographical and linguistic barriers began to disappear, revealing a strong unity of purpose for the common task.

Unlike Vatican II, the African Synod did not witness a sharp division between 'progressives' and 'conservatives'. The delegates moved rather toward an African sense of consensus in which the middle position provided a unifying element. They had not come to introduce innovations in the Church, but neither did they seem to feel it was desirable to oppose the liberative movement of Vatican II and post-Vatican II. Their mission was to emphasize those elements in the universal teaching of the Church that are most urgently needed by the Church in Africa. Thus, the synod was pastoral in its orientation and content. The delegates were pleased with their achievements, and united in purpose to implement the synod. This in itself was no mean achievement. Their unity of purpose can become a powerful incentive for African theologians and pastoral agents.

A second and more tangible achievement is contained in the concluding message of the synod. Drawing from this document, I will highlight ten contributions of the synod.

Inculturation

After talking about inculturation for the last forty years, after developing several theologies of inculturation and initiating several experiments in inculturation, the synod fathers gave clear and full support to the process and theology of inculturation. Evangelization consists of proclamation and inculturation, they said. The domain of inculturation 'is the entire Christian life'. The synod fathers strongly recommended dialogue with African traditional religion and with African cultural values and the guardians of those values.

From now on, the movement and process of inculturation have official approval and support. Those few bishops, members of the clergy and pastoral agents who, in the name of orthodoxy and defence of the faith, have been either opposed or indifferent to the movement now need to undergo a fundamental *metanoia*, a conversion, to join the consensus of the African Synod. African theologians and the many non-Africans who have been highly suspicious of the inculturation movement, alleging false motives to it, need a fundamental change in their attitudes. Those African Christians, especially among the elite and lay leaders, who prefer the status quo need to seriously rethink their position; they must learn to view Christianity as a message of life that changes in order to be relevant to all times, cultures and peoples. Those African theologians who have restricted inculturation to liturgy and other externals need the humility to accept that all aspects of Christian life must be inculturated. This enormous task must be undertaken in solidarity with one another.

Commitment to justice and peace

The themes of justice and peace, human rights and reconciliation, democratization and stability were undoubtedly most highlighted at the synod. It is important to remember the context of the synod: the tragedy in Rwanda happened just before it began, and it continued throughout the month of the synod. None of the bishops from Rwanda managed to attend the synod. With this sad context in mind, the delegates gave a lot of time and thought to justice and peace in Africa. Bishops fully recognized the great omission of the African Church:

> We have not always done what we could in order to form the laity for life in society, to a Christian vision of politics and economics. A protracted absence of the lay faithful from this field has led them to believe that the faith has nothing to do with politics. (Browne, 1996: 79)

This admission has vital importance. If the politics and economics of Africa are to change fundamentally, it is necessary to realize what has not yet been accomplished and to make urgent plans to rectify the situation. The bishops called on all Christians without exception to educate themselves on democracy. A lay Christian who participates in the democratic process becomes the sign of a Church that promotes justice and peace.

To achieve peace, we are called to work for justice, for there cannot be genuine peace without justice. 'Democracy should become one of the principal routes along which the Church travels together with the people . . . There is need for prophets for our times, and the whole Church should become prophetic' (Browne, 1996: 79). If these powerful statements are translated into action, they will have the power to transform the Church and society in Africa.

In the past, it was not easy to know or even guess whether African church leaders wanted 'prophets' in their communities. To challenge the Church in Africa to be prophetic has often been interpreted as an unwarranted challenge of its leadership. Conformity and uniformity seemed to be the only accepted norms, even in Africa's Catholic universities. Nonetheless, the synod has committed the Church in Africa to travel with the people along the road of democracy. This means the Church itself should become more democratic as an example of democratization.

The synod clearly rejected the inferiority complex that has been forced on the African Black people, the injustice of the North to the South, the Northern world view that maintains a structural inequality, the unjust terms of trade, the unjust price system, the massive sale of arms to Africa so that Africans may kill one another, and the unjust external debt that oppresses Africa and its people. This was a powerful message indeed, especially coming from the African bishops who in the past have been known to be timid in their condemnation of the North. Such a message is a good starting point for genuine dialogue with the North, for both Church and society.

The message to African political leaders, the military, and all those who embezzle public funds and carry out institutionalized corruption can be used to effectively challenge any future dictator in Africa. The synod's support to the current democratization process in Africa and to its consolidation should arouse every Christian and African of goodwill to play his or her active part. As a continent we must say No to war, oppression, racism, ethnic rivalry, inferiority complex, injustices, dictatorship and corruption.

Commitment to dialogue and ecumenism

Vatican II was based on a very strong commitment to ecumenism, religious dialogue and cooperation. Forty years after Vatican II, the Church in Africa has not progressed enough in this area. Fundamentalism has taken over in many churches, including the Catholic Church in Africa. Relations with Muslims have not been friendly, especially since the birth of Islamic fundamentalism in the Sudan and Nigeria and in most of the countries in North Africa. This is part of our context. The synod called for dialogue with African traditional religion, with the Coptic churches of Egypt and Ethiopia, the Anglican Church, the Protestant churches, the Muslims, and members of other religions. There was no specific mention of the thousands of African indigenous churches or the breakaway churches from the Catholic communion.

Ecumenism and religious dialogue have faced many obstacles in Africa because the introducers of the various religious traditions have often been fundamentalist in approach. In wanting to emphasize the difference between one tradition and another, they stressed the aspects that divide rather than those that unite. Poorly educated pastoral agents may fear the challenge and exposure to ecumenism and sincere religious dialogue. The economic poverty of the continent has also caused some religious traditions to oppose dialogue for fear of losing the little they have. The 'politics of religion' has also been a hindrance to dialogue, as some religions feel favoured and others discriminated against by the political system.

Yet without a culture of religious pluralism and peaceful coexistence, Africa can never be stable. Hopefully, this initial challenge of the bishops will be developed in the final text so that the Church in Africa can reflect on these issues and take the necessary action.

Church-as-family

The synod messages show clearly that the theme of Church-as-family was central to the bishops' thinking. The concept is repeated several times to underscore its importance and it is made clear that the Church-as-family must always be at the service of the entire community in Africa. African theologians should reflect on this theme. The bishops could have chosen the well-developed Vatican II concept, the Church as a communion or as people of God; they purposely chose Church-as-family. It would be interesting to learn how that theme gathered such overwhelming support.

Obviously, the bishops wanted to use the African family as a model or the model for being and living Church. This model includes everyone, baptized and non-baptized. It is the basis of unity and solidarity because it means sharing roles and involving every member. It emphasizes small communities and fits the ecclesiologies developed by several African theologians based on the African family, clan and tribe. Some theologians have gone further to develop the model of African blood brotherhood (and sisterhood). As the bishops pointed out, they owed much to African theological reflections on this point.

However, this does not hide the fact that the model of Church-as-family has some very fundamental problems that need clarification, if it is to serve the purpose for which it is recommended. First, we need to be clear about the type of family being envisaged. Is it the African traditional family, or the contemporary one? In any case, the African family, whether traditional or contemporary, is still very hierarchical. The father figure is still much feared by the other members of the family. The wife is not yet given full rights of equality, and for this reason the women's movement in Africa is very powerful. The rights of children are only beginning to be realized and respected. Therefore, when the Church-as-family model is recommended, it is important to agree that this does not mean any of the families that are not yet fully liberated. We must create a vision of an African family where equality is guaranteed, clear sharing of responsibility is accepted, the clear option for the disadvantaged members is made, and deadly tensions are eliminated.

The theology of Church-as-family is a double-edged sword. It can be profit- ably used but it may also lead to benign paternalism. We must be careful not to end up again with a pyramid structure of the Church instead of the circular one of communion. African theologians must take on the challenge of this theme and show how it can be used positively to create a new understanding of the African Church and society.

Commitment to theological research and the role of African theologians

One of the positive elements in the message is the bishops' clear recognition of the role of the African theologians and of theological research. African theologians were praised for their contribution to evangelization:

> The Synod knows that without the conscientious and devoted exercise of your function something essential would be lacking. The Synod expresses its gratitude and its encouragement to you to continue working with your distinctive role certainly, but in communion with your pastors. (Browne, 1996: 84)

The bishops acknowledged the importance of doing theology and theologi- cal research. They called on all major seminaries and higher institutions of learning to define with vigour and transmit effectively 'our cultures in all that they have that is viable and transmissible, being always careful to find the possible meeting points with other cultures' (Browne, 1996: 83).

It would be most useful to know how the bishops reached this consensus, given the fact that not a few of them have viewed African theologians with some suspicion in the past. African theologians had requested the synod, through the powerful words of Jean-Marc Éla, to recognize their service as a distinctive ministry within the Church. It is now a challenge to all of us to respond to the call, beginning with the very text of the bishops.

Active participation of the laity

The theology of active lay participation and of the family as the domestic Church obviously influenced the bishops. The United Nations Conference on the Family that was about to take place in Cairo (September 1994) also greatly influenced what the bishops had to say on family values. They agreed that the African Christian family should be evangelizing, mature in faith, educative of all its members, and serve as the active living cell of the local church. They challenged the laity to evangelize all strata of society and especially the political and economic sectors. The synod expressed the need for 'holy' politicians and political leaders. In sum, the laity must find its legitimate role in the Church-as-family and fill it.

Relevant formation of pastoral agents

The challenges of the synod can only be realized if the future and present pastoral agents are fully and properly trained. There is need to rethink the syllabi of our institutions to form pastoral agents. Inculturation, justice and peace, genuine dialogue and ecumenism, and effective methods of communication ought to be treated as core issues for serious study and reflection rather than as appendices.

Church support for liberation of women

The synod emphasized the liberation and support of all the formerly marginalized groups: women, youth, the poor, the sick, those with HIV & AIDS, refugees and displaced people. There was a greater emphasis, however, on women. The oppression of and discrimination against women were identified as one

> of the major forms of the structure of sin engulfing our African societies. To educate a woman is to educate a people. Your bishops and all those who participated in this holy synod are determined to take every measure to see your dignity fully respected. (Browne, 1996: 85)

These were powerful words, and if I were an African woman, I would certainly test my local church to see how serious it is in translating these words into real liberative action! One thing is clear: African women can look to the Church for support in their struggle for equality and equal opportunities. They can demand their distinctive roles in the Church and they can powerfully articulate their aspirations in Church and society. Should any church leader let them down, they should know it is the individual and not the Church as a whole that has done so.

Optimism for the future of Africa

Despite the many sad predictions for Africa and the present catastrophes in some parts of the continent, the bishops were optimistic for the future. This optimism is meant to challenge us to do whatever we can to save Africa, to liberate Africa, to develop Africa and love it.

An exemplary Church

It took courage for the bishops to fully recognize publicly that the African Church needs to make a critical examination of conscience. Justice and respect for human rights have sometimes been lacking within its internal structures, institutions and decisions. If the Church gives witness to justice, she recognizes that whoever dares to speak to others about justice should also strive to be just in their eyes. It is therefore necessary to examine with care the procedures, the possessions, and the lifestyle of the Church.

 ## Conclusion

In conclusion I cannot help asking the following questions:

- **Was the synod in Rome the climax** of the entire process or simply one of the important stages?
- **Will the Church in Africa establish an efficient organization** to widely discuss the outcome of the synod, or will it continue its usual way as it did during the preparatory stage?
- **Will there be a real commitment by all church leaders in Africa** to implement the message or are we to read beautiful words that will remain on paper?
- **Above all, will the African Church enjoy the freedom it needs to develop its unique identity** and contribute richly to the world Church?

It is too early to respond adequately to any of these questions, but the sooner those in the African Church consider them the better. Fearlessly, let us confront the challenges presented and begin a new evangelization of African society.

 ## STUDY QUESTIONS

1 In the first section of the chapter, Waliggo examines the preparation of the African Synod and concludes, 'We must change from a clerical notion of Church to an understanding of Church as a communion.' Explain the contrast between these two ecclesiologies, or understandings of Church. Why did Waliggo challenge the synod in this way?

2 What are Waliggo's main concerns about the methodology of the synod? On the basis of his critique, outline specific recommendations for the Church to improve in its future meetings, whether at the synodal or diocesan levels.

3 Summarize in your own words the ten indications of hope that Waliggo finds in the concluding message of the synod. On the basis of your experience of the Church in Africa (or elsewhere), to what extent do you share in these aspects of hope? Explain your answer.

5

Contributions and challenges of the African Instituted Churches in developing African theology

Thomas Oduro

 Abstract

The need and importance of putting Christian theology in African contexts has been a bone of contention among many African scholars and certain African Christian communities. African Instituted Churches (AICs) do not have many scholars to join the continental conversation, yet they have been at the forefront of developing African theology that is suitable, relevant and meaningful to African contexts while remaining faithful to the Bible. This chapter argues that the popularity and growth of the AICs cannot be divorced from their desire to contextualize theology. The chapter discusses the struggles and achievements of AICs in developing African theology without any conventional knowledge of formulating theology. It also highlights the development of an African theology of child-naming in the Church of the Lord (Brotherhood), an AIC in Ghana.

 Introduction

African Instituted Churches (AICs) have been defined as:

> congregations and or denominations (with or without any historical reference to the West) planted, led, administered, supported, propagated, motivated, [and] funded by Africans for the purpose of proclaiming the Gospel of Jesus Christ and worshipping the Triune God in the context and world-view of Africa and Africans. (Oduro, 2004: 8–9)

This definition, in a broader sense, takes into consideration Protestant churches that were not planted in Africa by Western missionaries. In a narrow sense, however, it excludes churches planted in Africa whose liturgies and practices are akin to Western churches. Churches that do not promote African personality are similarly not included in this genre.

The growth and impact of AICs in African Christianity have been tremendous. In fact it is generally believed that the immense growth of Christianity on the African continent cannot be recounted without taking into cognizance the growth and contributions of the AICs. Some scholars, while acclaiming the growth of the AICs over the mainline churches in Africa, claim that Pentecostal/charismatic churches have overtaken the AICs in popularity (Jenkins, 2002: 68–9). However, such claims are highly debatable for several reasons: the absence of current clear-cut statistics of the growth of African Christianity; the urban-centredness of the Pentecostal/charismatic churches vis-à-vis the rural-centredness and house-church status of many AICs; Western concepts of growth as against African concepts of growth; and other factors that go beyond the purpose of this chapter. The very fact that the AICs are still called 'mushrooming churches' provides veritable indication that they are still growing at a fast rate and, as a result, their growth is difficult to quantify.

Gone are the days when Christianity was ridiculed in Africa as 'the white man's religion' due to the foreign nature of some of the liturgies and practices of Christianity. Without deliberate planning, the AICs actually launched and championed the reformation of African Christianity in the twentieth century. This has changed the face and quality of Christianity in Africa. Consequently, there is now a thin line between the AICs and other Christian communities in terms of worship and liturgy. The following description of a worship service in an Anglican Church at Cape Coast, Ghana, clearly exemplifies the success and influence of these reforms:

> In the middle of the service a special collection was taken. The music which accompanied it consisted of newer African compositions, originally emanating from the African Independent Churches (AICs). There was much enthusiastic communal singing and dancing. The idiom of music was very much African, it gripped and grabbed the congregation each and all and none looked excluded. Joy was evident and palpable and, if we may add an interpretive word, there was every sign of the Spirit moving people. The atmosphere was electric, much different from what it had been as the worshippers were going through inherited English liturgy. (Pobee and Ositelu, 1998: 1)

AICs have become indispensable in African Christianity. Many scholars have acknowledged the significance of the AICs and described them in apt terms such as 'the signature tune of African Christianity' (Sanneh, 1989: 109), and a group of churches 'indicating the trend and direction of African Christianity' (Bediako, 1995: 113). Furthermore, the AICs' missionary zeal is not limited to Africa; they can also be found in many parts of the world. For instance, in 2001, the Church of Jesus Christ on Earth through the Prophet Simon Kimbangu, an AIC with headquarters at Nkamba, in the Democratic Republic of Congo, claimed to have congregations in the Republic of Congo, Angola, Gabon, Central African Republic, Zambia, Zimbabwe, Rwanda, Burundi, South Africa, Nigeria, Madagascar, Spain, Portugal, France, Belgium, Switzerland and England. Therefore, theologians have stated emphatically that the AICs are vital to African and world Christianity. John Pobee and Gabriel Ositelu conclude: 'There is no way we can talk of world Christianity, much less Christianity in Africa, without taking account of this genre of AICs' (Pobee and Ositelu, 1998: 5).

Theological distinctives of the AICs

What has created this popularity and influence of the AICs over other Christian communities in Africa and elsewhere? Many reasons are offered. Dedji Ayegboyin and Ademola Ishola list the following as some of the main characteristics of AICs with widespread appeal: emphasis on prayer, emphasis on the spiritual, interest in divine healing, attention to women, affection for freer forms of worship, stress on African world views, and dedication to evangelism and revival (Ayegboyin and Ishola, 1997: 27–34). While these factors cannot be doubted, we must note that it is not simply these emphases that attract people to the AICs. Rather, it is the African nuances, or interpretations and feelings, which shape these factors in the context of Christian theology and practice. In other words, it is the way these factors take on African colouring that makes them so appealing across the continent and beyond.

Let us take healing as an example, since scholars generally consider it to be a major characteristic of AICs:

> Indeed, sickness is by far the most common reason which people give for attending AICs. Testimonies of healing, soundness and miracles are heard from many about their answered prayers. In quite a number of cases those concerned claim that they first went to the hospitals, and or consulted traditional healers. They then resorted to an indigenous church when the foreign physicians and herbalists failed them. (Ayegboyin and Ishola, 1997: 29)

Similarly, Christian Baëta captured the following account from an insider's point of view:

> At an evening prayer meeting of this Church [Musama Disco Christo Church] in a small provincial town, the catechist began his address as follows: 'We are all in this Church because we have found healing here. But for this Church the great majority of us here assembled would not be alive today. This is the reason why we are here: is that not so?' To that question came from the congregation as answer, a unanimous and most decided 'Yes'. (Baëta, 1962: 54)

Healing in most AICs has been interpreted and applied according to indigenous world views and practices within African contexts. Prior to the success of the reformation of African Christianity, when African Christians fell sick and went to Western mission-planted churches, they were generally prayed for and asked to have faith in God. If they became increasingly ill, they were advised to seek medical care from either a hospital or clinic.

The AICs take exception to this kind of approach. In contrast, before prayer is said, those suffering illness are assured of the almighty God's power and readiness to heal. They are also admonished to have faith in Jesus Christ and to trust the healer who is to pray. They are then asked to repent and confess all hidden sins while trusting that God is prepared to forgive and heal. Only after this kind of preparation does prayer take place.

After praying, the healer purportedly declares God's revelation regarding what caused the illness and how it might be cured. The causative factors might be attributed to a charm, gossip about someone, a malevolent spirit, or witchcraft. The curative methods are usually elaborate and include the use of many elements. Allan Anderson mentions blessed water, special tea, walking sticks, ropes and strings, or strips of cloth worn around the body, copper wires, pieces of wood, and a sheet of paper as some of the elements used in healing and protection against evil forces in the Zion Christian Church. This is one of the largest AICs in South Africa with millions of members (Anderson, 2001: 101–2). The use of elements to heal is not peculiar to the Zion Christian Church; it cuts across many AICs. The healing process, at times, does not rest on the healer alone; the entire community of faith also gets involved. For example, sometimes another person might even fast in proxy, or as a substitute for the sick person.

This short description of an AIC healing process is theologically loaded. It reveals the AICs' theology of a holy God who utterly hates sin, yet loves those who put their faith in Jesus Christ. The stress on the causative factors reinforces the view that sickness is not God's original plan for humanity. Rather, an act against the will of God might have caused the disease. The act of asking sick persons to repent and confess sin implies that they might have brought the disease on themselves, thus making it possible for evil spirits to inflict the disease. Having faith in Jesus Christ, and trusting the directives of the healer, is another important theological element of the healing process. Jesus heals, yet he uses those with the gift of healing to effect healing. Thus the brief preparation for healing is equivalent to a whole semester's teaching in a seminary setting on the doctrines of sin, the Fall and its consequences, and salvation.

The use of elements in healing mostly has its roots in African traditional healing methods, although the Bible also records the use of certain elements in healing such as spittle mixed with saliva, water, handkerchiefs and oil. In Africa, sick persons who visit shrines for healing rarely return without being given something to use, either as a curative or protective element. In West Africa, the element could be a kola nut, a feather, herb, chewing stick, shea butter, etc. The practice of using elements to heal suits the empiricist world view of Africans – the use of something that can be seen and touched. The fetish priests and priestesses prescribe these elements when their gods purportedly possess them. Thus, they claim the gods reveal the elements. Similarly, AIC leaders prescribe the use of the elements immediately after prayer. These leaders therefore take their patients from the known to the unknown.

The prescription of the elements, they claim, propels the faith of the users in Jesus Christ rather than the elements themselves. The healing procedure and methods of the AICs, as explained above, are couched in African theology – a theology that is known to the people, which is relevant and meaningful to them. This is why those who are healed in AICs often remain members and invite others to go with their ailments in anticipation of being healed by Jesus Christ.

✳ A theology of child-naming among AICs

AICs have been at the forefront of doing African theology. An example is that of child-naming, an important event in many African communities. Below is a description of an attempt by the Church of the Lord (Brotherhood), an AIC in Ghana, to put child-naming ceremonies into Christian theological perspective.

The Church of the Lord (Brotherhood) is an AIC that defected from the Church of the Lord (Aladura), another AIC, in 1974. The Church of the Lord (Brotherhood) has congregations in Ghana, Belgium, UK, Germany, and France. It is among the largest AICs in Ghana. Even though the following child-naming ceremony practised by the church was inherited from the Church of the Lord (Aladura), Bishop Jonathan Atiemo, bishop of Accra Diocese, claims that the practice has been modified to suit Ghanaian perceptions.

In order to understand the child-naming ceremony, you must place it within the wider context of marriage and family life in Africa. Marriage is an institution that Africans highly honour. It is regarded as 'a requirement of the society, an obligation every man and woman must fulfill, a drama of life in which every man and woman must participate' (Gyekye, 1996: 76). In fact among many African communities, adults who reach marriageable age but refuse to marry are hardly respected by society, no matter how wealthy the man or woman might be. This view is buttressed by a Swahili maxim apparently geared towards bachelors: 'It is better to be married to an old lady than to remain unmarried' (Korem and Abissath, 2004: 76). Consequently, adults who are marriageable often face great pressure to marry without delay.

There are many reasons why Africans cherish marriage but the primary one is procreation. 'In an African view the whole or ultimate purpose of marriage is procreation – to produce children who will continue with the heritage and name of the family, so that the family does not diminish or disappear' (Gyekye, 1996: 83). Therefore, those who refuse to marry are viewed as enemies of society, or as those who do not want to perpetuate the family line. Formerly, infertility was attributed only to wives. Now, with the help of science, many Africans are becoming aware that husbands could as well be the cause of infertility in marriage. Barren wives and husbands with low sperm counts are equally humiliated in many African societies.

Childbirth and naming ceremonies are, therefore, joyous and important events in every African family. Besides legitimizing the marriage, childbirth marks God's deep blessing upon the couple and saves them from being humiliated by society. Giving a name to a child is the ultimate rite that publicly marks the child's entrance into the local community. Names in Africa are significant because they carry special meaning. For example, names might indicate the circumstantial or historical events occurring when the child was born (e.g. day of the week, time of day, conditions of famine or drought), or follow other cultural norms (e.g. naming after the couple's parents or ancestors).

We will now turn our attention to the child-naming ceremony in the Church of the Lord (Brotherhood). According to Bishop Jonathan Atiemo, the church prays for pregnant women any time that members meet to worship. They do so because of the dangers inherent in pregnancy and childbirth. Some members even fast in proxy for pregnant women when it becomes evident, through dreams and visions, that certain dangers lie ahead during childbirth. Giving birth to a child without any complication is therefore considered an answer to prayer and consequently a cause for rejoicing.

The church does not mandate parents to name children on specific days or at particular places after childbirth. Choosing a name for the child, as well as the date and venue for the rite, are the sole prerogative of the parents. The church simply fits the event in its calendar. The child-naming ceremony is usually done during the church service. According to Bishop Atiemo, this is in accordance with the biblical injunctions stated in Leviticus 12.1–8 and the fulfilment of the injunction by the parents of Jesus Christ as recorded in Luke 2.22–24.

On the day of the naming ceremony, the parents of the child attend the service together with friends and relatives. The following items are used in the rite to name the child: water, honey, sugar, salt, bell, candles, and leaves from a palm frond. Pastors pronounce a wish based on the significance of the item. The wish, which is a blessing stated in the form of a prayer, is said during the administration of the items. Pastors request parents to 'name the child' each time they are about to administer one of the items. Pastors repeat the name of the child before administering the item. They then address the child with a prayerful wish. The cycle of pastors asking the parents to mention the name of the child, then repeating the name, administering an item and making a prayerful wish goes on until the end of the ceremony.

The actual rite begins with the pastor going to where the parents are seated midway through the service. The child is then given to the pastor who asks the parents to 'name the child'. At the mention of the name, the pastor calls the child by the name and sprinkles water on the child, symbolizing cleansing from all spiritual filth during birth. A drop of water is placed in the mouth of the child, with a prayer to God to heal the child when sick and to assuage any thirst for any earthly thing. The pastor dips a finger into a cup of honey and applies it to the lips of the child. The honey symbolizes wisdom, and the prayer is that God would grant the child wisdom to be able to solve any puzzle in life with ease.

Granulated sugar is the next item. According to Bishop Atiemo, sugar cane is a plant that symbolizes durability. It is able to withstand fire and flood. The pastor therefore uses sugar in pleading with God to grant the child the necessary fortitude so that nothing in life will overwhelm him or her. The application of salt to the lips of the child signifies his or her indispensability to society. The pastor prays that the child would grow to become the salt of the earth (Matthew 5.13), useful to society to such an extent that decisions cannot be taken without his or her presence. The next step in the ceremony is the ringing of a bell seven times, signifying the call of God to worship. The pastor prays that the child would hasten to go to church whenever it is time for church service.

Seven candles are then lit and placed on a candlestick. The pastor lifts the candlestick over the child and prays that Jesus Christ, the light of the world, would lead the child throughout life. The child is also reminded of the need to become the light of the world (Matthew 5.14–16). Bishop Atiemo states that the seven candles stand for completeness; hence another wish is that the child would grow and die at a ripe age, completing whatever task needs to be done before being called to rest eternally.

The last article to be used is a leaf from a palm frond, which signifies victory. A prayer is said for the child to lead a victorious life on earth. The pastor takes the child to the front of the altar and prays that the child would turn to the Lord in prayer in times of need and any difficulty. The prayer ends in the name of the Father, Son and the Holy Spirit. The child is then given back to the parents to signify the end of the naming ceremony.

At this juncture members of the congregation express their joy by singing, clapping and dancing. They give an offering for the parents. The offering is considered as seed money for the child. The church does not take a share of the offering; whatever money is collected is given to the parents. The pastor asks the parents to use part of the money to buy a Bible for the child and to train the child in the Lord. Members of the church also donate other token items to the parents such as detergents, clothing, cash, talcum powder, lavender and towels. The parents in turn express their gratitude to God and the congregation. According to Bishop Atiemo, the ceremony unintentionally serves as an evangelistic tool since many relatives later register their names in the church in admiration of the ceremony. Bishop Atiemo asserts that every creature of God has its distinct significance; it is up to humanity to identify that significance and ask God to apply it to life (Bishop Jonathan B. Atiemo, personal interview, Accra, 21 May 2007).

This brief description of the naming ceremony of the Church of the Lord (Brotherhood) illustrates one AIC's attempt to put a very important event in African society into theological perspective. In the traditional religion of the Akan people of Ghana, for instance, only two elements are used to name a child – water and alcohol. The officiating elder puts a drop of water onto the lips of the child and tells the child, 'This is water.' The elder then puts a drop of alcohol onto the lips of the child and says, 'This is alcohol.' The child is then exhorted to make a clear distinction between water and wine when he or she grows up. In essence, the child is exhorted not to play by any double standard in life. 'This is water, this is alcohol', simply implies truthfulness and forthrightness. The naming ceremony of the Church of the Lord (Brotherhood) is therefore an enlargement and integration of a traditional religious practice within a Christian theological perspective.

Recently, the theology of blessings and curses has become increasingly important in African Christianity. Many Africans cherish verbal blessings from elderly people, particularly from parents, just as was done in the Old Testament patriarchal period. Whereas many parents pronounce blessings on their deathbeds, the naming ceremony of the Church of the Lord (Brotherhood) takes a different approach by pronouncing a blessing upon the child in infancy. Many people perceive that this blessing, uttered in the form of a prayer by no less a person than a pastor, at a place of worship and witnessed by many people, carries more weight than the parental blessings. With this emphasis on the theology of blessing at the outset of a child's life on earth, naming ceremonies have become even more meaningful and relevant to members of the Church of the Lord (Brotherhood).

 ## Conclusion: Theological contributions and challenges of the AICs

In spite of the significant growth and influence of the AICs, and widespread research into their origins, growth and life, AICs remain among the least understood Christian communities in Africa. Scholars have referred to them with various terms that tend to confuse people, such as 'syncretistic movements', 'witchcraft eradication movements', 'separatist churches', 'prophetic movements', 'nativistic churches', 'spiritual and Pentecostal churches' and many others (Pobee and Ositelu, 1998: 26–44). The numerous name-tags that scholars assign to AICs indicate the depth of their struggle to understand them.

In contrast, the manifesto of the Organization of African Instituted Churches, a continental body of the AICs, identifies more clearly from their own perspective why these churches were founded and how they do African theology:

> The Independent Churches were attempts by African Christians to live our Christian faith in our own national garb without an *a priori* theologizing. We sought to establish a Christianity of the Bible as we saw it, without Western additions and in harmony with our own cultural heritage. We attempted to come to grips with the traditional beliefs and practices and world-views implied; to make the Christian faith come alive to our own thought processes and culture . . .

> We African Independent Churches try to live Christianity with our own national clothing, in harmony with our own cultural heritage, seeking vehicles of worship that make the Christian faith alive to us as Africans.
>
> (Quoted in Pobee and Ositelu, 1998: 68–9)

So the *raison d'être* or the overall purpose of AICs is to use African world views, philosophies, languages and cultures to interpret the Christian faith and, to a certain extent, to integrate them into Christianity. Unless this is recognized, many scholars will continue to misunderstand and, as a result, misrepresent the AICs.

In their attempts to make Christianity more meaningful and relevant to their constituencies, AICs encounter some challenges. Notable among them is the formulation of theology without being guided by the experience of the wider Church – the problems the wider Church has grappled with and the resultant decisions that have been taken. There is also the challenge of analysing some cultural beliefs and practices and deciding what is compatible with Scripture and what is contrary to it. Another challenge is accessing theological education that provides a holistic view of culture and theology.

The greatest challenge, however, is the uncompromising attitude of some scholars who do not have the patience to study the AICs to understand their struggles and discern their contributions to African Christianity. Such attitudes have resulted in various forms of persecution of AICs. Nevertheless, the AICs are undaunted in their efforts to make Christianity authentically African.

Whenever people identify with an institution, seeing its relevance and practical applicability to their lives, they perceive the institution as their own and thus promote its growth. AICs have attempted, with considerable success, to rid Christianity of some Western cultural and philosophical embellishments, thereby making it more appealing to Africans. What remains is for African Christian scholars to further assist them in developing Christian theologies that are thoroughly African yet truly biblical.

STUDY QUESTIONS

1 Do you think there is need for Africans to plant, finance and manage their own churches without looking to the West for support? Why or why not?

2 The naming ceremony of the Church of the Lord (Brotherhood) is presented as an appropriate attempt to make the Christian faith relevant in Ghana. Identify similar attempts by local Christians in your own context to make the Christian faith relevant. Discuss whether or not these attempts are indeed appropriate. Why or why not?

3 What are some of the challenges that AICs face in their attempt to contextualize theology?

4 'The *raison d'être* or the overall purpose of AICs is to use African world views, philosophies, languages and cultures to interpret the Christian faith and, to a certain extent, to integrate them into Christianity. Unless this is recognized, many scholars will continue to misunderstand and, as a result, misrepresent the AICs.' Do you agree with this conclusion? Explain your answer.

6

Pentecostalism in Africa

J. Kwabena Asamoah-Gyadu

 Abstract

Pentecostalism and its charismatic variations have become the representative face of Christianity, especially in the Global South. It is a movement that appeals to what happened on the day of Pentecost in Acts 2, with the growth of the Church that followed, as events that God's Holy Spirit is replicating today. Thus Pentecostalism tends to focus very much on the experience of the Holy Spirit with manifestations of speaking in tongues, prophesying, healing, visions, dreams and revelations and other such Spirit-related phenomena. Wherever they are found, Pentecostal/charismatic churches also emphasize the need for Christians to read the Bible and to live lives of holiness in keeping with the Scriptures. The movement has contributed immensely to the growth of Christianity, particularly in developing countries. Thus at a time when many churches in the West are experiencing decline, Pentecostals, as Harvey Cox (1995) puts it, are changing the face of and reshaping spirituality in the twenty-first century.

 Introduction

Pentecostalism has been growing very quickly and spreading fast across many continents, including Africa south of the Sahara. This growth is evident in many ways. First, Pentecostal churches and movements have an impressive physical presence in African cities. Second, statistics provided by David B. Barrett in the *Encyclopedia of World Christianity* show that Pentecostals constitute a good percentage of the world's Christian population. Third, there is a significant rise in published academic research on different streams of Pentecostalism.

There are different types of Pentecostal and neo-Pentecostal or charismatic renewal churches and movements across the world. Together these new streams of Christianity, as we will see below, are reshaping Christian ministry, mission, spirituality, worship and theology in many parts of Africa.

Pentecostal churches in Africa, such as Ghana's Church of Pentecost, Nigeria's Redeemed Church of God and the Zimbabwe Assemblies of God Africa, run some of the largest denominations on the continent.

Within the last decade in particular, many African Pentecostal/charismatic movements have also developed into transnational entities by establishing congregations and networks in the major cities of the Western world. To this end, some of the largest Pentecostal congregations in Europe are also founded and led by Africans. One of the best known in this category is Nigerian Pastor Matthew Ashimolowo's Kingsway International Christian Centre, London.

Additionally, African Pentecostals dominate in religious uses of the media. Books, video and audiocassette recordings of Pentecostal sermons and services are available for purchase by the wider public. All these developments indicate that Pentecostal/charismatic churches and movements lead the present Christian growth in Africa.

Defining Pentecostalism

Theologically, Pentecostalism has usually been associated with four main emphases: belief in Jesus Christ as Saviour; belief in Jesus Christ as Baptizer in the Holy Spirit; belief in Jesus Christ as Healer; and belief in Jesus Christ as the King who will soon return to judge the world. Due to the strong emphasis on moral purity and new life, some scholars add a fifth theological category, that is, the sanctification work of Jesus Christ as seen in the High Priestly prayer of John 17. Although fairly representative of what Pentecostals believe, these four or five themes do not necessarily exhaust the theological emphases of Pentecostal Christianity.

It is important to note that Pentecostalism is a very experiential movement that does not articulate its theology simply in terms of creeds and doctrines. Indeed, it is very rare for Pentecostals to recite the Apostles' Creed as part of worship, but that does not mean that they do not believe what it articulates as the substance of the Christian faith. Pentecostalism has an oral theology: that is, it is expressed through songs, dances, testimonies, dreams and visions, and 'the message', as the sermon is usually called in Pentecostal churches. The sermon, even when it is outlined on paper, is considered 'a message' from the Lord.

Thus one of the most distinctive characteristics of Pentecostalism is that it places emphasis on experiences of the Spirit. This gives Pentecostal worship a spontaneous, expressive and dynamic quality usually absent from the liturgically ordered worship services of historic mission denominations. A definition of Pentecostalism must also consider the fact that it appeals not simply to experience, but also to the Bible. Pentecostalism is a movement that prides itself in attempting to recover biblical patterns of being Christian for the contemporary Church.

In the pursuit of this agenda, Pentecostal/charismatic Christians are concerned primarily with the experience of the Holy Spirit as part of normal Christian life and worship because they find it in the word of God. In the Apostles' Creed, Christians confess 'I believe in the Holy Spirit', but for Pentecostals, belief must be complemented by experience. The idea is to make the biblical teaching on the outpouring of the Holy Spirit, as prophesied in Joel 2.28 and as experienced by the apostles on the day of Pentecost, a paradigm or model for contemporary Christians. The book of Acts records that on the day of Pentecost, the Spirit, as promised by Jesus, was poured out on the apostles and they began to speak in other tongues 'as the Spirit gave them ability' (Acts 2.4). These events are critical to the identity of the Pentecostal movement.

Pentecostals generally believe that repentance must be followed by an ardent search for a second experience, baptism in the Holy Spirit. The key text is found in Peter's response to those who enquired about what to do following his sermon on the day of Pentecost:

> *Now when they heard this, they were cut to the heart and said to Peter and to the other apostles, 'Brothers, what should we do?' Peter said to them, 'Repent, and be baptized every one of you in the name of Jesus Christ so that your sins may be forgiven; and you will receive the gift of the Holy Spirit. For the promise is for you, for your children, and for all who are far away, everyone whom the Lord our God calls to him.'* (Acts 2.37–39)

The last sentence is important because modern-day Pentecostals insist that the promise of Pentecost was not only a historical event, but also an experience that must be sought by Christians of every age. The umbrella term 'Pentecostalism' may therefore be defined as any stream of Christianity that emphasizes Christian salvation as consisting of conscious personal acceptance of Jesus Christ as Saviour, followed by a subsequent experience called 'baptism of the Holy Spirit', which, it is thought, must manifest in what theologians call *glossolalia*, or 'speaking in tongues'.

This doctrine, also called the 'doctrine of subsequence' or the 'doctrine of initial evidence', is an important defining characteristic of Pentecostalism. The openness to the experience of the Spirit means that Pentecostal/charismatic churches and Christians accept, value and consciously encourage certain manifestations that are understood to be signs of the presence of the Holy Spirit within and among God's people. These manifestations include speaking in tongues, prophecies, visions, healing, miracles, and signs and wonders in general.

The additional expression 'charismatic' derives from St Paul's reference to *charismata pneumatika*, meaning 'gifts of the Spirit', in his expositions in 1 Corinthians 12—14. Thus in 1 Corinthians 12.7, for example, St Paul says to the Church: 'To each is given the manifestation of the Spirit for the common good.' Gifts of the Spirit are graces with which God endows his children in order that the Church can function in a way that testifies to his presence among his people.

 The rise of Pentecostal Christianity in Africa

The rise of Pentecostalism in Africa was preceded by the work of several indigenous prophets who led revivals across the continent from the early years of the twentieth century. These prophets challenged Africans to throw away their traditional resources for seeking supernatural help and turn towards the living God of the Bible. God alone, they taught, was able to rescue people from the fear of witchcraft, medicines, and principalities and powers that are familiar to the African religio-cultural world. The prophets in question included William Wade Harris, a Kru man from Liberia who worked in Ghana and La Côte D'Ivoire, Garrick Sokari Braide of the Niger Delta, Joseph Babalola also of Nigeria, Simon Kimbangu of the Congo, Isaiah Shembe of South Africa and others. A number of these prophets did not found churches, as such. However, their revivals led to the rise of what became known in South Africa as Zionist churches, in Ghana as Spiritual churches, and in Nigeria as Aladura, that is, 'praying churches'. These are churches that are known in the literature as 'African independent' or 'African initiated' churches (AICs).

There is a continuing debate as to whether the AICs should be described as Pentecostal churches or not. The various positions will not be rehearsed here. Yet it is obvious that the single most important phenomenon that defined the character of the early AICs was their keen interest in seeing the power of the Holy Spirit among God's people, as they read in the Scriptures translated into African languages. The major difference between the AICs and African Pentecostal/charismatic movements and churches lies more with attitudes towards African culture, as Allan Anderson explains:

> Although the AICs can be called 'Pentecostal', many of them have few connections with classical Pentecostalism and are very different from it in several ways. There are external differences like the use of healing symbolism including blessed water, many other symbolic ritual objects representing power and protection, forms of government and hierarchical patterns of leadership . . . the use of some African cultural practices and the wearing of distinctive robes or uniforms. They also differ fundamentally in their approach to African religions and culture, in liturgy, healing practices and in their unique contribution to Christianity in a broader African context. (Anderson, 2004: 105)

It must be added, though, that with time, the differences between AICs and African Pentecostals have become blurred. For example, many of the Pentecostals now use such therapeutic substances as olive oil and blessed water for their healing ministries. The African world view that also attributes misfortune and sickness to witchcraft and evil powers, as I will point out later, has also very much become a part of African Pentecostal discourse. Healing camps have emerged among Pentecostals that serve the same purposes as what the AICs refer to as 'mercy ground' or 'prayer gardens', where people retreat to ask for God's intervention in their existential problems.

Further, although we cannot describe the AICs as 'Pentecostal' without qualification, they, like modern Pentecostals, are keen to emphasize the power and experience of the Holy Spirit as a missing factor in historic mission Christianity. Thus, during worship in a typical independent church, certain 'activities' and 'signs' that are attributed to the presence of the Holy Spirit among worshippers are expected to occur. Christian G. Baëta describes these from the perspective of Ghana's Spiritual churches:

> These activities and 'signs' include rhythmic swaying of the body, usually with stamping to repetitious music (both vocal and instrumental, particularly percussion), hand-clapping, ejaculations, poignant cries and prayers, dancing, leaping, and various motor reactions expressive of intense religious emotion; prophesyings, 'speaking with tongues', falling into trances, relating dreams and visions, and 'witnessing', that is, recounting publicly one's own experience of miraculous redemption. (Baëta, 1962: 1)

These 'signs', including the emphases of the AICs on exuberance and Spirit-led worship, and healing and prophecy as means of divine revelation and communication, are also all present in contemporary African Pentecostalism. So here in the area of the experience of the Holy Spirit, the spirituality of the AICs and that of African Pentecostal/charismatic movements seem to cohere, or come together. In a sense, as far as African Christianity is concerned, there are obvious continuities between the spirituality of the AICs and that of the Pentecostals.

Types of Pentecostal movements

There are three broad types of Pentecostal/charismatic churches and movements in Africa: first, we have the classical Pentecostal denominations. Some of these, such as the Assemblies of God, the Church of the Four Square Gospel, Apostolic Faith Mission and Elim Pentecostal, were established in Africa through missionary activities of North American and Western European Pentecostals. Historically these Western mission-related classical Pentecostal churches have their roots in the 1906 Azusa Street revival led by the Black Pentecostal, William J. Seymour.

Africa has generated its own brand of classical Pentecostal churches and these include the Church of Pentecost in Ghana and the Deeper Christian Life Church of Nigeria. The Christ Apostolic Church, found in Ghana and Nigeria, and the Zimbabwe Assemblies of God Africa also belong to this category. The main distinguishing characteristic of a classical Pentecostal church is that it usually holds fast to the doctrine of 'initial evidence', insisting on 'speaking in tongues' as the single most important mark that a person has been baptized by the Spirit of God. Some have their roots in North America. However, the majority of classical Pentecostal churches operating in Africa were initiated locally; foreign assistance often came later.

Second, there are the churches that could be referred to as new Pentecostal churches or neo-Pentecostal churches (NPCs). At the moment these constitute the fastest-growing stream of African Pentecostalism. In various parts of Africa, the NPCs go by different designations such as 'born-again churches', 'charismatic churches' or 'prosperity churches'. They have proliferated within the last three decades and their chief characteristics include an attraction for Africa's upwardly mobile youth, a penchant for mega-sized urban-centred congregations, internationalism, English as the main medium of expression, a relaxed and fashion-conscious dress code for members, innovative appropriations of modern media technologies, a well-educated leadership (not necessarily in theology) and, as compared to the AICs in particular, a very modern outlook.

These churches are initiated by indigenous people but there is also a lot of North American influence on their approach to Christianity. This influence is seen particularly in the use of the media and in the gospel of material prosperity that they preach. Paul Gifford has described these extensively in three of his recent publications: *Christianity and Politics in Doe's Liberia*, *African Christianity: Its Public Role*, and *Ghana's New Christianity*. In Uganda, for example, the new Pentecostal phenomenon has overshadowed that country's version of older AICs, the *balokole* or East African revival movement. We are also told that the new Pentecostal communions are 'mushrooming in luxuriant fashion' (Gifford, 1998: 157). Allan Anderson's *African Reformation* and Asamoah-Gyadu's *African Charismatics* also discuss the history and theology of these NPCs.

The major names within the field of NPCs include Mensa Otabil of the International Central Gospel Church in Ghana; David O. Oyedepo of the Word of Faith Mission International or Winners' Chapel, also of Nigeria; and Andrew Wutawanashe of the Family of God in Zimbabwe. Historically, the major African influence on the NPCs was the late Archbishop Professor Benson Idahosa of Nigeria. He was the protégé of several North American televangelists including the now infamous Jimmy Baker of the defunct PTL ('Praise the Lord') Club. Archbishop Idahosa trained a number of the early leaders of NPCs through his Christ for All Nations Bible School in Benin City, Nigeria. His model of prosperity-oriented and media-savvy Pentecostalism, which he picked up through his North American networks, was followed by many of the leaders he trained.

In the introduction to the edited volume, *Between Babel and Pentecost: Transnational Pentecostalism in Africa and Latin America*, André Corten and Ruth Marshall-Fratani speak of Pentecostalism on the two continents as a kind of 'New Reformation' of the twentieth century. Pentecostalism, they write, 'projects a new vision of the world, responding in particular to processes and promises of modernization' (Corten and Marshall-Fratani, 2001: 1). That sort of Pentecostal orientation is very much evident in the Christianity of the NPCs. Unlike the classical Pentecostals who sometimes 'retreat from the world' and view material things as obstructions to the kingdom of God and true spirituality, NPCs see material things as God's blessing for Christian commitment and as God's reward for the faithfulness in the payment of tithes and offerings.

Third, within the African Pentecostal family, there are charismatic renewal movements and trans-denominational fellowships. The charismatic renewal groups usually function within existing mainline denominations in order to help renew them from within. Their main emphases are Bible study, prayer and the integration of charismatic renewal phenomena into mainline-church Christianity. The lack of such 'spiritual' activities, they preach, has led to 'dry denominationalism' within the churches. In other words, renewal groups attempt to make available those Spirit-inspired phenomena found in Pentecostal churches within their own non-Pentecostal denominations.

The trans-denominational fellowships are like the charismatic renewal groups but they exist outside the boundaries of denominationalism and provide spaces for like-minded believers with shared experiences of the Spirit to fellowship outside church control. The most popular ones include the Full Gospel Businessmen's Fellowship International, Women Aglow, and Intercessors for Africa. These, together with itinerant international Pentecostal preachers and prophets, have taken over the religious landscape as the new faces of African Christianity.

So in Africa today, we do not only have major Western mission-related Pentecostal denominations, such as the Assemblies of God originating from the USA, but also African ones which are born out of local initiatives. Additionally, we have noted, African Pentecostal churches have become a dominant force in Western Europe and North America. The fact that African religions have emerged in Europe, not as primal or traditional forms but in terms of Christianity, is itself evidence of the growing strength of the Christian faith in modern Africa.

 ## The African factor in Pentecostalism

Rudolf Otto in his work, *The Idea of the Holy*, laments the inability of 'orthodox Christianity' to recognize the value of the non-rational aspect of religion, thus giving the 'idea of the holy' what he calls a 'one-sidedly intellectualistic approach' (Otto, 1950: 3). Pentecostalism is a response to such cerebral and 'orderly' Christianity. Wherever it has appeared, the Pentecostal movement has defined itself in terms of a recovery of the experiential aspects of the faith. Pentecostalism does so by demonstrating the power of the Spirit to infuse life, and the ability of the living presence of Jesus Christ to save from sin and evil.

This is even more so in African cultural contexts where fear of witchcraft and curses is common. Religion in Africa is thus a survival strategy. In this type of religion, spirit possession with its emphasis on direct divine communication, prediction, explanation, intervention in crises and religious mediation is central to religious experiences. The ministries of healing and deliverance have thus become some of the most important expressions of Christianity in African Pentecostalism. The charismatic renewal movements also practise the ministries of healing and deliverance widely within their mission churches because such ministries are in high demand among ordinary members. Many aspects of the world views underlying the practice of healing and deliverance, especially the belief in mystical causality, resonate with African philosophical thought and inform Pentecostal theology on the continent.

 ## African Pentecostal theology

First, there is in African Pentecostal theology a keen emphasis on transformation. In the early years, most of the people who left mission churches to join Pentecostal ones always cited 'compromised' Christianity in the former as one of the major reasons for leaving. Not only did people accuse mission churches of tolerating immorality in the church but they also point to the continued reality of members resorting to traditional religious ways of solving problems. Pentecostalism, with its emphasis on being born again, thus became an alternative religion to mission denominations. The trend is in keeping with the distinguishing mark of the Pentecostal movement, which is the offer of a direct and particularly intense encounter with the Holy Spirit. Thus, in a study of Zimbabwe Assemblies of God Africa, David Maxwell describes how from the outset Pentecostals are taught to expect and seek change, and to expect an 'experience of the sacred'. In services, he notes, they are repeatedly told 'you will never be the same again' or 'you will go home transformed'. 'There is a constant emphasis on permanent internal revolution . . . There is a continued emphasis on holiness, or good character. Born-agains are exalted to live moral and disciplined lives' (Maxwell, 2006: 195–6).

Pentecostals generally teach that a true encounter with God introduces profound changes in the lives and circumstances of those who experience God's self in the power of the Spirit. The Holy Spirit, God's empowering presence, is the one who facilitates the direct character of the encounter. A sense of transformation thus takes place at the personal and communal levels including a new dynamism in worship that is also inspired by the Holy Spirit. The foremost theological emphasis of Pentecostal/charismatic Christianity is therefore the transformative encounter with God who is 'holy' and who is 'spirit'.

In the African context, participants in Pentecostalism keenly testify of their new life in Christ. They often stress the transition they have made from resorting to traditional resources of supernatural help to becoming sincere Christians who believe in God alone through Jesus Christ. It is not uncommon for converts from traditional religions to bring items from those religions to have them publicly destroyed as testimony of the transition from the 'world' to Christ. Corten and Marshall-Fratani explain that in Pentecostal/ charismatic Christianity, conversion or 'getting born again' is still conceived in terms of radical transformation of the self through rupture with a sinful past. An intensely private and emotional experience, they note, gives rise to a moment of great personal freedom and empowerment, where the possibility of 'all things becoming new' opens itself up for the first time to the individual (Corten and Marshall-Fratani, 2001: 6–7).

Second, African Pentecostal theology is a theology of empowerment. The born-again experience empowers believers to lead new lives, and the experience of the Spirit endows them with the confidence and authority they need to overcome the devil, the flesh and other evil powers. The theology of empowerment is further evident in the prayer for spiritual gifts. The state of being a born-again believer means the individual has also become a 'vessel of honour', that is a potential recipient of spiritual gifts. These gifts, when they are received or identified, enable beneficiaries to exercise different ministries within the body of Christ. The recognition of personal spiritual gifts explains why Pentecostalism is sometimes defined as a participatory type of Christianity. It gives practical expression to the Protestant principle of the priesthood of all believers by facilitating the use of spiritual gifts in the life of the church.

In Pentecostalism therefore, there is emphasis on the empowering effects of the gospel of Jesus Christ. This introduces a relationship between transformation and empowerment. The core of the new experience is that it redefines personality and reinvents identity as the born-again develop new visions, fresh life goals and ethics, which constitute a rupture from a sinful past. Thereafter, people pray earnestly for the gifts of the Spirit with which they can function as 'ministers' among God's people. The special anointing of the pastor is recognized but, generally in Pentecostalism, ministry is not necessarily the preserve of the leader alone. Charisma is virtually democratized in order to make the church charismatically functional.

Another way to appreciate the empowering effects of the Pentecostal experience is through the ministry of healing and deliverance. Wherever Pentecostalism has appeared, healing tends to be a major factor that draws people into it. This is even more so in Africa because health and wholeness are generally sought for within religious contexts. Here religion is expected to deal with the effects of evil caused by demonic spirits, curses and witchcraft. Evil powers, represented by evil eyes, demons, witchcraft and curses, result in all sorts of misfortunes – sickness, failure, childlessness and other setbacks in life.

The world view underpinning the practice of healing and deliverance in African Pentecostalism therefore tends to be a synthesis of traditional religious ideas and an understanding of the ministry of Jesus Christ as a healer and exorcist. Much is also made of St Paul's reference to the fact that

Christians wrestle not against 'flesh and blood', but against 'principalities' and 'powers' (Ephesians 6.12, RSV). The basic theological orientation of the healing and deliverance phenomenon is the belief that demons may either possess a person and take over his or her executive faculties or simply oppress people through various negative influences. Whether human crisis has resulted from satanic possession or oppression, African Pentecostal/charismatic churches and movements provide the ritual contexts for dealing with the fears and insecurities of the afflicted.

Third, a successful implementation of a healing and deliverance ministry, it is believed, paves the way for good health, success and prosperity in life. In short, Pentecostals preach a holistic concept of salvation. The encounter with the transformative and healing ministry of the Lord makes possible the realization of God-given abilities and potentialities in life. This is sometimes referred to as 'dominion theology'. In the dominion or prosperity theology discourse, there is continuity between coming to Christ and experiencing a redemptive uplift that is evidenced partly through the possession of the material comforts of life. Neo-Pentecostals in particular preach that there are links between being born again and the realization of personal ambitions in life in terms of success and prosperity. This relationship is well articulated by Corten and Marshall-Fratani:

> The emphasis on miracles of health and prosperity which are at the heart of the new wave implies a new relationship between the experience of conversion and the conception of salvation . . . Salvation is now absolutely this-worldly, and the evidence of new life has become as much material as spiritual. Moral rigor and strict personal ethics have not been superseded, yet the notion of transformation has been broadened to include the possibility of material change in everyday life. (Corten and Marshall-Fratani, 2001: 7)

Thus it is possible to view the deliverance theology, for example, as a response to the shortfall of faith preaching. Africa is a country that is home to some of the world's most deprived people and communities. Once the gospel of prosperity does not work, some preachers then explain the shortfall in terms of faithlessness or the work of demons against a person's prosperity. When things are not going well, these appeals to the works of demons and witches come in handy as explanations. Thus African Pentecostal prosperity theology may have some ground to recover in respect of its weak theology of suffering and, to some extent, its neglect of the lessons from the cross of Christ.

Be that as it may, the cross of Christ is not just a symbol of weakness, but also one of victory over sin, the world and death. Pentecostals draw attention to the fact that the gospel is about restoration, so it is expected that the transformation of the personality will be manifest in personal health and well-being. Thus salvation is seen as holistic and includes spiritual as well as physical abundance. The process of restoration is not individualistic as people are encouraged to disengage from generational curses through fasting, prayer and personal ministration. Salvation is here given a holistic meaning that includes a sense of well-being evidenced in freedom from sickness, poverty and misfortune as well as in deliverance from sin and evil.

Pentecostalism and African public life

In Africa today Pentecostal/charismatic churches may be found throughout major cities. They often meet in converted cinema halls, refurbished abandoned factories and warehouses, or newly constructed large and modern chapels with fashionable architectural designs that members appropriately designate 'auditoriums'. The involvement of Pentecostal/charismatic Christianity in Africa has been felt at all levels of African civil life including economics, education and politics. In the past, African Pentecostals were accused of neglecting involvement in social life. Indications are that this has changed within the last two decades. In Ghana, for instance, Pastor Otabil's International Central Gospel Church has built a university college, and an information technology facility for a children's home in Accra, the capital. One of the most prominent tertiary institutions in Nigeria now is the Dominion University built by Bishop Oyedepo's Winners' Chapel.

In the political arena, the NPCs in particular have played both functional and dysfunctional roles. In African countries such as Ghana and Zambia, politicians have courted the friendship of popular charismatic leaders in order to take advantage of a movement with a massive youthful following to achieve political ends. In Ghana, Bishop Duncan-Williams virtually served as 'chaplain' to the authoritarian Rawlings regime of the 1980s. The former president of Zambia, Frederick Chiluba, not only declared Zambia a Christian nation when he took office in 1991, but he also constantly put in appearances at Pentecostal crusades and conventions. In the 1980s when leading churchmen from the historic mission churches joined the opposition in challenging Daniel Arap Moi's dictatorial regime, leaders of some Pentecostal churches, notably the Gospel Redeemed Church, publicly upheld Moi as a God-appointed leader who had brought freedom of worship to Kenya.

In spite of these critical observations, the influence of African Pentecostals on the region's politics has not all been negative. It is on record that in the midst of the turmoil accompanying transitions to democracies in sub-Saharan Africa through the 1990s, the Pentecostals rallied in prayer for their nations, interceding as some of the prophets of the Old Testament did, in order to save the countries from bloodshed.

 Conclusion

In his seminal work on AICs, *Bantu Prophets in South Africa*, Bengt Sundkler noted that these movements reveal what Africans, when left to themselves, considered important in Christian faith and in the Christian church (Sundkler, 1961). This observation is equally true of the Pentecostal/charismatic churches and movements we have discussed in this chapter. What people consider important in religion and theology are the things that address their deep-seated spiritual and physical needs. Encounters with the spiritual world are important elements in African religiosity. These encounters might be perceived as evil powers seeking to destroy people, water spirits working against efforts at public morality, or the performance of ritual in order to solicit help from good powers. The Pentecostals have created alternative religious centres in which African Christians can worship and serve God in ways that directly address the concerns that they bring to religion. In continuity with the African religious paradigm, Pentecostal/charismatic Christianity has proved successful in Africa because of its openness to the supernatural and its oral forms of theology that resonate with traditional African piety. Yet the primary intention of the practitioners is to be biblical. As we have seen, this theology is expressed in several ways including emphases on God's power of transformation and personal empowerment.

 STUDY QUESTIONS

1   What are some of the passages in the Bible that are usually quoted to support the rise of the Pentecostal/charismatic movement?

2   Name and discuss briefly the key manifestations of the Holy Spirit associated with Pentecostalism.

3   In what way has Pentecostal/charismatic Christianity influenced styles of worship in non-Pentecostal and historic mission churches in your community?

4   In your opinion what can non-Pentecostal churches learn from their Pentecostal/charismatic compatriots?

7

African Christian spirituality

Laurenti Magesa

Abstract

Spirituality is understood in the following discussion to mean the human attempt to relate to and with Transcendence or God. As such, it is a universal phenomenon, common to all human beings. However, approaches towards this goal differ among persons and communities, and so you can distinguish various spiritualities. After a brief general presentation of what 'spirituality' involves, this chapter tries to show (a) the distinction between African indigenous and Western Christian spiritualities, and (b) some points of contact between them. The purpose is to explore some outlines for a genuine African Christian spirituality for contemporary Africa.

The nature of spirituality

Spirituality is a universal human activity involving human recognition of, and relationship with, Transcendence. Both these aspects of spirituality require and evoke two conditions in the human heart and mind: dependence and gratitude. These attitudes are closely related to one another. Dependence, as a spiritual condition, flows from human awareness of Transcendence as being the ultimate Power over creation. Apart from this Transcendence, nothing else is possible, including life itself.

On the other hand, gratitude is a consequence of dependence. Since human beings see that life exists, and that for whatever reason Transcendence has not as yet chosen to exercise the power to destroy it, they conclude that Transcendence is benevolent towards human beings and creation in general on which human life depends. Therefore, both dependence and gratitude imply a relationship of supremacy and trust between human beings and Transcendence. This relational process is what spirituality consists in. It is an activity that implies four questions related to one another, as parts of a whole:

- **Who or what is Transcendence?**
- **Where is Transcendence?**
- **How do we relate to Transcendence**, and for what benefit?
- **What is the human being's final end or fate?**

To begin with, Who or what is Transcendence? For spirituality and religion, this is the core aspect of the cluster of questions. In order for the human mind to grasp reality of any kind, it must name it. Therefore this question attempts to give Transcendence a name. Indeed, virtually all religions have their own names for Transcendence, which are basically descriptive analogies since it lies beyond our human senses.

The second question – Where is Transcendence? – is closely related to the first. Human beings exist in space and can only conceive reality in terms of location and space, whether physical or mental. Thus, Transcendence is thought of in terms of locality, using names or descriptions of divine space such as 'heaven'. This question also involves the issue of whether Transcendence is one or many, and whether there are 'associates' of Transcendence. All transcendences are conceived of in terms of spirits or other non-physical existences.

The next question – How do we relate to Transcendence? – involves certain practical attitudes and behaviour. That is why in popular understanding, when we talk about spirituality – as in 'So-and-so is a very spiritual person', or 'Such-and-such a group of people follows such-and-such school of spirituality' – reference is usually to observable religious attitudes and behaviours. In other words, what is the attitude to Transcendence of the individual or group in question, and how do they visibly express it? At this level we can then discuss similarities and difference among various spiritualities. On this basis we can begin to construct an African Christian spirituality, which is the main task of this chapter.

Still, there is a further issue at stake. One of the main reasons human beings try to relate to Transcendence concerns the question, What happens after I die? Since death cannot be avoided, organized religion tries to assure its followers that there is an answer to this question, and that its particular answer is the right one. Although the answer to this question lies in the future, it still guides the present. How I will be after this life directs how I must live this life. Therefore all forms of spirituality involve concepts of morality, since we act in the present with an eye to what is to come.

 # Distinctions between Christian and African indigenous spiritualities

The major distinction

Let us first note the most fundamental distinction between Christian and African indigenous spiritualities. Then we will describe how it shapes people's attitudes and behaviours within the two religious approaches. The basic difference lies in how each spiritual tradition approaches Transcendence, which from now on we will call God. While Christianity emphasizes the 'vertical approach' – my or our direct relationship with God – African indigenous spirituality stresses the 'horizontal approach' – relationship with God through the community of persons. Although these orientations are not necessarily mutually exclusive, the emphasis is clear enough to make the distinction extremely significant.

Characteristics of Christian spirituality

The Christian God is a personal God. For Christians, God became a human being in Jesus Christ. This doctrine of the incarnation is central to Christian spirituality. Since God in Christ became one of us and 'lived among us' (John 1.14) as Immanuel ('God is with us', Matthew 1.23), God can be approached directly by human beings any time. He can also be approached, if need be, without intermediaries.

Indeed, of the many branches of Christianity, the Catholic and Orthodox traditions are about the only ones that give importance to deceased holy people – called saints – as mediators between humans and God. Many Protestant traditions hardly do so. In fact, one of the most serious doctrinal points of difference between Catholicism and Protestantism has been the place Catholicism ascribes to Mary, Mother of God, as *mediatrix* (or mediator). Protestantism generally interprets the Letter to the Hebrews to mean that only Christ, because of his dual nature as human and divine, is mediator. However, the focus of our question here is how this perception of the human being's direct relationship with God affects Christian spirituality.

Morality is a case in point. How do Christians approach morality? What is morality for them? In classical Western spirituality, morality is seen as primarily personal, often in individualistic terms. It pertains mostly to my 'feeling good' within myself as a result of how I perceive myself to have behaved before God. It is the 'before God' that ultimately counts in Christian morality over and above 'before others'. This represents the key characteristic of a 'guilt culture': I have sinned, and I stand before God convicted. Consequently, I feel guilty. The way to erase my guilt is to put things right between God and me. The status of my relationship with other people comes as a consequence of my relationship with God. This is ethics from above, as it were.

Christian prayer and worship reflect this ethical stance. As we have just noted, if the central concern of morality is to stand in right relationship directly with God – as classical Christianity interprets the biblical notion of 'righteousness' – then prayer and worship are understood to be disciplines meant to serve this purpose for the individual and community. God has power to act for good in human life and the world, but God will act positively only when humans show obedience to God's commandments as interpreted by the Church. Prayer and worship are for the purpose of ensuring

God's favour, which, if withdrawn, spells doom all around. This leads us to the Christian notion of 'salvation', the goal of morality and spirituality.

What is salvation in Christian terms? Salvation is to be with God at the end of earthly life. The opposite of salvation is damnation, which is life in the absence of God, seen as an unbearable condition for the human spirit. It is referred to as 'hell' in Christian literature and doctrine across denominations. But heaven or hell in Christian understanding comes as a direct consequence of being either in the right or wrong relationship with God in my earthly life. Again, this relationship is determined by my willingness to acknowledge God's greatness and power through prayer and worship. Asceticism as self-denial, self-control and personal sacrifice, therefore, count positively as basic aspects of spirituality because they are ways of recognizing divine greatness and power. They are ways to 'conquer' the body, as it were, and 'get out' of it. Throughout Christian spiritual history in the West, there is a strong hint of the physical body as evil; the more you distance your 'self' from it through self-inflicted pain and sacrifice, the more spiritual you become. Rather than immersing yourself into life in the world, certain traditions of Christian spirituality suggested that the ideal is to escape from it.

Characteristics of African indigenous spirituality

On the contrary, immersion into the life of the world through participation in your community is the very core of African indigenous spirituality and morality. In African religion we find the closest link, perhaps of any religious tradition, between spirituality and morality (see Magesa, 1997). Here spirituality is indeed understood to be morality, and vice versa. From this perspective, spirituality and morality relate to behaviour in the world before the community. The question is not directly what God wants of me, but what the community through our tradition expects of me. In wrongdoing I do not stand guilty before God, first of all; rather I stand ashamed before or in the midst of my community, one that is directly injured on account of my behaviour. Thus, African indigenous societies have been described as shame cultures. Not that guilt-feeling is totally absent in these cultures' sense of wrongdoing (or sin), but it is secondary. In other words, it follows after shame, that is, after wrongdoing has been known and established by the community to which you belong and are accountable.

Yet, to avoid hasty and wrong conclusions about African morality and spirituality, it is crucial to understand what African religious thought understands by community. 'Community' in African indigenous thought is inclusive, embracing the totality of creation: living humans, the 'living dead' or ancestors, the yet-to-be-born, and also tribal land and property. The individual stands, morally and spiritually, before and in the midst of the totality of this community (see Bujo, 1998, 2001). For African spirituality, therefore, the process of 'redemption', if we may speak of it as such, is within the order of creation, not outside of it.

Notice that God and (evil) spirits, the Transcendence and transcendences, are not immediately included in the list. In African religious thought, God's magnificence means that this divine reality lies beyond any intellectual understanding: God is God and God acts as God wills, and it helps little to speculate on why. Towards God, silence is the proper attitude. However, God, as the source and origin of everything in existence, is the ultimate sustainer of the human community through the agency of the ancestors. Despite not being immediately involved in human affairs, God and God's sovereignty over the entire existence – including the ancestors – stand in no doubt in the African religious view. God is acknowledged as the Transcendence above and beyond all transcendences, and nothing of value can be said beyond that.

As for the ancestors, however, we may rationally understand the reasons for their behaviour towards humanity because it is similar in character to ours. The ancestors remain part and parcel of the living, as do potentially the yet-to-be-born. Thus, marriage and birth occupy a prominent place in African ethics and spirituality because these life events assure the continued survival of the individual and community through the yet-to-be-born. The ancestors are reborn in their descendants and the descendants are assured of becoming ancestors through incarnating their forebears in this way. Perpetuation is therefore seen as the basis of community, the supreme good. Since tribal land and property play an indispensable, practical role in this perpetuation, in terms of sustaining life, they are included in the understanding of community.

The sense of spiritual mediation is strongly present in African religious thought. Except in very exceptional circumstances when the ancestors 'fail' humanity, so to speak, by not granting the needs the community expects and asks of them, God is not directly approached in prayer and worship. The ancestors are the normal recipients of prayer and sacrifice as immediate representatives of God, who are closest to the community and who have obvious vested interest in its perpetuation. Studies in African religion have now established beyond any shadow of doubt that Africans do not worship their ancestors. Through prayer and sacrifice, they venerate them. They show reverential respect for them as the more powerful part of the community on account of their proximity to the divine entity and wisdom.

Voluntary asceticism and self-denial for their own sake do not feature prominently in African indigenous spirituality. Suffering, especially if self-inflicted, is accepted only if it serves to strengthen the vital force of the community, such as in the process of initiation and other rites of passage. Otherwise it is seen as a negative reality because it undercuts the ideal of the fullness of life. Indeed, African spirituality entails immersion into life, and maximum enjoyment of life whenever possible. There is no ideal of fleeing the world here. Rather, the emphasis is on embracing the world and preserving the harmony of the cosmos as created by God. Only then can the vital forces within creation work together in harmony for the sake of the survival of the community. This is what leads to life with the ancestors, which is the individual person's highest achievement.

Towards African Christian spirituality

With the above discussion in mind, it is now possible to suggest the foundations of an African Christian spirituality. The main principles are methodological, doctrinal and pastoral. They include dialogue, identity, inculturation, Christology, and prayer and worship.

A dialogue of equals

One of the most important methodological pillars for constructing an African Christian spirituality is dialogue between classical Christian spiritual approaches and African indigenous ones. The goal of the dialogue is not to collapse both spiritualities together into one single approach to God, as is sometimes mistakenly thought in discussions about inculturation. It is important to bear in mind that different spiritualities can coexist, or dwell together, in the Christian religion without rending apart its fabric of faith. Rather, in coexistence they can enrich one another. The history of Western spirituality itself shows this with its many different approaches to the divine reality (see Mursell, 2001).

The task of the dialogue is rather to remove basic contradictions that have contributed to the widespread problem among African Christians known as 'dual religious consciousness'. This occurs when Africans follow two contradictory religious approaches either at the same time or at different times, depending upon their current needs. In contrast, inculturation invites a healthy dialogue between Christian and African traditions that explores how they contribute positively to one another. Ultimately, this approach shows respect for cultural identity.

Identity

While two paths can sometimes lead to the same destination, in the end, two paths that are totally different cannot. The question for African Christian spirituality is to determine which elements from the two spiritual traditions finally come together and lead to the God of Jesus Christ. The word 'determine' is used purposefully here, for it is a process of selection based on our present understanding of a particular culture in relation to the revelation of Jesus. Today it is common knowledge that our understanding of revelation is never neutral; at the best of times it is influenced by cultural prejudices and sheer ignorance of what God's word really means as it is addressed to people in their circumstances. Yet these prejudices disturb the identity of individuals and peoples, which authentic spirituality must never do. It is extremely important to be aware of this if inter-religious dialogue (here between African religion and classical Christianity) is to be honest and helpful. So, then, what is the appropriate method in this dialogue?

Inculturation

Historically, two methods have been used in Africa to introduce Christianity. The first, adaptation, has been the most popular until recently, but in the end it is quite oppressive or unfair. Basically, it tries to find elements in both Christianity and African religion that agree or seem to agree in expression or practice. These common elements then form the basis of African Christian spirituality, theology and pastoral practice. The difficulty with this approach, however, is that it begins with the Christian understanding as the most important, and African viewpoints must always conform or 'adapt' to it. Therefore there is no genuine dialogue because Christianity is not truly willing to learn from African religion. Although this method is still used by some people, most African theologians and church leaders do not find it very helpful in encouraging African Christian communities to become truly African and truly Christian.

The second approach shows much more openness for genuine dialogue and respect for people's cultural identity. Since the 1970s it has been officially adopted by the African Catholic Church as the only appropriate approach, and African Christian theology in general has encouraged it. This is the incarnation or inculturation method, which has deep roots in the Christian faith. Just as God became human in Jesus Christ to bring about the liberation of humanity – thus 'incarnation' – the Christian faith must also enter deeply into any culture and become truly part of it – thus 'inculturation'. There is indeed no other way for Christianity to take root anywhere. Otherwise, it remains superficial, simply added onto a culture without the possibility of truly influencing it positively, and vice versa. This situation produces what we have already described as dual religious consciousness in people, where they feel deeply alienated both spiritually and pastorally. The history of world Christianity is one of either successful or failed inculturation. In other words, faith either becomes integrated with culture or alienated from it.

Christology

How, then, can the God of Jesus Christ be understood in Africa? In other words, is there a place for Jesus in African culture and world view? If so, which images should be used to present him so that both his person and message may be understandable within the religious experience of the African people?

We must first of all acknowledge one fact: Jesus as a divine–human person does not fit naturally, as it were, in African indigenous religious thought.

However, we must quickly explain that this is true not only for African cultures, but for all cultures. The Scriptures say that Jesus enters the world as a new 'Word', or a new revelation, and a key challenge to individuals and groups. People must accept Jesus as an extraordinary Guest bearing new 'good news'. They must also understand their faith in him, first of all, as a gift from God, or what is theologically described as divine grace. Yet, this is precisely the point of the incarnation and inculturation: for Jesus to be known, believed in and genuinely accepted, he must be incarnated and inculturated into the receiving culture. He must be talked about in the local language, called by indigenous names and painted in local features, so that he is no longer a stranger but 'one of us'. This is extremely important for African Christian spirituality. It dictates African Christian spirituality, or in other words, how Africans can 'comfortably' approach Jesus and relate to him.

The Graeco-Roman language used words and symbols to describe Jesus and his mission, such as 'Saviour' and 'Redeemer'. However, these descriptions hardly inspire and challenge African persons to relate to him as one who brings the Good News of God for them. But if African spirituality concerns God's entrance into the world through Jesus in order to bring fullness of life, how does Jesus do so for Africans? Salvation and redemption are categories relevant to guilt cultures, indicating the guilt from human sinfulness before God. In the shame cultures of Africa, however, the issues that prevent fullness of life are a result of humans failing to behave well before others. These issues include practical matters that bring pain and suffering, such as witchcraft, disease, lack of offspring, and disharmony among people and between human beings and the rest of creation. The language that makes Jesus Christ relevant to these situations will not necessarily be the same as the language of guilt, or of salvation and redemption. In general, the images used to explain the reality of Jesus from the perspective of guilt are rather abstract and theoretical, while those from the viewpoint of shame will be more concrete and practical.

Is this realistic? Is it orthodox? Are not the language and images of Scripture, like salvation and redemption, revealed by God himself and therefore sacred? To answer this question, we have to consider the historical development of the Christian Scriptures and the different forms of language employed by the scriptural authors under the guidance of the Holy Spirit. In the New Testament, for example, Graeco-Roman philosophical and imperial language and symbols were used to explain Jesus and his mission. In fact, Jesus could not have been explained and understood in any other way in the circumstances. If this is the case, it is essential that African languages and images communicate Jesus in the same way for contemporary Africans. The question is indeed not asked in amusement: 'What language does God speak?'

In African religion and Christianity, the language referring to God as Father, Creator, all-powerful, all-knowing, and so on, really causes no great difficulty for African Christian spirituality. However, it is the language about Jesus that needs to be brought down to earth to accept African interpretations of his mission in the world. African theology has studied this quite thoroughly, and many different analogies are now accepted as expressing the person and mission of Jesus appropriately in African thought-forms and experience (see Mugambi and Magesa, 1989; Schreiter, 1991; Gibellini, 1994; Stinton, 2004). These analogies include Jesus as Proto-Ancestor or Ancestor par excellence, Jesus as Healer (*Nganga*), Elder Brother, Chief, and Master of Initiation. Since these figures and their activities are central to African life, it is appropriate to interpret Jesus and his mission analogically, or in similar ways, to express how he brings fullness of life to the African world.

Prayer and worship

Understanding Jesus in local images influences our approach to prayer and worship, the most important concrete expressions of the spiritual life. If Jesus is to Africans an Ancestor, Healer or Elder Brother, Chief, or Master of Initiation rather than Redeemer or Saviour, prayer takes on different forms and approaches from the Western types. For one thing, prayers become more active than passive. Prayer becomes a conversation, not in theory but in actual fact. Since ancestors are still considered part of the human community, ongoing conversation with them is natural and vital for the individual and the community. Even when an ancestor seems to fail us, we are free to respond with disappointment, complaint, argument, frustration, or even anger. Likewise, approaching Jesus as Ancestor invites this kind of openness and honesty in prayer as conversation, while still standing in submission to him.

For Africans, the ancestors provide and sustain the community's life, since they are in immediate contact with God and with humanity. Naturally, they are the main recipients of prayer and veneration, and therefore the main partners in our spiritual conversation. However, in African Christian spirituality, Jesus as Proto-Ancestor or Ancestor par excellence becomes the main focus of prayer in this ancestral hierarchy. From this perspective, Jesus is the one who gives power to our human ancestors, enabling them to extend kindness and care to us. So, clearly, the highest form of reverence – that is to say worship proper – is reserved exclusively for Jesus alone and for the God whom he represents. African Christian spirituality must not attribute this honour to human ancestors however exalted, and in actual fact, indigenous spirituality does not do so. It must be emphasized that whatever power human ancestors possess is only derived power, coming from God through Jesus Christ. For example, the elders of a community, people with civil authority, or experts in different fields of knowledge are only honoured secondarily, because they derive their power from Jesus through the ancestors.

Healing and deliverance

We must also mention how prayer is expressed in healing and deliverance, which are of prime importance in African spirituality. We have noted that the central mission of Jesus is to bring fullness of life to the world, and that Christian spirituality is based on this goal. Human beings obtain the life that Christ offers not only when they are freed from the invisible chains of hatred, anger, malice, pride and contempt for God and one another – in a word, from wrongdoing – but also from the visible chains of disease, poverty and ignorance – the concrete results of human failing. Jesus' message aims to break all of these bonds so that there may be abundance of life. According to the Scriptures, Christian prayer and activity are deficient ('useless' and even 'offensive' to God, as the prophetic literature puts it) if they do not address these issues.

Yet what drives African indigenous spirituality, as we have also indicated, is similarly to obtain abundant life in this world, and in concrete terms. This spirituality clearly declares that shortcomings in this area – lack of offspring, food and other material needs necessary for life, and especially illness of whatever kind – are bad, a sign of disfavour from the ancestors and God, and an indication that something is wrong within the community. Misfortunes therefore provide an obvious call for prayer and repentance. For life to be restored in abundance, sickness must be healed and any power that threatens life must be expelled. In this way, humanity will be delivered from suffering and grow towards wholeness.

It seems that the only issue for African Christian spirituality regarding healing and deliverance is not 'why?', but 'how?'. It is not why we should heal but how do we approach healing and deliverance? Of course, Jesus Christ must have a central role in African Christian spirituality, for he is, in the end, the one who is the most potent Vital Energy for us. Can Jesus sometimes give his power to the ancestors directly? Does he give power through them to certain 'elders' to bring about healing and deliverance in our communities? We must answer positively, for how else does the power of the God of Jesus become manifest among us? It is through his creation, through medicine, counselling, peacemaking, prayer, and so on, that we often come in direct contact with him. God grants certain people his power to heal bodies and souls together, and therefore these individuals must be counted among the elders. They themselves, if they are Christians, must realize that they are fulfilling a spiritual task to which they are called by Jesus himself.

 Conclusion

It seems clear that the long-standing divide between Christian spirituality and African indigenous spirituality has mostly been exaggerated. The problem is that classical Christianity has used Graeco-Roman, and later European, philosophical categories to express spirituality from a Western world view, while excluding categories from other world views. Perhaps this is the biggest obstacle in constructing African Christian spirituality because African indigenous categories are neither respected nor accepted. Concretely, however, the so-called divide is not very big at all. African Christians must simply realize that the goal of all spirituality is human communion with God, and that this communion may be achieved in different ways. For all Christians it is, of course, through the agency of Jesus Christ. But only those categories that definitely contradict Jesus' message of love and fullness of life need to be removed from both classical Christian and African indigenous spirituality in the process of constructing an authentic African Christian spirituality.

? STUDY QUESTIONS

1 What are some of the major distinctions between African indigenous and Christian spirituality? What is the degree of difference between them?

2 To what extent is it possible to construct an African Christian spirituality based on the essential similarities between the two? Using this approach, describe some of the key characteristics of African Christian spirituality.

8

Distinctives of African ethics

Bénézet Bujo

Abstract

Bénézet Bujo's chapter contributes a valuable overview of African ethics, particularly in distinction from Western ethics. First, Bujo explains how African ethics are founded upon the African understanding of humanity in its relation to God, the human community, and the cosmos. Second, he introduces African morality by outlining the practice of 'palaver', the traditional council that deals with community matters. This communal interaction forms the context for examining the relation between corporate and individual being and behaviour, as well as the notions of freedom and conscience. Bujo then explores the relevance of African ethics to three contemporary issues: human rights, the elderly, and abortion and euthanasia. Finally, he concludes by emphasizing the overall aim of African ethics in promoting abundant life, and cautioning against globalization that denies a plurality of cultures in constructive dialogue with one another.

Introduction

An understanding of African ethics is fundamental to understanding the inculturation of Christianity in Africa today. Therefore, this chapter examines certain aspects of African tradition, particularly those that distinguish African ethics from Western ethics. From the outset, we must point out that most African scholars agree on the unity of religion – and ethics – in sub-Saharan Africa. While there are differences among African religions, these are generally related to practice (e.g. customs, rites) rather than the substance of the religion itself. There is a great affinity of religious thought throughout all of Black Africa, so we will speak about it in the singular rather than the plural.

African thought centres on life. Life is only understood in relation to God, who is the origin and sustainer of the human community and the cosmos. This human community has three dimensions: the living, the dead and the yet-to-be-born. To begin with, we examine how this understanding of God and humanity forms the foundation of African ethics. We then deal with the origin and nature of ethical norms, or those moral principles that guide human conduct. We conclude by demonstrating, through a few examples, the relevance of African ethics in the modern world.

 # The foundation of African ethics

In order to comprehend African ethics, we must appreciate its foundation in African anthropology, or understanding of humanity. African thought combines two fundamental themes about humanity: its three-dimensional community and its relation to the world, or the cosmos, as a united whole. While these aspects of African tradition are generally acknowledged in theology and philosophy, they are not yet adequately recognized in ethical reflection.

 # Humanity in three-dimensional community

If African morality focuses primarily on inter-human relations, this does not exclude God from consideration. On the contrary, traditional African thought simply assumes God's existence, even if God is rarely mentioned. African myths, stories and proverbs indicate that without God, nothing exists, and that God is present in the lives of individuals and communities. Many African names clearly reflect God's perceived role, especially names in Rwanda and Burundi. For example, *Imana* indicates God and *Habyarimana* means 'God alone begets'. When given to a child, this name signifies that life originates in God alone, not in human strength. Similarly, among the Bahema of Congo-Kinshasa, there are children called Byaruhanga, which means 'God's property'. The idea of God as the originator of life is so fundamental that among the traditional Banyarwanda and the Barundi, parents do not go to bed in the evening without leaving a little water in a jug. Since they believe that God creates life at night, they leave water for God to wash his hands after the work of creation.

So although God is by no means absent from everyday life, African ethics concentrates its attention primarily on the individual and the community. The fundamental goal of African morality is to promote life in this world by doing God's will, which has been handed down through the ancestors. Pleasing God and the ancestors means living in harmony with the three-dimensional community of the living, the dead and the yet-to-be-born. This community forms an organic whole, as explained further in the next section. It is not based on some kind of contract, but rather on deep bonds rooted in a covenant. The covenant is generally grounded in a 'natural' blood relationship with extended kin, although it can possibly be formed through symbolic rites other than birth, such as a blood pact.

While African tradition deeply values kinship ties, it also recognizes the common origin of all humans. Therefore, there is an obligation to see each person as a member of a universal human community in which every individual lives and attempts to be moral. The Baluba of Kasayi, in Congo-Kinshasa, bring this to light through their expression, '*Muntu-wa-Bende-wa-Mulopo*', which means 'Human from *Bende* from God'. In other words, every human being comes from *Bende*, who comes from God. *Bende* here signifies the common origin of humans and of the cosmos, an origin that makes sense only with reference to God. Consequently, this affirmation means that the community is not only three-dimensional, but four-dimensional, since it includes God as the ultimate foundation.

Here, a key distinctive emerges in relation to Western ethics. The modern Western world view is largely based on the Cartesian philosophical concept, *cogito ergo sum*: 'I think, therefore I am.' This famous phrase from French philosopher René Descartes sums up the importance of rationalism in the West. In other words, reason is what defines human beings and their moral action. In contrast, the traditional African concept would be *cognatus sum, ergo sumus*: 'Because I am related to the others, not only I, but also we, together, exist.' Therefore interpersonal relations constitute the basis for ethics, both for the individual and the three-dimensional community.

Another consequence emerges from this African concept: in everyday life, people live within a certain duality that implies a threesome. In other words, masculinity necessarily relates to femininity, and both imply in turn a third dimension, the child. The human being is whole, only as man and woman summoned by the unborn child. This child is the representative of the yet-to-be-born and at the same time the messenger of the ancestors. This perception will bear upon concrete ethical norms, which we will return to in the last section. For now, we must underscore another important dimension in African anthropology, namely, the problem of the relation between humans and the cosmos.

 ## Humanity in relation to the cosmos

In African religion and ethics, everything in the world is intimately connected. All the elements in the universe are related to each other in an interlocking way. One cannot touch one of them without causing the whole to vibrate. Humans are not only part of the cosmos, they are also a microcosm within the macrocosm, or a miniature version of the universe. Black Africans belong at the same time to the world of the living, the dead, and the yet-to-be-born, and they can identify with spirits, animals, plants and minerals. They know that they exist within the vital flux of all creation, which ultimately connects them to the Supreme Being, God, the source of all life.

Thus, in traditional African rites and medicine, there is an encounter between human life and 'cosmic' life (plants, minerals, etc.). In this encounter, humans attempt to work out the tension between life and death. If they wish to secure life's victory over death, they must identify their allies and opponents in the cosmos. Thus, for instance, the cosmic elements used in traditional medicine, even if they are merely minerals, dry wood, or animal bones, are not inanimate realities but are endowed with life-giving power.

The transmission of vital energy applies not only to the medicinal realm, but also to the abundance of life found in nature as a whole. This explains the respect the African has for all of nature. For example, a widespread practice across Africa concerns sacred trees, such as the *ficus* tree which the Bahema of Congo-Kinshasa plant on the tomb of the head of the family. This tree is considered sacred for it represents the one who is buried there, and its branches symbolize the deceased's many descendants. Thus, it represents the life of the family in the African sense. Consequently, it is strictly forbidden to desecrate the tree by cutting it down or by removing any of its branches, twigs and leaves. While this practice may seem primitive and irrational to the Western rationalist, it illustrates ancestral wisdom regarding the life–death tension that prevails throughout the world.

 ## Standards of conduct

Since the community is of the utmost importance in African morality, the matter of establishing norms, or standards of conduct, can only unfold within the context of the community. In what follows, we will outline what we think is essential to understand moral action in Africa. We will begin with 'palaver', the traditional council that deals with community matters. We will then examine the relation between communal action and personal life, which will include a brief presentation of the concepts of person, freedom and individual conscience.

The palaver

In order to understand the role of the palaver, one has to keep in mind the function of words in African communities. The word is powerful. It can be medicine or poison, with the power to bring life or death. Words are said to be 'edible' or 'drinkable'; one 'chews' and 'digests' them. If badly chewed and digested, they can destroy the individual, even a whole community, whereas in the opposite case they bring life.

Palaver functions when people re-examine the meaning of received words. First, there is therapeutic palaver, which is a dialogue between the traditional healer and the patient, or his or her circle. As noted before, the community is a collection of relations where everything influences everything else. Therapeutic palaver aims to detect the causes of illness or malaise, based on how communal relations are experienced and expressed. Therapy will not simply administer medicines without taking into account the patient's life situation. Rather, the aim will be to revive him or her, primarily by recreating life-enhancing relations. To do so, the sick person, the doctor and the community as a whole must hold a palaver where together they digest the badly chewed and undigested words in order to deprive those words of their deadly venom, and then imbue them with vital force. The administered medicines will be able to take effect only after good relations are restored.

Second, there is the family palaver. Behind closed doors, people deal with problems of the family in its African sense, encompassing the living, the dead and the yet-to-be-born. Family palaver is the foremost place for developing domestic ethics. It covers a wide variety of topics because it seeks to contribute to the growth of the life of the extended family in all its dimensions. The problems it deals with may be about sharing property, considering the future, appointing or removing a person responsible for a given area, tackling family feuds – the list is endless. Family palaver aims to restore harmony within the community by bringing together those in conflict so they learn to listen to each other again. Aside from resolving contentious cases, it seeks to maintain healthy and harmonious relations within the community and to nurture ongoing mutual support. No wonder most palavers end by celebrating their reconciliation with a hearty meal!

Third, an administrative palaver is called if a family palaver fails to solve a problem, or to address issues relating to the wider community. This palaver has a more political character and may apply to several clan communities. Whereas the traditional doctor (male or female healer) presides over a therapeutic palaver and an elder oversees a family palaver, the political leader – whether a chief or king, or a council of elders – leads the administrative palaver. In each case, those who preside over the palaver must not be arrogant and authoritarian, and they must never humiliate or silence any participant. On the contrary, they are to be attentive to everyone in order to discover the wisdom in what each has to say. The concern for wisdom means that poetic language, symbolism, proverbs, parables and stories are often used in palavers to express fundamental insights about life.

The concept and practice of palaver thus shapes certain distinctives of African ethics in relation to Western ethics. Following the Cartesian philosophy introduced above, with its emphasis on reason and individuality, Western ethics becomes grounded in natural or moral law. In contrast, African ethics are derived primarily from the community and governed by what enhances abundant life for all. Therefore, differences emerge in the way various ethics are developed. In Western discourse ethics, only those capable of rational argumentation can participate in the discussion, to the exclusion of children or the mentally challenged or others whose interests can only be represented by an advocate. In Africa, the palaver is to embrace everybody and to establish meaning even through the symbolic actions and gestures of those who lack the standard level of language.

Another difference from discourse ethics concerns the palaver's religious dimension. God and the world of the ancestors form an integral part of palaver, whereas they are excluded from consideration in discourse ethics. This is not to say that participants are not allowed to be critical, but the power of reason has its limits, unlike in Western ethical discourse where reason is held to be supreme. Likewise, the dimension of sin radically sets apart African palaver, where religion features significantly, from Western discourse ethics.

Furthermore, discourse ethics generally contents itself with establishing ethical norms at the 'formal level' without caring about their concrete application. By contrast, African ethics does not stay at the level of formal principles, but is concerned with the application of the norms proposed in the course of palaver.

Some observers have drawn a parallel between this African style of community-based ethics and the Western model of communitarianism. Both models stress that the individual is always to be understood in relation to the community in which all endeavour is undertaken for the common good. But there are important differences between the two models. In the Western conception it appears that as far as moral action is concerned, the individual, though bound to environment and group, will not feel obliged to make personal decisions with reference to the community. The community might influence the individual, but it does not determine their personal life. By contrast, in African ethics community is all-important, so much so that even deceased members are involved in decisions. The whole community participates in helping the individual before, during and after making a decision so that it will be put into practice – always for the sake of the community.

It must also be said that the communal character of African ethics does allow for innovation. Traditions that no longer encourage abundant life must be abolished and new ones must replace them. That is what palaver is all about. In addition, African communitarians know how to avoid ethnocentric isolation. Communities are not isolated from one another but remain open to cultural influences. Since every human is believed to come from God, he or she is entitled to respect, whatever their clan or ethnicity.

Although African ethics shares some characteristics with Western models, such as natural law ethics, discourse ethics, and communitarianism, it clearly differs from them in many respects. Above all, its relational character in all aspects – involving God, the spirits, the world of the living, the dead, the yet-to-be-born, even the cosmos as a whole – makes it a unique system.

However, another question arises. If community shapes so much of African ethics, and if every decision cannot take place without its input, to what extent can one still talk of individual responsibility?

The concepts of person and freedom

It is not uncommon to hear criticism of the influence that the group exerts on the individual. Undoubtedly, some deplorable events have tarnished African tradition. However, this tradition's ideal should not be compromised by such breaches. As African morality is essentially based on interpersonal relationships, there can be no atomized activity separate from other people who constitute a community, even beyond death. It is impossible to talk of freedom in the sense in which modern Western philosophy conceives it, that is, in each individual's highly personal self-determination. This notion is also central to Roman Catholic morality, and to human rights activists who want to protect individuals from the tyranny of groups.

As for Black African ethics, since individuals can only exist within the 'us', it is impossible for them to fulfil their potential outside of the community. To grasp this concept, one must understand the notion of person in Africa, which consists in the interdependence between the individual and the community. This interdependence goes beyond biological continuity and a shared spiritual heritage, to entail the uninterrupted interaction between all of a community's members – those alive, dead, and yet-to-be-born. Thus, to be called a 'person' does not simply require being a member of a community, but actively participating in mutual, interpersonal relations. In other words, individuals only become persons if they do not isolate themselves but act together with the entire community.

Participation in this common life is so essential that even the dead depend on it to safeguard their growth as a person. Becoming a person is thus a perpetual process that does not end at death. Personal identity in the realm beyond this life depends on ties to the earthly community and to those still to come; from the beyond one lives in interaction and in harmony with the members of the three-dimensional community. This conception explains Africans' veneration for their ancestors. Even though ancestors can no longer suffer, they still have certain needs, such as hunger, thirst, love, the sense of justice and peace. They can be worry-free only if the community of the living does not forget them or cause them harm.

In addition, in order to ensure happiness for ever, continuity in the descendants has to be secured. For this reason, the yet-to-be-born occupy an important place in the community. In fact they already deserve to be called 'persons' because, even before they have taken shape, they embody the living and the dead in the future and carry everybody's hopes.

Western societies tend to see too much of the negative side of freedom, in the sense that one wishes to free oneself from any obstacles that prevent self-fulfilment. However, in African societies, individual freedom is possible only through participation in the community's life, or within 'being-with-the-others'. In other words, freedom cannot consist only in being free from, but rather in being free for and with. Furthermore, my freedom as an individual can be real only if I free the community at the same time. Likewise, the community can enjoy true freedom only if it allows me to be free as an individual. Strong and abundant life for all is possible only in this continual interaction.

It is obvious that in a community where individuals must never exercise self-determination without consideration for other members, questions concerning individual conscience will not pose themselves as they do in Western morality. In Africa, the individual conscience is not the ultimate decision-making authority, but rather has to be discussed in palaver, the authority by which the community examines the words hidden in each person's heart. These 'chewed' and 'digested' words must resurface in order to be ruminated collectively, so that they can manifest their life-giving quality. The process of subjecting an individual's conscience to regular evaluation by the elders effectively 'normalizes' it, and it becomes part of the collective communal conscience. To have a clear conscience is to be fully integrated in the communal conscience. This conception of communal conscience is of immense importance because in the end it excludes the type of fundamentalism that is driven by a private agenda. Individual freedom that is not integrated into the community is a bomb that can cause tremendous damage.

The relevance of African ethics

In what sense does African tradition still have relevance in the modern world? Is it a bygone tradition lost in the mists of time? On the contrary, African ethics, steeped as it is in the three-dimensional community, is of interest to the modern world in at least three areas: human rights, the elderly, and abortion and euthanasia.

Human rights

The Western interpretation of human rights, which begins with the individual, has little impact on the African model. For Africans, any individual right deserves to be so called only insofar as it does not lose sight of the common good. A typical example is the right to own property. In Africa, the property of the individual belongs also to the community. He or she must maintain it for the general good. It is noteworthy that in many African communities the notion of poverty is somewhat different from that in the materialistic West. In Africa, the goal is not to possess things but to form relationships. One is not poor because one possesses nothing material; true poverty consists in having no human relations, having perhaps lost one's parents or other family members, for example. Even concerning material things, the point is not to 'possess' them in the Western sense but to have relationships with them. This is evident in African languages, such as Swahili and Lingala, which lack the verb 'to have'. Instead, the term literally means 'to be with'.

A similar argument holds true for children's right to education. Children belong not only to their parents in the Western sense, but to the whole clan community. The right to education must therefore involve this community as a whole and not limit itself to the parents alone. When in modern Africa one talks of human rights' violations, it is absolutely necessary to take into account the context as we have just described it.

Issues concerning the elderly

In modern society, particularly in the West, young people tend to regard the elderly as a burden. Advertising praises eternal youth. As everything centres on profitability, the elderly are relegated to oblivion, since they are perceived to be of little use to society. In contrast, the elderly are treated with great respect in Africa. By virtue of their long experience they are considered a source of wisdom. Even though they can no longer generate biological life, they continue to strengthen the life of the whole community through their wisdom. Teaching through experience is not about transmitting technological knowledge, for instance, because young people can be experts in this. The experience African tradition speaks of is at a more existential level, providing technology with its soul. A technology devoid of wisdom is dehumanizing and leads to death. From the African point of view, a society that dispenses with the experience of the elderly ruins itself because it will not be able to identify the forces of life and death in the cosmos. We only have life in its various manifestations thanks to our elders. Even if they can no longer hand down their wisdom to us, it is our duty to demonstrate our gratitude and to share with them our presence in order to increase their vital force on their painful path to the ancestors.

Issues concerning abortion and euthanasia

The subject of the elderly is closely related to discussions about the beginning and end of life. Stormy debates on the status of the embryo reveal many divergent opinions on the determination of the precise moment at which one can refer to it as being a person. The various arguments often hinge on discerning potential for mental development, such as the appearance of the 'large brain' which supposedly indicates that the embryo has evolved towards an 'autonomous' human being.

In African tradition, it would be futile to have such a debate since the embryo, or foetus, belongs to the world of the yet-to-be-born and is fully integrated into the community of the living and the dead. It therefore lives within the love of the visible and invisible community. The foetus is the hope of the living and of the dead that survive in it, not only on the biological level but also as it enriches the community, increasing life in its broad sense. Though the foetus is yet incapable of providing any service, it acts as the ancestors' messenger, connecting them to their descendants on earth. From this perspective, the embryo is indeed a person whose life must absolutely be respected since there is a continuous interaction between the living, the dead and the unborn.

Likewise, the Western debates about euthanasia are not found in most African traditions. In Black Africa, caring for the dying is considered crucial. It consists in providing for their needs and conveying to them their ongoing importance, despite their physical condition. It also entails reminding them that they continue to develop personally even through suffering. Dying persons restore their being through interpersonal relations with those caring for them and, in turn, the sick and the dying deepen the personalities of those around them as they become more aware of life's highs and lows. Thus, in the way that they accept their suffering, the sick and the dying contribute to the edification of the living. A dying person's last days are a chance for everyone to enrich one another and to become even more conscious of their respective identities.

On this basis, euthanasia as it is understood in the West, far from protecting human rights, in fact violates them. It annihilates a person's identity. In its original meaning, euthanasia should consist in helping the dying to feel accepted by their family circles, as the African tradition seeks to do.

 Conclusion

Our study is only an overview, which by no means claims to exhaust the ethical questions in Black Africa. From what has been said, however, it appears that African ethics has its own logic, which deserves to be respected in intercultural and inter-religious dialogue. While the general tendency in the world is towards globalization, the inclination to deny African culture its identity, either reducing it to a monoculture or assimilating it into a global ethos, is a form of neocolonialism. The aim of African ethics is to promote life in abundance, which is only possible if one respects diversity within cultures. Far from being an impoverishment, diversity is a valuable opportunity for enrichment. Globalization, on the other hand, is a cultural cloning seeking to impose a monoculture that can be oppressive. The world will be able to enhance life and find peace only if we respect the plurality of cultures in dialogue with one another.

? STUDY QUESTIONS

1 Bujo summarizes the basis of African ethics as follows:

The fundamental goal of African morality is to promote life in this world by doing God's will, which has been handed down through the ancestors. Pleasing God and the ancestors means living in harmony with the three-dimensional community of the living, the dead and the yet-to-be-born.

Discuss what this statement means. How does it compare with your understanding of Christian ethics?

2 According to Bujo, what is an African palaver? Describe the different kinds of palaver Bujo outlines, and how these reflect standards of conduct in African ethics.

3 Summarize the key distinctives of African ethics in relation to Western ethics. What insights do you find from African ethics that might enhance your understanding of Christian ethics?

9

African women's theologies

Isabel Apawo Phiri and Sarojini Nadar

 Abstract

Isabel Phiri and Sarojini Nadar begin their chapter with the fundamental premise on which African women's theologies are built: humanity is made up of male and female beings, and both expressions of humanity must partner together in a balanced way for the whole community to experience fullness of life. Phiri and Nadar then demonstrate how women's experience is a chief cornerstone for feminist theology, yet this experience is significantly shaped by the contexts in which women live. Focusing on developments in Africa, the authors discuss issues regarding terminology and methodology, before identifying and critiquing seven key features of African women's theologies. They conclude by underlining the richness and diversity of these theologies, while lamenting the ongoing marginalization of African women's theologies within mainstream theology. Phiri and Nadar therefore appeal for African women's theologies to be acknowledged as an effective starting point for the kind of liberation theologies required to address the many crises in Africa.

 Introduction

Feminism has become the shorthand for the proclamation that women's experiences should become an integral part of what goes into the definition of being a human. It highlights the woman's world and her world-view as she struggles side by side with the man to realise her full potential as a human being ... Feminism then emphasises the wholeness of the community as made up of male and female beings. It seeks to express what is not so obvious, that is, that male-humanity is a partner with female-humanity, and that both expressions of humanity are needed to shape a balanced community within which each will experience a fullness of Be-ing [*sic*]. Feminism calls for the incorporation of the woman into the community of interpretation of what it means to be human.

(Oduyoye, 1986: 121)

This quote is by Mercy Amba Oduyoye, a Ghanaian theologian and founder of the Circle of Concerned African Women Theologians. Her statement introduces what African women theologians are seeking to do: that is, to take women's experiences and contexts seriously in their theologies. Our aim in this chapter is to demonstrate how experience and context influence the way in which women across the globe engage with theological reflection. We also summarize some of the important features of African women's theologies, highlighting the positive and negative aspects of each feature.

 ## Experience and context in women's theologies

The chief cornerstone of feminist theologies lies in experience. Feminist theologians have always maintained experience as a legitimate starting point of any theology. Ironically, it is on this issue of experience that African, Asian, African American, and Latin American women felt the need to name their theologies differently. Although some believed that all women share similar universal experiences, most recognized that these experiences were shaped by particular conditions of culture, gender, class and race. So for example, African American women contend that feminism, which first arose among white middle-class women, has not fully addressed their experiences of race and class discrimination, particularly their history of slavery and colonialism. Instead, feminism tends to focus more on gender than on race and class. To distinguish their own experiences, African American women began to use to term 'womanist'.

Similarly, women across the globe began to recognize that they had often taken different sides in colonialism and imperialism and had not possessed a common cause.

Therefore, it is necessary to point out the conditions from which feminism arises. Even if it means continuously using extra adjectives as in 'poor Latinos', 'Black middle-class women', 'white working-class women', it is worth it so that people don't feel excluded or robbed of an ability to identify with the category 'women' because they feel appropriated rather than addressed by feminism. In other words, although there are similarities between the oppressions that women experience, you cannot universalize their oppression. As Sarla Palkar argues:

> Western feminists tend to universalise patriarchy and thereby homogenise women, especially the Third World women . . . but the problems and the subjectivities may differ according to their national, historical or local contexts. The ideological construction of women in India, say, is not the same as that of a woman in Argentina though both of them are supposed to belong to the Third World.
> (Palkar, 1996: 20–1)

Feminist theologies therefore highlight the need to consider specificity and location of experience. In what is now popularly known as the 'third wave of feminism', experience is being taken more seriously than ever. Women from the Global South are beginning to make their voices heard, whether through postcolonial discourse, cultural hermeneutics or Marxist–feminist critique. Never before has the point been made so forcefully, that gender is linked closely with issues of race (e.g. in womanist scholars such as Delores Williams), of class (e.g. in Latin American scholars such as Ivone Gebara), of interfaith encounter (e.g. in some Asian feminist scholars such as Kwok Pui-Lan), or of culture (e.g. in African women scholars such as Mercy Oduyoye). Even within Africa, it is impossible to universalize African women's experiences. A case in point is the South African context, where the experiences of white women have been markedly different from those of their Black counterparts.

Given the strong argument for the specificity of experience, it is important to state at this point the specificity of our own experiences. Unfortunately, it would be impossible to tell our entire stories. Rather, what we want to highlight here is the significance of our gender struggles towards the kind of research we undertake. We come from different backgrounds.

Isabel Phiri is a Chewa from Malawi, a Presbyterian, living and working as an academic in South Africa. Her present location in South Africa can largely be attributed to her struggles as a feminist, both in her church and university context in Malawi, where she was violently barred from the church and the university for raising issues of gender justice in Church and society.

Sarojini Nadar is a fourth-generation South African Indian woman. She grew up during the time of apartheid, in a low socio-economic Pentecostal church in the racially segregated 'Indian' dormitory township of Phoenix, north of the coastal city of Durban. She now belongs to a Lutheran church in Chatsworth, also a previously designated 'Indian' township, south of Durban. Like Phoenix, Chatsworth remains predominantly Indian. The move from a Pentecostal to a Lutheran church has not changed the gender struggles she experiences almost daily with patriarchal theology deeply entrenched in the so-called 'Indian' church. The hardships she experienced in a patriarchal society after the death of her father, and her subsequent sexual abuse as a child, are what primarily drive her feminist agenda. Seeking to find solidarity with those who suffer similar fates, she strives to understand, analyse and change the systems of domination and abuse of power.

Both authors of this article are committed to the struggle for gender justice through the Programme of Gender and Religion, in which we both teach at the School of Religion and Theology, University of KwaZulu-Natal, South Africa. Our theologizing is necessarily influenced by the fact that both of us are in positions of relative privilege, due in part to our education and economic standing. Nevertheless, we consider ourselves 'activist-intellectuals' through our involvement with organizations such as the Centre for Constructive

Theology, our churches, and in most recent times with multinational corporations that invite us to conduct workshops on issues of gender, culture and HIV & AIDS. Together, we have also conducted Bible study workshops with churches. We constantly aim to raise awareness of gender justice, and ultimately to transform the patriarchy that is prevalent both in our churches and society. Additionally, we work closely within the communities in which we live and work, in municipal areas of eThekwini (Durban) and Msunduzi (Pietermaritzburg), in the Province of KwaZulu-Natal. True to feminist ideals, we see our task as not just the intellectual one but the activist one as well.

Finally, we are also committed members of the Circle of Concerned African Women Theologians (hereafter, the Circle). Indeed, Phiri has recently served a five-year term as the Chair of the Executive Members who provide leadership to the Circle across the continent. While it began in 1989, by 2006 the Circle had a registered membership of 617 members on the African continent and in the diaspora, distributed as follows: 465 anglophone, 93 francophone, and 59 lusophone. The Circle is an important space for women from Africa to do communal theology based on their religious, cultural and social experiences. It draws its membership from women of diverse backgrounds, nationalities, cultures and religions. Its central vision is to empower African women to contribute critical thinking and analysis towards the advancement of human knowledge.

Features of African women's theologies

So far we have raised some of the concerns of feminist theology around the world. We now want to focus on certain issues and developments within African women's theologies.

One of the fundamental issues that the Circle has faced concerns terminology, particularly whether or not to identify our theology with the controversial term 'feminist'. Some Circle theologians, especially from the anglophone region, have been reluctant to adopt this term, while others, especially the francophone theologians, are less so. Responses vary depending on how the term is understood and used. Yet if Oduyoye's basic definition of feminism is upheld, as quoted at the beginning of this chapter, then most Circle women should have no problem calling themselves feminist.

Another concern, related to terminology, is that of methodology in doing feminist theology. On the one hand, we acknowledge our need as African women theologians to broaden the theoretical basis of our work. Although many of us were trained in the tools of Western theologies, we have yet to fully critique their meaningfulness within our context as African women. Together with this, we need to establish ourselves differently (although with similar agendas) from the feminist cause which we perceive as being largely Western, white and middle-class. On the other hand, Isabel Phiri has argued that:

> despite the differences in terminology, all women would like to see the end of sexism in their lives and the establishment of a more just society of men and women that seeks the well-being of the other. The women go further to seek justice for all the oppressed including the environment.　　(Phiri, 2004: 156)

Oduyoye outlines a number of important characteristics that distinguish African women's theologies from other contextual theologies (Oduyoye, 2001). She first points out that African women have inherited various European and American theologies, including missionary and feminist/ womanist theologies. However, African women keep a critical distance from them, since their priority is to communicate African women's own understanding. By delineating seven key features of African women's theologies, we propose to explore how African women theologians have developed their own theological understanding.

Feminist cultural hermeneutics

One of the primary defining features of African women's theologies is their focus on culture as a source of theology. Of course, African male theologians also focus on culture as a way of redeeming African identity, which Christian missionaries often demonized in their aggressive efforts to evangelize Africa. Generally, however, African women theologians find that their experiences of culture are excluded in projects such as inculturation. In other words, when describing or analysing culture within the inculturation process, the experiences of African males are often taken as the norm and standard. Therefore, African women began to make a strong case for their experiences to be included within African theology. This is now popularly known as an 'irruption within an irruption' in the Ecumenical Association of Third World Theologians and other similar alliances.

The term 'hermeneutics' is usually reserved for the discipline of biblical studies, where it basically refers to how the Bible is interpreted. African women theologians speak of 'feminist cultural hermeneutics' as a tool for analysing both the biblical practices of culture and the various cultures within Africa. In the process, 'women are developing cultural hermeneutics for the appropriation of Africa's religio-culture, which constitutes a resource for envisioning the will of God and the meaning of women's humanity' (Oduyoye, 2001: 18). By so doing, feminist cultural hermeneutics has sought to face the 'challenge of struggling with one's culture, while fencing off those waiting to use our culture to under-rate us. Cultural hermeneutics seeks a critique from within and not an imposition from without' (Oduyoye, 2001: 18).

For example, African male biblical scholars proposed the project of inculturation. This arose within the broader context of the Black consciousness movement, with its call towards Black people to be proud of their Blackness, their cultures and their heritage. Kenyan theologian Musimbi Kanyoro responded seriously, yet critically, to the call by proposing her own version of a feminist cultural hermeneutics. She suggested that women make the

Bible and their culture speak to each other and analyse the issues that arise in the conversation.

African women theologians have therefore developed feminist cultural hermeneutics as a method of analysing various issues within African culture, including that of sexuality. Although sexuality has been widely engaged in feminist discourse in the West, it is usually discussed in the context of sexual orientation and reproductive rights. In contrast, African women theologians discuss sexuality in the context of rites of passage, including childbirth (women's sexuality in the context of giving birth), menstruation (purity and impurity laws), circumcision (male and female), marriage (the patriarchal constraints within marriage and the different forms of marriage), and even death (practices such as widow-cleansing, etc. See Oduyoye and Kanyoro, 2006). In order to analyse these issues accurately, it is not possible to use general and abstract theories which do not apply to the specificity of such cultural practices. African women theologians are therefore careful to specify concrete contexts in their writings, instead of making generalizations about the whole of Africa. The tool of feminist cultural hermeneutics helps us to do this.

A good example of this can be found in the work of the Black South African biblical scholar, Madipoane Masenya, who has established a new approach towards interpreting the Bible she calls *bosadi*, or 'womanhood'. Masenya aims to read the Bible from the perspective of the specific Northern-Sotho cultural sensibilities of womanhood. She asserts that the methodology is an 'African women's liberation' model which seeks to highlight the oppressive elements in African culture and in the biblical culture, while retrieving the liberative elements in both these cultures. She also asserts that this model of hermeneutics highlights the values of *ubuntu* ('I am because we are') and family. Her context as a South African scholar also compels her to include the interplay of post-apartheid, racism, sexism, classism and African culture in her hermeneutical model. Her desire to move away from a Western model of theologizing to a more African one can be seen in the way in which she charts a shift from naming her work originally as Black feminist theology within feminist theology, later as African womanist hermeneutics, while finally settling on a *bosadi* hermeneutic. However, Masenya's work has been criticized for almost excusing oppressive elements of culture in her attempt at inculturation.

African women have certainly taken the cultural debate, which is central to inculturation, to another level by developing feminist cultural hermeneutics. Indeed, culture is an integral part of our lives and identities. The focus in feminist cultural hermeneutics is on retaining those aspects of African culture which are liberative, while rejecting those which are oppressive. The criterion for assessing cultural elements is the standard of abundant life for both women and men: those things which are life-affirming are retained and promoted, while those which are life-denying are rejected. Yet the focus on culture, while establishing a separate space for African women to theologize, can also have the adverse effect of 'exoticizing' African women's discourses. In other words, the African women's theologies may be considered so unusual that they are not taken seriously within mainstream theology.

Narrative theology

African women's theologies are primarily narrative theology. Oduyoye (2001: 16) describes this method as follows:

> In their theological reflections, women of the Circle proceed from the narrating of the story to analysing it to show how the various actors in the story see themselves, how they interact with others, and how they view their own agency in life as a whole . . . The next stage is to reflect on the experiences from the perspective of the Christian faith – a conscious implementation of biblical and cultural hermeneutics are at work in this process.

It must be noted, though, that narrative theology is not exclusively 'owned' by African women theologians. In fact, it is a widely developed method used by feminist theologians across the world and in other disciplines besides theology. What distinguishes African women's narrative theologies is that they use the plentiful stories, proverbs, myths and sayings that already exist in African cultures, as sources of theologizing from a woman's liberative perspective.

A danger in over-reliance on this method, though, is that sometimes narrative theology is not considered to be academically rigorous. Academic rigour requires that we read and engage with the works of other scholars. Nonetheless, as Oduyoye asserts, African women theologians do not have 'to begin with reading other people's works, indeed most of the time the impulse to theologize is generated by experience or praxis. African women's theology does not end in documents' (Oduyoye, 2001: 18).

Theological and social advocacy

A third feature of African women's theologies is their focus on the transformation of society. This is where the Circle membership's commitment to advocacy for change is unmistakably witnessed. Through their application of feminist cultural hermeneutics, African women theologians:

> identify what enhances, transforms or promotes in such a way as to build community and make for life-giving and life-enhancing relationships. The concern is not limited to the articulation of statements of faith. Women do theology to undergird and nourish spirituality for life.   (Oduyoye, 2001: 16)

This focus on the transformation of society places African women's theologies firmly within the field of liberation theologies. Such theologies generally seek to conscientize communities of people, or to make them aware of their oppression as the first step towards overcoming it. Classical Latin American liberation scholars such as Gustavo Gutiérrez and Miguez Bonino, who are well known for championing the cause of the poor and oppressed, spend half their time in the academy and the other half living and working among the poor.

The Circle achieves its advocacy goals primarily through theological institutions. It has prioritized theological education for women, and also designed and implemented theological curricula which include feminist theology and gender studies. The Circle seeks not only to include these subjects as a separate discipline, but also to mainstream gender concerns in the theological curricula. The Circle believes that by empowering the future leaders of the church and faith institutions, it is also empowering those selfsame communities, since these are the people who will do the work on the ground. In addition, the Circle has advocated more female faculty members and women students being prioritized in theological institutions.

Finally, between 2002 and 2007, the Circle declared HIV & AIDS to be a major priority in research and advocacy for change and empowerment. Given the gendered nature of HIV & AIDS, particularly in Africa, the Circle compelled its members to reflect theologically on the AIDS pandemic and to empower communities through conscientization. Since religion is often a vehicle for promoting stigma and discrimination, the Circle prioritized its educational role in addressing these matters. The education provided comes out of deep theological reflection on the context of HIV & AIDS in Africa. This theological reflection has also borne fruit in mainstreaming HIV & AIDS into the theological curriculum of institutions.

Communal theology

The fourth feature of African women's theologies is what might be called a 'theology of relations'. Here the focus is on replacing hierarchies with mutuality. Since African culture is very community-oriented, African theologies must be sensitive to the needs of others and to the well-being of the community as a whole. Therefore African women theologians take their communities very seriously in their work. We have already alluded to our own personal roles in conducting empowerment workshops for women in our communities. Likewise, Kanyoro emphasizes the importance of doing theology in community as a contribution which African women make in the field of theology.

The Circle intentionally provides space for women to do communal theology of a scholarly type through its structures of chapters and conferences. For example, in the Pietermaritzburg Chapter of the Circle in South Africa, those women who have experience in research and publishing mentor those who have less experience, including students.

Another type of scholarly communal theology can be found in the work of the Nigerian biblical scholar, Teresa Okure. Okure insists that the task of African feminist hermeneutics is not simply the liberation of women alone, but the entire community. Also, the liberation of women does not mean the oppression of men. She further argues that feminist biblical scholarship in Africa is made up of both scholars and non-scholars, highlighting her commitment to popular readings of the Bible and to the community at large.

One problem that can be raised with this 'theology of relations', or communal theology, is the need to balance it with a 'theology of gender justice'. This is because sometimes the needs of the community are promoted at the expense of gender justice. In addition, when one speaks of a 'theology of relations', the environment should be included. However, there is limited scholarship within Africa that demonstrates eco-feminist theological reflection. Perhaps this could be an area of future research for African women theologians.

The Bible and African women's theologies

Fifthly, the Bible is a central source of theologizing in African women's theologies. As indicated above, the Bible is often used in dialogue with African culture and religions. Several studies have shown parallels between the biblical cultures, especially those found in the Old Testament, and Africa. Having found 'Africa in the Bible', many inculturation scholars have been at pains to point out that Christianity indeed contains elements of African culture within it. These findings strengthen the case against the missionaries' demonizing of certain African cultural practices such as polygamy, which contributed significantly to the rise of the African Initiated Churches (AICs).

Given these parallels between biblical and African cultures, the Bible has become a rich source of doing African theology. African women began to protest against the often oversimplified and uncritical way in which cultural practices in their communities, such as those concerning purity and menstruation, polygamy, or inheritance, found justification from within the Bible. At first, this analysis was simply a means of protest rather than a systematic analysis of biblical texts using the tools of biblical criticism. Soon, however, there were a growing number of women, trained in classical biblical studies, who applied the tools of biblical criticism in their interpretation of the Bible.

As a result, African women theologians take issue with the simplistic parallels that are often drawn between biblical and African cultures, especially those regarding women. They often appeal to the story from the Gospel of Mark of Jairus's daughter being raised from the dead (Mark 5.21–42) as a key metaphor for their own liberation from oppression. Indeed, a vital centre for African women's theology, the Talitha Qumi Centre in Legon, Ghana, is named on this basis.

Race, class and gender

A sixth feature of African women's theologies is the importance placed on issues concerning race and class, that is, in addition to those of gender. Once again, this situates these theologies within the broad scope of liberation theology. The work of the Botswana-born biblical scholar, Musa Dube, makes this very clear. Dube's methodology, which she calls 'postcolonial feminist hermeneutics', is one of the most theoretically advanced methodologies to come out of African women's biblical scholarship. She focuses primarily on the oppressive nature of the Bible toward women, which she views as a multilayered reality. Her particular interest is in the role of the Bible in promoting gender oppression as well as imperial domination. The task of feminist postcolonial criticism is not simply to hold a 'pity-party' for the wrongs of the past; rather, it is to actively engage with the continuing effects of the past, thereby working towards the transformation of the present. In this respect, Dube has produced profound readings of texts which focus on the interconnection of imperial and gender discourses. An important contribution in this regard is her reflections on Ruth in 'Divining Ruth for International Relations' (Dube, 2001).

Interdisciplinary and multi-faith theologies

Besides Christianity, the African continent is home to other religions including African Religion, Hinduism, Islam, Judaism and Sikhism. Therefore, these religions are included in the theologizing of the Circle, as illustrated by its multi-faith membership. Moreover, African women theologians have taken the interfaith nature of the African community seriously, although most work has been done in the disciplines of Christianity and African Religion. Since it is predominantly African Christian women who have engaged in these disciplines, their tendency is to use African Religion only in the service of Christianity. Dube has made the excellent observation that while African Religion has always been subject to the saving grace of Jesus Christ, it has never been taken seriously as an independent entity. Hence scholars like Nokuzola Mndende, who operate solely within the confines of the discipline of African Religion, have fought for it to be recognized as a self-sustaining discipline within the Circle. Thus they methodologically separate from the project of Christian theology.

Despite the fact that the multi-faith work of the Circle is currently limited in scope, the work of African women theologians is nevertheless interdisciplinary in nature. Although a wide range of disciplines are present, including the history of Christianity, biblical studies, religious studies and practical theology, African women's theologies still remain a marginal project within the overall field of theology. We would submit, therefore, that African women's theologies should not only be acknowledged as an authentic discipline, but also be mainstreamed into all theological disciplines.

 Conclusion

In this chapter, we have attempted to reveal the richness and diversity of African women's theologies. We recognize, however, that together with other feminist theologies, African women's theologies remain a marginalized discipline within mainstream theology. Indeed, it may be the most marginalized! By highlighting the methodological and theoretical perspectives that undergird their work, we hope to challenge the notion that African women's theologies are not an authentic discipline within theology. Rather, much of the groundwork has already been laid, and we are now simply stacking the building blocks of this theology of liberation.

Unfortunately our inherited forms of Western theologizing are clearly inadequate to respond meaningfully to the present crises that plague Africa, including HIV & AIDS, poverty and gender injustice. For example, Tinyiko Maluleke has argued that in the face of the HIV & AIDS pandemic, the Church has been rendered 'theologically impotent'. He thus makes a concerted plea for us to return to a variety of theologies of liberation in order to effectively respond to these enormous challenges. We submit that African women's theologies are a good place to start.

 ## STUDY QUESTIONS

1 How would you define 'feminism'? How does your understanding of feminism compare with that of Phiri and Nadar?

2 Explain why feminist theologies differ among African, Asian, African American and Latin American women. Describe the kind of feminist theology, if any, you encounter in your own context.

3 Discuss each of the seven key characteristics of African women's theologies presented in this chapter, noting its positive and negative aspects.

4 Phiri and Nadar conclude that African women's theologies are a good starting point for responding effectively to the present crises in Africa such as HIV & AIDS, poverty and gender injustice. Do you agree? Explain your answer.

10

The challenges of ecumenism in African Christianity today

Hamilton Mvumelwano Dandala

 Abstract

In identifying the challenges of ecumenism in Africa, Hamilton Mvumel-wano Dandala begins with the arrival of Christianity in Africa and the con-fusion that was often created when missionaries introduced new rites of worship and fostered rivalry among Christian missions. He traces the birth and development of ecumenism in Africa, highlighting the role of the All Africa Conference of Churches (AACC) since its foundation in 1963 to its ninth General Assembly in 2008. Over the decades, the AACC has advocat-ed the Church's responsibility in addressing socio-political and economic issues. Nonetheless, Dandala argues that the Church has not achieved the unity it sought in establishing the AACC. He therefore calls Christians to consolidate the voice of the Church in oneness and authenticity, and to take prophetic action on behalf of those who are suffering, for example in Zimbabwe. Only then will the Church fulfil the mission of Christ, extending love, hope and reconciliation.

 Introduction

Dr Zachariah K. Matthews was an outstanding academician and political activist, as well as a strong Christian leader in South Africa. He campaigned keenly for the formation of an ecumenical body in Africa (Utuk, 1997). He willingly acknowledged the many positive contributions made by mission-aries, yet also pointed out the injustices that accompanied their work. Con-sequently, Matthews was convinced that the gospel had to be removed from the hands of missionaries so that Africans could appropriate it authentically for themselves. His message was that there were African values that had once been incorporated in the Christian practices, but these were eventually lost and should be brought back into the Church.

It would be wrong for anyone to think that when Christianity was first introduced in Africa, it found a people with no systems of belief and worship. In the words of John Mbiti, 'Africans are notoriously religious' (Mbiti, 1969: 1). In other words, there was a firm conviction that any occurrence – whether good, such as birth or plentiful harvests, or bad, such as famine, natural calamity, or death – did not happen just by chance. Rather, some force that was beyond human conception was responsible for it. Indeed, such an occurrence was reason for elaborate celebrations, either to rejoice at the good tidings or to appease the gods so they would not inflict further harm upon the people.

As Christianity came to Africa, a marriage occurred between the two 'cultures' – African celebrations and worship, and the gospel of Christ. This marriage gave birth to the unique package of spirituality and celebration that African Christianity is today.

It is also interesting to note that there was no uniformity in the 'celebrations and worship' (cultures) throughout the entire continent of Africa. Neither was there any uniformity to be found within the borders of the newly created African countries. While this was a testament to the wealth of the diversity of cultures in Africa, it also provided an avenue for the colonizers to amplify, or exaggerate, the diversity among neighbouring cultures. This eventually disrupted the near harmonious coexistence and respect for one another's celebration and worship practices. Indeed, relationships among cultures became worse with the arrival of different Christian missions. These various missions came under different names and they introduced different celebration rites during their worship services. Of course, this created confusion for Africans, who naturally entered into some of the rivalry found among Christian missions.

The birth of ecumenism in Africa

It is not surprising therefore that in 1958, church representatives from 25 African countries met in Ibadan, Nigeria, in a conscious effort to bridge these differences. Yet the conference took place at a time when the continent was grappling with challenges of liberation, independence and decolonization. This led to the decision to form an umbrella body that would become the prime ecumenical thinking agent and common voice for the churches in Africa. Five years later in Kampala, the All Africa Conference of Churches (AACC) was born.

Dr Don M'timkulu, one of the founding fathers of the AACC and its first General Secretary, declared the following about the first General Assembly in Kampala in 1963:

> The All Africa Conference of Churches Assembly in Kampala is undoubtedly the most historic single event that has taken place within the life of the churches of Africa during this century. It marked the end of an epoch – the end of the

missionary era with its mission churches; but it also saw the fruition of those missionary labours as the new autonomous churches of Africa triumphantly declared their acceptance of the responsibilities that now were theirs, and began carefully to chart the course that lay ahead.   (AACC, 1963: 4)

The objectives of the assembly were:

- **to address the colonial situation** in the spirit of nationalism permeating the political scene at the time;
- **to define the selfhood of the Church in Africa;**
- **to discuss Christian responsibility** in Africa's economic development;
- **to establish a theology** of African nation-building;
- **to emphasize the Christian concern for the family** among the churches; and
- **to discuss a Christian's responsibility to his or her community.**

The themes of its General Assemblies since Kampala indicate that the AACC has continued to focus on fulfilling these objectives, including the theme of economic liberation of the continent after South Africa became free in 1991:

- **Abidjan, Ivory Coast (1969)** – Working with Christ
  Focus: building the African nation, indigenization of the Church
- **Lusaka, Zambia (1974)** – Living No Longer for Ourselves but for Christ
  Focus: evangelization, liberation theology, conflict resolution (moratorium on foreign missionaries and aid)
- **Nairobi, Kenya (1981)** – Following the Light of Christ
  Focus: more active involvement of the youth, laity and women in the Church, conflict resolution (Sudan)
- **Lome, Togo (1987)** – You Shall be My Witnesses
  Focus: human rights violations, hunger, poverty, urbanization, Africa's debt, and the refugee crisis
- **Harare, Zimbabwe (1992)** – Abundant Life in Jesus
  Focus: peace and reconciliation (Rwanda & Burundi), ending apartheid in South Africa
- **Addis Ababa (1997)** – Troubled but Not Destroyed
  Focus: church expansion, political liberation, interfaith relations, conflict resolution in the Great Lakes region
- **Yaounde, Cameroon (2003)** – Come, Let Us Rebuild
  Focus: rebuilding broken communities, the refugee crisis, interfaith dialogue on matters of peace and reconciliation in Sudan and the rest of the Great Lakes region
- **Ninth Assembly Maputo, Mozambique (2008)** – Africa Step Forth in Faith
  Focus: the Church's responsibility to participate in the renaissance in Africa, the fast-changing socio-political situation, just and sustainable development, and environmental preservation.

Not much gained

Despite these efforts, the continent continues to experience challenges which indicate that all of us – governments, the civil society, individuals and the Church – have not yet been able to achieve the continent we are looking for. Indeed, the Church itself has not yet found the unity it sought to achieve at the time when the AACC was established. The authenticity and oneness of the voice of the Church is still not consolidated.

There are obvious questions around the consolidation of the voice of the Church. The challenge is for the Church to review its tendency to segment itself from the communities it serves into 'us' and 'them'. Denominations in the same locality must be challenged to address the situations of their people in unison, because their congregations live in the same socio-economic and political context. In sharing a common social context, these churches are affected by the same problems such as HIV & AIDS and poverty. It thus becomes essential that in responding to these challenges, the Church seeks to unite the people for a common response. To emphasize denominational divisions in such circumstances is to undermine the mission of the Church to bring healing and transformation to the situations that the people face. It is always regrettable when the Church continues to convey a puritanical attitude that 'we' of a certain Christian tradition are closer to God and holier than 'they' of another tradition or community, or that 'we' are right and 'they' are wrong.

The challenge is for us to ensure that the Church does not subscribe to socio-economic and political positions that have made the ground fertile for conflict. The Church has to constantly seek to apply the measure of love, justice and truth in the struggles of the continent today. It cannot lose focus on the matter of the liberation struggle, which has only changed its face from politics to economics. The rich and powerful continue to impose policies upon the poor and weak, with total disregard as to whether such ideas have any positive outcomes for the poor.

Prophetic action

The Church in Africa has to apply its mind to the issues of prophetic action. This means that the Church must accept the challenge to be an advocate of those who are suffering. The nature of prophetic responsibility requires the Church to speak powerfully to those who wield power, be it political and/or economic. The Church must accept that the difficulties that the continent faces are complex because of the international interests that often characterize them. So wherever problems may appear to be straightforward, the Church must try to understand all the dynamics involved so that it can speak both with authority and adequate understanding of the issues.

One place for concrete ecumenical action today is in Zimbabwe. The problems in Zimbabwe are very complex. Very often this situation has been dealt with as a straightforward case of human rights abuse by the current government of that country. However, a little historical reflection will indicate that there is a legitimate gripe in that country against its colonial masters, the United Kingdom. Several facts are beyond dispute:

1 The fact of the unjust distribution of land during the colonial era;
2 The limitations that were imposed by the Lancaster agreement on the Zimbabwe government, were it to try to resolve the problem; and
3 The unfulfilled obligations in compensating for the reclamation of the farms.

On the other hand, the reality of the suffering caused by the Zimbabwean government's response to these problems, in its attempt to resolve them, cannot be denied.

It has to be acknowledged, then, that the prophetic witness of the Church in the Zimbabwean situation is questionable. The Church has left itself open to the accusation that it is not actually being prophetic, in the sense of standing up for justice and responding in the name of God to all the suffering of the people in Zimbabwe. Rather, it has simply echoed what may be seen as the interests of the United Kingdom. Otherwise the question may be rightly put to the Church as to why it never raised its voice with equal vigour against the suffering caused by the unfair land distribution in Zimbabwe. As the Lord Jesus calls on his disciples to be as wise as serpents and as harmless as doves, so must the Church be – particularly in Africa where we face so many conflicting interests.

The churches in Zimbabwe must be hailed for recognizing the need for balance and honesty in their attempts to respond prophetically to their context by establishing the Ecumenical Peace Initiative for Zimbabwe. In this initiative they sought to probe and analyse the whole situation, taking into consideration the entire history that has led their country to the current impasse. They decided that both the unjust distribution of land and the subsequent human rights abuse were critical factors that they had to speak to with power, in an even-handed manner. Anything less would have been political expediency, unworthy to be understood and categorized as prophetic witness. Perhaps what is even more laudable is the fact that the Church in Zimbabwe tried to straddle the divides within its own ranks to arrive at this position. They attempted to find unity among themselves as part of the process. In other words, they realized the extent to which the witness of the Church depends on the unity of the Church. The Zimbabwean situation therefore demonstrates that the task and mission of the Church is to constantly search for the voice of integrity in its witness.

 Conclusion

This situation is not uniquely Zimbabwean, for much of the continent has found itself sharing similar experiences to those of Zimbabwe. The temptation for the Church to echo popular voices is the biggest threat to the authenticity of its prophetic witness. Popular voices may coincide with the voice of the Church, or even awaken the Church to what it should have long seen. However, using its own criteria from biblical and Christian tradition, it has to constantly ensure that its voice represents the synthesis of the gospel and each situation. Again, because of the competing interests that impact the African continent, it cannot be denied that the challenge for the Church is to carefully read the signs of the time and to speak and act appropriately.

Coupled with this is the need for the Church to consistently seek to lead a life of righteousness in its own affairs. When the Church surrenders itself to a life that contradicts its own message, it disembowels its own mission. It is thus necessary for the Church to subject itself to a spiritual audit that has social ramifications for its life and work.

We, the Church in Africa, must therefore seek courage to hear and speak the truth, search for justice, and embrace one another with love. Indeed, this is a call to Christians throughout the entire world. We cannot stand by helplessly and watch, or take divisive positions, as our people slide into more and more bitterness, frustration and conflict. The mission of Christ for the Church is that of giving hope and love while reconciling one to the other.

? STUDY QUESTIONS

1 According to Dandala, why did African Christians feel the need to establish an ecumenical body like the AACC?

2 Discuss the objectives of the AACC and the key themes addressed throughout its nine assemblies from 1963 to 2008. Which themes are most relevant to your own context?

3 Do you agree with Dandala's verdict that not much has been gained through the ecumenical movement in Africa? Why or why not?

4 How might you help to strengthen ecumenism in your own area?

Part 3

The Church in the world

11

Interfaith relations in Africa

Johnson A. Mbillah

 Abstract

Given the reality of religious plurality in Africa, Johnson A. Mbillah contends that churches must engage in interfaith relations based on collaboration and cooperation in attending to human needs. He advocates constructive engagement with other faith communities for peaceful coexistence and for the holistic development of humanity. Mbillah develops his argument in relation to three main issues. First, regarding the churches and interfaith relations, he outlines theological rationale for interfaith relations and sets forth key principles for such engagement. Second, he examines the essence of interfaith collaboration, particularly in relation to Christian–Muslim relations, and highlights the need for cooperation in peace-building. Third, he tackles thorny issues in interfaith relations including those related to politics, African identity, and the imperatives of Christian mission and Muslim *Da'wah*. He then concludes by urging theological institutions to incorporate interfaith relations in the formation of church leaders so as to enhance the theology and practice of interfaith relations in future.

 Introduction

The continent of Africa is known for its vast religious landscape, with most Africans being deeply religious people. Christianity and Islam joined the primordial African religions, commonly referred to as African Traditional Religions, thus producing Africa's triple religious heritage. This triad of religious pillars was then transformed into Africa's rainbow of religions with the addition or growth of other faiths such as Judaism, Hinduism, Sikhism, Jainism and the Baha'i faith.

In the recent past, Africa's rainbow of religions has extended further into a mosaic of religions, as variants of the religions above joined 'the pioneer religions' in seeking to attract African followers. Today new religious movements parade themselves all over the continent. Given these developments, there is no doubt that religion plays a pivotal role in shaping the actions and/or inactions of many Africans.

The growing religious plurality in the African continent means that Africans have multiple identities. In the past, for example, people spoke primarily about ethnic identities (as the more appropriate term for 'tribal identities'). In the present situation, however, someone might say, 'I am Kenyan, a Kikuyu, and a Christian of the Presbyterian denomination.' Another might say 'I am Ethiopian, an Oromo and a Muslim', possibly adding that he or she belongs to the Tijaniyya Sufi fraternity. This maze of possibilities for defining an African's identity can be enriching and rewarding if harnessed properly. Equally, however, the multiple identities can be troublesome and destructive if not harnessed properly.

In this chapter we reflect on what the churches in Africa must do to ensure that the mosaic of religions are appropriately harnessed to bring about collaboration and cooperation in attending to human needs and concerns. We also advocate for what we, in the Programme for Christian–Muslim relations in Africa (PROCMURA), call constructive engagement with other religious groups for peace and peaceful coexistence for the holistic development of the human family. This entails seeking ways to celebrate our common humanity in the spirit of our God-given inalienable rights and freedoms, and being responsible for our actions or inactions. We shall not shy away from issues that may be seen to be controversial in interfaith engagements, but rather highlight them and raise questions for further reflection.

The chapter addresses three key issues, as follows:

- **the churches and interfaith relations in Africa**;
- **the essence of interfaith collaboration and cooperation**;
- **thorny issues in interfaith relations**: what shall we do?

❊ The churches and interfaith relations in Africa

Religious diversity has existed throughout the ages. Our Christian understanding of God, made clear by his self-revelation in Jesus Christ, affirms that religious diversity never came about without God's knowledge. We cannot say that God brought about our religious diversity, but certainly it arose with his knowledge, at best with his permission and at worst against his will. Whatever the case may be, religious diversity has been part and parcel of the entire human family, including the African religious heritage.

Christian theology states that God grants human beings the freedom to choose the religious path that they wish to tread, but they are responsible for the choices that they make. With this understanding, the churches in Africa must be tolerant with the religious variety around them since this diversity is bound to continue until the end of time. A credible question for the churches to ask, therefore, is not how to eradicate religious diversity (for that may mean attempting to eradicate the God-given freedom of human beings), but how to relate constructively with others in this religious diversity.

The churches in Africa, like elsewhere in the world, inherited a certain stream of Christian tradition that discouraged relationship with peoples of other faiths. In some cases it was virtually taboo to do so. Many have asked, 'What has belief got to do with unbelief?', or 'What has Christianity got to do with "paganism"?' The common, traditional Christian approach to religious variety has been to bring those outside the household of Christ to Christ – to convert them. More recently, an emerging trend has essentially advised, 'Leave them alone; let us relate and not convert lest we give the impression that Christianity is true and the other religions false.' These two approaches, as well as other emerging trends, have created different camps within Christianity as far as interfaith relations are concerned.

The two main camps ('convert them by all means' and 'leave them alone') need to face the existential reality as it is, and not as they would imagine or wish it to be. For the truth of the matter is that those who see conversion as the ultimate or only objective of interfaith relations have to answer the crucial question: What happens if that objective is not achieved? In other words, if you present the gospel to a person of a different faith who decides to remain in his or her faith, what do you do to still remain friends and good neighbours as narrated in the story of the Good Samaritan (Luke 10.25–37)?

For those who are anti-conversion, the question also remains as to whether conversion is in essence an activity of the human person or of the Holy Spirit. If it is of the Holy Spirit, as demonstrated in the story of Cornelius (Acts 10.1–48), for example, who are they to limit the activity of the Holy Spirit? In any case, the reality of the African religious environment shows that significant numbers of people are converted from one faith to another, just as many people choose to remain within their original faith.

What Christian proponents of interfaith relations advocate is that we talk with, and not just about, people of other faiths. We do so because of our faith in Christ who challenges us on what merit there is if we love only those who love us (Luke 6.32). In other words, what merit is there if we take for neighbours only those with whom we share a religion?

Interfaith relations in the African way

In many African societies, especially at grass-roots levels, families live together in the same households with interfaith and intra-faith differences. They eat together, work together, celebrate the diverse religious festivals together, share in the joys of birth and the sadness of death, and jointly work towards the development of the community. This phenomenon, which may be described as practical theology brewed in the African pot, demonstrates long-standing African spirituality that focuses on existential matters over dogma. Thus the bedrock of African religiosity is to 'live and let live' with religious diversities in harmony.

Therefore, engaging in interfaith relations in Africa today is not a matter of introducing anything new. Rather, a central concern is how to curb the growing intolerant religious spirit that blows around the world, including parts of Africa such as Nigeria and Sudan to a greater extent, and other countries to a lesser extent. To put it in another way, we need to revitalize our societies, which were previously tolerant of religious diversity, and protect them from the wave of religious intolerance that would rather see us live by the law of the jungle: 'eat or be eaten'.

To engage effectively with people of other faiths, churches in Africa must first put their own houses in order regarding intra-faith relations, or relations among the various Christian traditions. Only then can they agree on the way forward in interfaith relations for peace, harmony and human development. What this means in practice is that all church denominations in Africa must be encouraged to get involved in interfaith relations so as to build bridges of understanding for harmonious relationship.

Interfaith relations from a position of faith

'Interfaith relations' means 'faith meeting faith', or people of one faith meeting others of another faith. In practice it is not, and should not be, a meeting aimed at compromising or watering down the beliefs of any faith with the hope of striking a mean and concluding that all faiths are the same. Of course, if all faiths were the same, there would be no need for interfaith relations.

Recently, some international interfaith relations meetings seem to suggest, whether overtly or covertly, that Christians should do away with their cardinal belief in the uniqueness of Christ since this may be offensive to those of other faiths. Therefore, the charge goes, Christians who hold this belief may hinder the success of the interfaith meeting. This challenge raises the issue of context in interfaith relations. The undisputed objectives of interfaith relations, namely peace, harmony, development and sharing our common humanness (*ubuntu* in South Africa), are noble and must be vigorously pursued. However, historical experiences and cultural differences mean that interfaith relations from one continent, region or country cannot be exported wholesale to another continent, region, or country. They may be shared in other areas, to enrich or inform, but they should not be transposed as if they were the norm everywhere.

The present situation, in which some Christians imply that biblical truth should be watered down to enhance interfaith relations, is not acceptable to many Christians in Africa and elsewhere. It will be a disaster for interfaith relations if those from any faith attempt to explain away their cardinal doctrines for the sake of peace and harmony. The quest for peace and harmony among faiths is possible only if we are able to acknowledge that there are major differences in our belief systems. Instead of agonizing over them, we must accept our differences and seek to live harmoniously despite them.

Perhaps the best illustration of how we need to approach interfaith relations in Africa comes in a conversation between Dr Nnamdi Azikiwe, the first President of Nigeria, and Alhaji Ahmadu Bello, a premier and Saurdauna of Sokoto in the mid-1960s. The two leaders met to discuss growing tensions between coalition partners in the central government (the Northern People's Congress and the National Council of Nigerian Citizens). These tensions brought into the open divergences between the majority Muslim north and the majority Christian south which were degenerating into ethno-religious antagonism. In the cause of dialogue to restore some understanding, Dr Azikiwe is quoted to have said to Ahmadu Bello, 'Let us forget our differences.' Ahmadu Bello replied, 'No, let us understand our differences . . . By understanding our differences we can build unity in Nigeria' (Gambari, 1992: 98). This short conversation between the two leaders indicates the real grounds for carrying out interfaith relations in Africa: accepting our differences and living with such differences in peace, not in pieces.

Having set out the principles under which interfaith relations have to take place in Africa, I will now turn my attention to areas of collaboration and cooperation to improve the human condition in the continent.

 # The essence of interfaith collaboration and cooperation

It is important for Christians to collaborate and cooperate with those of other faith communities in Africa to address issues of common concern. However, if we are to scratch where it itches the most, we must make the interface between Christianity and Islam high on our agenda. These two religions command the largest following in the continent. They have also shown throughout history and at the present time that they can be the best at building peace and stability in the continent (and the world at large). Yet they can equally be the worst at creating or fanning conflicts and strife.

As missionary religions that have succeeded in gaining adherents in Africa, Islam and Christianity may produce greater tensions to come if their respective adherents are not proactive in collaborating and cooperating to improve on the human condition across the continent. To this end we would like to briefly outline key areas that the churches in Africa need to explore carefully in pursuing collaborative interfaith actions.

Peace and peaceful coexistence

Success stories of interfaith cooperation emerged in Sierra Leone and Liberia, where religious leaders took ground-breaking initiatives that contributed immensely to restoring peace. What is not adequately recognized is that in the case of Liberia, there were attempts to publicize the war as one between Christians and Muslims. Fortunately, the Christian leaders of the country worked hard to defuse the tension that was generated. They teamed up with Muslim leaders so that together they formed an inter-religious council to work towards peace in the land.

This example clearly indicates that interfaith collaboration is possible only when there is peaceful coexistence between and among faith communities. Religious leaders can be agents of peace in the continent only when they are themselves at peace with one another. Faith communities involved in violent conflicts have no moral ground whatsoever to mediate in other conflicts, such as those that are ethnically or politically motivated.

In Africa, people of faith continue to listen to their religious leaders and, in most cases, take directives from them. Therefore religious leaders of all faiths must capitalize on this advantage in order to collaborate for peace in a continent yearning for peace.

Our programmes for peace must seek to consolidate peace in peaceful situations, and to promote peace-building in situations of strife. The programmes must also be continual, to avoid the situation of churches only cooperating with other faith communities in times of tension. Rather, peace is a process that must be worked at all the time.

Religious rights and peace

The most difficult aspect of interfaith relations for peaceful coexistence in Africa is that of religious freedoms and rights. The religious rights claimed by some can be viewed as the violation of others' religious rights. Nowhere is this more evident than in Nigeria and the Sudan, where the introduction of the *shariah* (Islamic law) in its totality contributed in large measure to violent conflicts between Christians and Muslims.

The irony of such situations is that both parties, Christians and Muslims, argue in defence of their God-given rights. Muslims argue that it is their God-given right to introduce the *shariah* in its totality to govern themselves, while Christians argue that it is their God-given right not to live under the *shariah*. Similarly, faith communities in Kenya, Tanzania, and to some extent in Uganda have to deal with debates on entrenching *Khadi* (Muslim) courts in their respective country's constitution. These are issues that can and do divide religious people, especially Christians and Muslims.

In the churches' bid to work for peace with people of other faiths, issues such as those mentioned above are bound to arise from time to time and to poison relations. Therefore, the critical question is not so much how to prevent such issues from emerging, but how to deal with them when they do arise.

One of the most important areas of PROCMURA's work is fostering a spirit of understanding between Christians and Muslims. The aim is to ensure that when conflicts occur between them, they are addressed in a nonviolent manner. The churches must always look to Jesus Christ who is himself the Prince of Peace (Isaiah 9.6), and who is recorded as having said, 'Blessed are the peacemakers, for they will be called children of God' (Matthew 5.9). Insofar as it is possible, let us work hard to ensure that we live peaceably with all our neighbours (Romans 12.18).

Other areas of collaboration and cooperation

There are several areas that require appropriate interfaith cooperation, especially if these are concerns across the religious divide. Two such issues include the HIV & AIDS pandemic, and what has come to be known as female genital mutilation. In view of the devastating impact these continue to have across Africa, it is crucial for Christians and Muslims to work closely together in addressing them.

Since some issues are more sensitive and controversial than others, it is advisable for interfaith relations to first approach those that are less controversial. This lays a foundation for then tackling, in a peaceful manner, those issues that are more thorny.

 ## Thorny issues in interfaith relations: what shall we do?

In the introduction to this chapter, we indicated the multiple identities of African people. We now explore how these multiple identities, as they relate to faith, create divided loyalties and thus lead to the segmentation of African societies.

The formation of the African Union signifies that Africa's diversity, which includes religious diversity, should not stand in the way of Africans being united. Churches must carefully examine three main areas for interfaith action towards justice, peace and development of the continent: politics, African identity, and Christian mission and Muslim *Da'wah*.

Politics

In the realm of politics, there is now a widespread tendency to categorize African heads of state according to their religious affiliations, especially Christian and Muslim. This is a dangerous trend which can easily lead to 'religious tribalism', where adherents of one religion or another vote for a presidential or parliamentary candidate because they share a religion and not because the person is competent to govern.

The forefathers and foremothers of Africa's modern political landscape identified themselves as Africans irrespective of their religious affiliations. In this light, Leopold Senghor, a devout Catholic, could be voted in as the President of Senegal, a predominantly Muslim country. Not long ago, President

Bakili Muluzi, a Muslim, was elected as President of Malawi, a majority Christian country. If this noble trend is to continue, interfaith programmes must embark on political education that emphasizes unity of purpose and development among Africans despite their belonging to different faith communities. Politicians must likewise be cautioned against religio-partisan politics.

African identity

From PROCMURA's experience, one crucial issue is the question of African identity in relation to the universality of the Christian and Muslim faiths. The fact that Africans have multiple identities can evoke the question as to whether they are African Christians and African Muslims, or Christian Africans and Muslim Africans. In other words, which aspect of an African's identity takes priority over other aspects, or calls for greater allegiance? For example, after the events that took place in the United States on September 11, 2001, Christians and Muslims in Africa took sides with those involved in the conflict, to the extent that violent confrontations erupted in some parts of the continent.

Christianity is a universal religion that recognizes all its followers as belonging to the body of Christ. Likewise Islam teaches the universal *Umma* (community) to which Muslims all over the world belong. It is truly unfortunate that this sense of universal belonging found within both faiths then creates negative perceptions towards those of the other faith, especially on the basis of conflicts occurring elsewhere in the world. In the case above, political conflicts between the West and the Arab world have set Africans against each other.

Therefore interfaith relations in Africa must ensure that the universal nature of Christianity and Islam is viewed constructively. We must avoid conflicts that arise from making alliances with those with whom Africans share faith, even if they are far away, and enemies of those who live close by but do not share the same faith. Rather, our common humanity as people of faith, both in Africa and beyond, should be harnessed to bring about peace and development instead of antagonism and destruction.

Christian mission and Muslim *Da'wah*

Christian mission, including witness and evangelism, and its near equivalent in Muslim *Da'wah*, are imperatives for the two faiths. The question therefore is not whether Christian mission and Muslim *Da'wah* should be carried out, but how they should be done so as to avoid polemics, stereotypes and derogatory remarks about the other. This is an important area for establishing positive interfaith relations.

It must be said that any form of mission or *Da'wah* that does not transform lives for the better, but rather provokes tension and conflict, should be regarded as a deformation of these faiths. Is it not possible, for example, for Christian and Muslim religious leaders in Africa to establish a guiding ethic for recommending their respective faiths without defaming the other? This would seem to be a crucial priority for interfaith relations.

 ## Conclusion

This chapter has examined interfaith relations in Africa, particularly between Christians and Muslims. The focus has been on what the churches in Africa must do to engage constructively with Muslims for peace and peaceful coexistence for the holistic development of the human family.

In conclusion, we must underline that the future of interfaith relations in Africa rests on our theological institutions. Ecumenical and denominational theological colleges and seminaries need to incorporate interfaith relations in the theological formation of priests and pastors. This will help the future leaders of our churches to critically examine our inherited theologies, so as to construct an African theology of interfaith relations.

 ## STUDY QUESTIONS

1 What are some of the key challenges to interfaith relations, according to Johnson A. Mbillah and according to your own experience?

2 Do you think that engaging in interfaith relations means that you must compromise, or water down, your own religious beliefs? Argue your case in relation to Mbillah's view.

3 Why is peace-building so foundational in interfaith relations?

4 Explain the three 'thorny issues in interfaith relations' that Mbillah identifies and addresses. What relevance do these issues have to your own experience of interfaith relations?

12

The problem of evil and suffering: theological reflections from an African perspective

Isaiah M. Dau

 ## Abstract

In this chapter, Isaiah M. Dau offers theological reflections on the problem of evil and suffering from an African perspective. He first examines African cosmology in relation to the problem of evil and suffering, including an attempt to differentiate between natural and moral evil. He then investigates prayer-songs, laments, and funeral dirges, expressed in traditional African contexts, as a way of facing the tragic reality of suffering, evil and death. Finally, he concludes with theological implications regarding the problem of evil and suffering, drawn from the framework of the incarnation as the Christian answer to the problem of evil and suffering. He affirms the cross, community, personal character and hope as the basis of transcending and transforming suffering and evil into the highest good possible in this life.

 ## Introduction

Suffering is a fact of life for many people today. It touches us in many ways. We see and hear of people who suffer. In recent times, Africa has witnessed a great deal of suffering. The genocide in Rwanda that claimed hundreds of thousands of lives is still fresh in our minds. The wars in Somalia, Sierra Leone, the Congo and Burundi, to mention a few, have shattered many dreams and destroyed many lives. The war in Sudan, extending for nearly five decades, has caused massive death and suffering.

In the midst of this suffering, the Church has experienced tremendous growth as many people have come to believe in God, renouncing their traditional African deities. For these believers, the continual war and suffering raise serious questions relating to the meaning and purpose of suffering. Why does suffering exist? What is the purpose of suffering? Why does God allow suffering? If he is all-powerful, why does he not remove it altogether? Could there be some value in suffering and, if so, is suffering the only means of obtaining it? Can one still experience God as almighty and loving even when suffering strikes? This chapter seeks to examine some of these questions concerning the problem of evil and suffering, and to offer a Christian response from an African perspective.

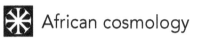

African cosmology

The African view of evil and suffering is one component of a complex but holistic cosmology, or view of the universe. This cosmology consists of a hierarchy, or cosmic order, from God to spirits or divinities, ancestors, the living dead, the living, the unborn, animals and plants, etc. In this world view, reality is a coherent unity. Good and bad, blessing and misfortune, comfort and suffering, joy and grief, success and failure, life and death, are all part of the existential reality. Far from being fatalistic, the African world view accepts that life is sometimes unfair and bitter. Although this world view does not accept suffering and evil as normal, it still recognizes that these are realities of life that must be faced and resisted. Thus, the African view recognizes suffering and evil as the unfortunate lot of humanity, even though God did not originally intend this to be so.

African peoples are therefore very aware of evil in the world and they endeavour to fight it in various ways. Yet the problem of evil as it is discussed in the West does not arise in the African concept of deity. For Africans, the Supreme Being is the Creator, the source of life. But between the Creator and humanity lie many spiritual powers both good and bad, such as gods, spirits, magical forces and human witches, which account for the strange happenings in the world.

The origin of evil

In African traditional thought, the origin of evil is not explained but taken as fact. Many African peoples categorically reject the idea that evil originated from God. Some, like the Vugusu of Kenya, believe that evil originated from spiritual beings or divinities. According to Francis Deng, the Dinka of Sudan believe the *jak* (independent spirits), as opposed to *yieth* (ancestral spirits), cause destruction and suffering (Deng, 1972: 122–3). These divinities, or spirits, were created by God but became evil only when they rebelled against God and began to do evil. Deng further observes that in the Dinka world view, *jak* act as God's police. They bring God's judgement on those who do wrong.

What is more, there is human responsibility in how evil came to exist. Evil is thought to originate as a result of human transgression of a divine command. While the exact content varies from one ethnic group to another, there is widespread belief across Africa that in the beginning, God and humans lived together on earth and communicated frequently. However, on account of some misconduct by one man and one woman, God left the earth and went to live in the sky, leaving humankind always trying to reach him without success (Smith, 1950: 7–8). A story of 'the Fall', somewhat similar to the biblical one in Genesis 3, is thus found in different forms in African oral traditions as an attempt to explain the origin of evil, suffering and death.

Therefore, in many African societies, God is not the origin of evil for God neither does evil nor harms anyone. The spirits are either the origin or agents of evil (Mbiti, 1990: 199). For example, the 'living dead', or the spirits of those recently deceased, are believed to bring fear and evil to the living. If they are improperly buried, neglected or disobeyed, they take revenge and punish the offenders. The living, therefore, bear the consequences of their own actions when they experience evil and suffering because they fail to give honour to the living dead.

However, there are times when evil and misfortune are attributed to God. As the one who knows all things, God may be held responsible for epidemics and afflictions. Yet, at the same time, it is believed he is the only one who can deliver from evil and misfortune. Thus, in traditional African thought, God may be exonerated of evil and yet also be implicated. Whatever the case, the traditional African will not generally reject God if evil, suffering and misfortune overtake him or her. Rather, he or she will cling to God even more in spite of evil and suffering. People may, however, complain to God and ancestors for the suffering or evil that comes upon them, but they will virtually never accuse God of any moral wrongdoing (Smith, 1950: 30). God cannot be charged with wrongdoing because moral responsibility is always placed on the shoulders of humanity (Magesa, 1997: 50).

Moral and natural evil

At this point, we must distinguish between moral evil and natural evil. First, moral evil arises in the context of communal relationships and it concerns matters of virtue and character. The Nuer and the Dinka people of Sudan, for example, highly value conformity to the norms of behaviour in the family and the community. Failure to conform is a serious offence that may result in a curse or even death. People are considered to be neither inherently evil nor inherently good; being good or evil depends on their conformity to community norms.

African people generally believe that good follows right conduct, while bad follows wrong conduct. None can escape the consequences of his or her actions, whether good or bad. Essentially, this means if a person keeps in the right, he or she will avoid serious misfortunes. However, that person may not avoid misfortunes that come upon the individual or the community (Pritchard, 1956: 17). No one can avoid suffering, but God does not punish those who wrong others unknowingly.

Significantly, the consequences of a person's actions are accepted only when they are exposed. There is no concept of personal sin that is not connected with a person's conduct in the community. Hence suffering in any form is always attributed to something or someone in the community. Usually, that somebody is a witch, sorcerer or magician. 'The witch', as David Bosch rightly notes, 'is sinner par excellence, not primarily because of his or her deeds, but because of the evil consequences of those deeds: illness, barrenness, catastrophe, misfortune, disruption of relationships in the community, poverty and so on' (Bosch, 1987, 50).

In traditional African moral ethics, sin and evil cannot exist in human experience except as perceived in people. It is people who are evil or sinful, whether or not they are aided by invisible forces. For even when evil forces cause harm, it is because evil people use them to attain their own ends (Magesa, 1997: 162). Thus, all that happens in African traditional society may be explained mystically or naturally, sometimes resulting in sustained communal suspicion and fragmentation. This is what constitutes moral evil in traditional thinking.

Second, there is natural evil in the form of droughts, epidemics, floods and other natural disasters that may not be directly attributed to human activity. Such calamities produce suffering and misfortune, yet once again, nothing in African society simply happens without being caused by somebody or something. Consequently, Africans seek possible explanations for whatever happens to humans. In this process, individual and communal soul-searching, or even witch-hunts, often occur in an attempt to find those responsible. The evil eye or the evil heart or the evil mouth – all due to jealousy, rivalry, hatred, or even ancestral anger – may be possible causes for examination whenever suffering and tragedy strike (Fortes, 1987: 211–17).

 # Facing evil, suffering and death

African people are generally not passive in the face of suffering. They try to do everything possible to take away suffering and restore health and harmony to the individual and the community. To do this, they offer sacrifices, libations and prayers to God and divinities to solicit their help. Sometimes this help is obtained; other times it is not. When it is not obtained, people resign themselves to the mystery of evil and suffering. This is perfectly in line with African traditional thought, which readily accepts that life is full of things that we cannot know or explain.

This being so, suffering is, nevertheless, not accepted as normal. Africans wrestle with it in their continual search for the real meaning of life as it relates to God and the presence of evil. In traditional African religion, God is the complete Other Being, the absolute sovereign one, external to his creation,

so far removed in his glory as to be unapproachable except through intermediaries. At the same time, he is also thought to be present among humans as
expressed symbolically in creation stories (Smith, 1950: 27).

This tension in the traditional understanding of God is particularly shown
when humans encounter suffering and adversity. We see this in the following prayer-songs and funeral dirges of African religions, especially those offered in times of anguish. The first of these prayer-songs is precipitated by
the loss of a loved one. The bereaved, in self-focused lament, charges *Imana*
(God) with treating him unjustly:

> As for me, Imana [God] has eaten me,
> As for me, he has not dealt with me as with others.
> With singing I would sing,
> If only my brother [or whoever the deceased was] was with me.
> Sorrow is not to hang the head mourning,
> Sorrow is not to go weeping (for that will not take away sorrow).
> As for me, Imana has eaten me.
> As for me, he has not dealt with me as with others;
> If he had dealt with me as with others, I could be as Scorner-of-Enemies.
> Woe is me!   (Guillebaud, 1950: 198)

Being eaten by *Imana* implies, among other things, being dealt with unjustly
by a God who is presumed to be good and just. It betrays the feeling that
the loss of one's relative is like one's own death. But *Imana* is not a subject
of rejection here. He is being indicted for he has given to others what he has
not given to the plaintiff. Only the plaintiff has been forgotten and hence
his protest.

The ring of his complaint echoes in the following prayer-song by another
individual who is also suffering grief of some kind, possibly sterility or the
loss of a child:

> I do not know what Imana is punishing me for: if I could meet with him, I
> would kill him. Imana, why are you punishing me? Why have you not made me
> like other people? Couldn't you even give me a little child, Yo-o-o! I am dying
> in anguish! If only I could meet you and pay you out! Come on (Imana), let
> me kill you! Let me run you through with a sword, or cut you with a knife! O
> Imana, you have deserted me! Yo-o-o! (Woe is me!)
>   (Guillebaud, 1950: 198–9)

Heaviness of heart has prompted this individual to draw battle lines to fight
Imana. Like suffering Job in the Bible, the lamenter demands to know why
Imana is punishing him or her. The strong language used expresses both
faith in God, and anger with him: faith, in the conviction that God is present
even if his presence is not felt, yet anger that he does not seem to intervene
when he is needed most. Both the notions of faith and anger, in this context, denote a process of spiritual journey that leads to mature knowledge
of God and freedom to express deep human feelings to him. A human person dialogues and even argues with God as if he or she were face to face

with him. As Mbiti points out, this is an outstanding dimension of African spirituality that should be carefully cherished, not ignorantly dismissed (Mbiti, 1975: 44).

We must hasten to point out that there are no atheistic overtones in this prayer. In traditional African society, there is room for complaining, quarrelling or even fighting with God, but there is no room for atheism. Belief in God and other divinities is an inherent part of daily life for all in the community. It is thus virtually impossible, in a typical traditional African society, to be part of the community and fail to be part of its religious system. Therefore, practising atheists can hardly be found, even when suffering and adversity abound and when answers to the problem of evil are lacking. Yet wrestling with the problem of evil and suffering in relation to faith in God is a continual reality, as shown in the prayer-songs.

Traditional African societies also grapple with evil and suffering in facing the unavoidable reality of death. When death strikes, dialogue between human beings and God is clearly heightened. Africans regard death as the climax of evil because it takes away life. They acknowledge that when a person dies, God has let him or her go. Although they believe that a person goes to another land when dying, they still find death frightening. They also consider dying childless to be the worst imaginable thing that can happen to a person, for a man even more than a woman. However, they think that dying at a good old age, after raising a family, is not such a bad thing, since the deceased has left offspring to perpetuate his or her lineage.

Nevertheless, death still generates strong feelings that are expressed through prayers and songs. These convey deep sorrow, agony and bewilderment, and are uttered to register protest. Africans often lament, or even blame God and other spiritual realities, for not keeping life as they are supposed to.

For example, consider the following prayer-lament from the Congo:

> O great Nzambi [God], what thou hast made is good, but thou hast brought a great sorrow to us with death. Thou shouldest have planned in some way that we would not be subject to death. O great Nzambi, we are afflicted with great sadness. (Mbiti, 1975: 98)

This prayer is a thinly veiled rebuke to *Nzambi* for making people subject to death. However, it does not indicate doubt in God's goodness or in his created order. The wish that God had planned things better so that people were not subject to death is a natural one, expressing bewilderment at the mystery of evil and suffering. Yet the fact that one can pray at all, at such a time, is in itself an affirmation of faith in God. The release of emotions such as deep anger and sorrow is an important part of the healing process for the bereaved.

Prayer-laments associated with death also convey acceptance that it shall ultimately overtake all people, while asserting that it should not call too soon. This thought is clearly presented in the following song-lament, along with the idea that death is not the end of life but the beginning of another life:

> Would it were not today!
> God, you have called too soon!
> Give him water, he has left without food;
> Light a fire, he must not perish of cold.

Addressing the dead person:

> Prepare a place for us,
> In a little while we shall reach [you],
> Let us reach each other.
> (Mbiti, 1975: 98)

The plea for death to wait a little while is a universal cry, found especially in Africa if the deceased has not fulfilled such vital obligations as marriage and bearing children. This lament reminds God that the departed, who 'has left without food', has not lived long enough to enjoy his or her life. Yet that is the nature of death – it comes when it is least expected, as a debtor or thief in the night. The belief that beyond the grave there exists a land of the dead where people eat and drink is reflected in this lament. Hence, the deceased is not really considered dead, but gone to that land. Finally, there is the clear hope of soon being reunited with the departed in that land.

The idea that death is a journey to another world is also expressed in funeral dirges. In the following dirge, the departed is told not to betray secrets of this world to those in the other world:

> Do not say anything,
> Yaa Nyaako [name of departed], do not say anything.
> If you did your speech will be long.
> When you arrive, do not tell tales.
> Yaa Nyaako, do not tell tales.
> If you did, your tales will be long.
> (Nketia, 1955: 122)

Once again, the prayer reveals the conviction that death is not the end of life. It also implies that life in this world is similar to the one in the other. People there are capable of talking and even letting out secrets, just as they do here. This belief neither minimizes the suffering and sorrow brought about by death, nor explains the mystery of death; the sense of deep uncertainty and bewilderment remains.

Another dirge expresses this lingering wonder, and even anger at the Creator, in the face of death:

> When the Creator created things,
> When the Manifold Creator created things,
> How did He create?
> He created bereavement.
> He created sorrow,
> The sorrow of bereavement.

Alas! Drinking vessels!
Alas! Drinking vessels!
Alas! Drinking vessels!
Anno Ofori [name of deceased] that spells death to others,
I could shoot myself on account of this event.
(Nketia, 1955: 124)

Thus the mystery of suffering and evil, especially as manifested in death, remains as elusive as ever. Again, it is confronted, not explained, in African traditional religions. The songs, prayer-laments and funeral dirges express both faith in God and anger with him, for his presence and absence are experienced in the reality of suffering.

 Theological implications and conclusions

The problem of suffering and evil generates diverse interpretations across cultures and communities. There is no human system of thought that adequately resolves this problem to the satisfaction of all. Yet theological reflection from an African perspective reveals striking similarities between traditional African views and biblical views. Both faith traditions see reality as a totality, as an integral whole. Both assume, rather than explain, evil and suffering. Both do not reject God on account of human suffering and evil. Both maintain the language of protest against suffering and evil, as expressed in song, lament, prayer and funeral dirges. Those discussed above from African traditional religions are similar to the dozens of biblical psalms of lament (e.g. Psalms 10, 12, 22) and prophetic oracles (e.g. Habakkuk 1.2–4, 12–17).

Besides these similarities, there are also differences that must be addressed by African Christian theology. For example, from the biblical perspective, traditional African views fall short of admitting that suffering and evil are indications of something terribly wrong in our nature as human beings. The Bible calls this sin, an irresistible force capable of alienating us from God and from one another, so that we miss the goal of life for which we were created. This is the force that moves us to do evil and to inflict suffering upon one another. Therefore, we as human beings need to be delivered not only from the evil that may afflict us, but also from the evil that we might inflict on fellow human beings. From a biblical viewpoint, therefore, the answer to the problem of evil and suffering lies in the redemption provided in Jesus Christ. In that sense,

the ultimate solution to the problem of evil must lie in the fact that the God who created the world is also the God who redeemed it; the creator is himself in Christ the bearer of all creation's sin and suffering as he is the bringer of the redemption that shall be. But only the Christian can know that Christ has explained suffering in the act of defeating it.   (Richardson, 1983: 195–6)

125

Consequently, redemption through a suffering God is the only truly Christian response to the problem of evil.

As the Christian answer to the problem of evil and suffering in the world, the incarnation is no explanation as such, but rather provides a framework in which the believer may respond positively to the problem. Because God came to humanity in Jesus Christ and identified with us in all that we may suffer, we can now seek to transcend and transform it rather than be destroyed by it. This is essentially the theology of the cross, which is also a theology of suffering. God does not observe our suffering from a safe distance but comes down to us and participates in it. Consequently, the cross is the supreme demonstration of God's solidarity with us in this world of suffering. The cross of Christ will always stand as a powerful reminder that God was prepared to suffer in order to redeem the world, and that he expects his people to share the same commitment as they participate in the task of restoring the world to its former glory (McGrath, 1995: 15, 26).

The cross directs our gaze away from contemplating our own anguish and suffering to the God who shares in our suffering and transforms it. The death of Jesus Christ on the cross brings us face to face with the wonder of God's sacrificial love, so that we gain the strength and courage to deal with our own suffering. The cross reminds us that the power of death has been broken. Although evil and suffering are still pertinent realities in this life, the cross clearly points to their ultimate defeat and elimination in the future. Then God will usher in a new order of things where there will be no more suffering, tears and death.

It must also be said that the cross reminds the believer that suffering is a necessary part of following Jesus. Disciples of Jesus are not only called to believe in Christ, but also to suffer for him. Indeed, Jesus declared that following him meant taking up our cross and carrying it, with all the sufferings and the difficulties that go with it.

As mentioned briefly above, the cross spurs us on to respond to the suffering of others as God responded to our suffering. Since the suffering of any human being grieves the heart of God, those who have experienced God's redeeming love need to extend the compassion of Christ to those in pain. Attending to the practical needs of those who suffer clearly demonstrates the message of the cross: that God has not abandoned them in their pain and misery. When we thus convey the message of the cross in practical love and compassion, we empower those sufferers to transcend and transform their suffering.

Furthermore, within the framework of the incarnation, we also find the unconditional love and the valuable support of the community of faith. Christians have not always had a 'solution' to the problem of evil; rather they have had a community of care that has made it possible for them to absorb the destructive terror of evil that constantly threatens all human relations (Hauerwas, 1990: 53). Within the warmth and care of our community, we come to know at the time of suffering what it means experientially to have our burdens carried.

Finally, suffering within the framework of the incarnation has the capacity to shape our character. Suffering produces perseverance, and perseverance character. This shaping of a resilient Christian character through the things we suffer enables us to endure and to be steadfast in the midst of trials. In addition, we are inspired by a living hope that suffering and evil will be ultimately defeated when our redemption in Christ is fully consummated. This hope is stronger than death and it is absolutely invincible in the face of evil and suffering. Thus, with the assurance of God's presence and his suffering with us, the love and care provided by the community of believers, and our focus on building a resilient character comforted by hope, we are empowered to transcend and transform suffering and evil into the highest good possible in this life.

 ## STUDY QUESTIONS

1 According to African religions, what is the origin of evil? What part does human responsibility play in relation to suffering?

2 What is the difference between moral and natural evil? Why is it important to distinguish between the two?

3 How do traditional African societies respond to evil, suffering and death? How do these responses compare with your own reaction to evil, suffering and death?

4 Explain how Dau interprets the incarnation of Christ as a framework that allows Christians to respond positively to evil and suffering. Discuss the insights he presents in relation to your own experience of suffering.

13

Christian identity and ethnicity in Africa: reflections on the gospel of reconciliation

Philomena Njeri Mwaura

 ## Abstract

In this chapter Philomena Njeri Mwaura explores the problem of ethno-centrism, which challenges Christian identity and the authenticity of the Church in Africa, despite a century of tremendous growth. Tracing the New Testament markers of Christian identity as transformation in Christ, love, unity and embrace of the other, she argues that only a people who are secure in their Christian identity are able to be authentic witnesses to the gospel. Paul's teaching on the ministry of reconciliation is an imperative in diverse contexts where ethnic, national and religious identities are in conflict and competition. The Church must be equipped for this ministry by being prophetic, vigilant, intrusive and in solidarity with the marginalized.

 ## Introduction

The notion of human identity, or even identity crisis, has become one of the most salient issues of our time. People have become much more aware of their identity, whether as individuals, ethnic groups, or nations. Yet what exactly is identity? How is it formed? And how does it relate to the gospel and to world mission today?

Human identity generally refers to our specific individuality or distinctiveness in relation to others. Identity gives us a sense of who we are, and how we are located in the world around us or what links we have with others. Our identity is formed not only from our common humanity, but also from other sources including our particular nationality, race, ethnicity, social class, gender and religion. It is produced and regulated within our culture through the language and symbols used to represent who we are. Positively, our identity can create bonds of solidarity and collaboration with others, even those across barriers such as nationality and ethnicity.

However, human identity is often marked by polarization between 'inclusion' and 'exclusion', 'insiders' and 'outsiders', 'us and them'. Negatively, then, the quest for identity now takes place within a world of competing identities. People often try aggressively to consolidate their own identity against others, or in fear of being absorbed by other identities. A clear example of this is fundamentalism, whether political, economic, or religious, with its allied actions of militarism and even terrorism. Therefore identity can be a positive source of one's own sense of selfhood and empowerment, or it can be a negative source of tension and conflicts with others.

Missiology must address these challenges posed by identity, since it is an academic discipline that deals with Christians' interactions with 'the other'. This 'other' might be an individual, a cultural or religious group, or a nation. How do Christians engage with others in their social, political, religious or geographic locations in such a way that we do not exploit, marginalize, absorb, or threaten their security? Moreover, Christian mission is founded upon theological themes such as salvation, reconciliation and liberation, and authentic Christian witness promotes justice, peace and unity. These theological teachings are inherently related to issues of identity, such as otherness, difference and diversity. For example, reconciliation with God necessarily demands reconciliation with other people, and this requires recognizing their differing identities. So the question arises, how do we share the good news of Jesus Christ amidst diverse cultural identities?

In view of these questions, I intend to explore the issue of Christian identity from its New Testament foundations and the challenges posed to it by other identities. I will examine Christian identity from the African experience which has been characterized by conflicts between Christian, ethnic and national identities. As a result, questions have arisen regarding the authenticity of African Christianity, which has witnessed tremendous growth in the last seventy years but has not been perceived to result in total human and social transformation. To address this fundamental problem, we must examine how Africans express or live out their basic Christian identity in their social-cultural milieu. How can African Christians reconcile the conflicting identities they experience? What role does reconciliation in Christ play in the process? And what recommendations are there for fostering Christian identity amid diverse and conflicting ethnic identities within the Church in Africa? It is my conviction that only people who are secure in their Christian identity are capable of authentic witness to the gospel and its transforming power.

 # New Testament teaching on Christian identity

The New Testament teaches that Christians gain a new identity in Christ. For example, 1 John 3.1–2 emphasizes that because of God's great love, believers are not only called God's children, but 'that is what we are'. Christ, as the Son of God, shares his identity with us so that we become sons and daughters of God, and brothers and sisters with one another. Paul adds to this Johannine view by proclaiming and celebrating that we are God's adopted children, and therefore heirs of God and co-heirs with Christ. This adoption is experienced through the gift of the Holy Spirit, God's life principle poured into the hearts of believers which makes us cry 'Abba! Father!' (Romans 8.15). Through baptism, we become united with Christ both in his death and in his resurrection from the dead. We thereby receive the gift of eternal life and enter into a new relationship with Christ that frees us from sin (Romans 6.3–8). This divine adoption makes us 'a new creation' in Christ, with a transformed identity that transcends and supersedes our old fundamentally human identity (2 Corinthians 5.17). It also means that whether we are 'Jews or Greeks, slaves or free', we are baptized into the one body of Christ, united by the one Spirit (1 Corinthians 12.13).

The two New Testament writers are therefore in agreement that as believers,

> our basic inalienable Christian identity is that we are God's children through baptism, bearing God's life and marks within us. God seals and stamps us as his own through the seal of the Holy Spirit, God's life principle or seed (*sperma*) (1 John 3.9).   (Okure, 2007: 175)

This Christian identity applies to every believer regardless of nationality, race, ethnicity, class, age, gender, or church affiliation. Therefore all Christians acquire a new identity of equality that transcends all other human identities, and that neutralizes all other identity traits that tend to discriminate based on race, class, sex, etc. (Galatians 3.28; Colossians 3.11).

The question then arises: are Christians today aware of their basic identity in Christ? Or have other identities defined by nationality, ethnicity, class, age, gender, or church affiliation overruled this basic identity? In order to discern which identities are being manifested, we need to establish the fundamental markers of Christian identity.

The New Testament is very clear that if we claim to 'live by the Spirit', we need to 'be guided by the Spirit' and manifest 'the fruit of the Spirit' (Galatians 5.22–25). In other words, we must demonstrate our Christian identity by our way of life, as Ephesians 4.22–32 spells out. The fundamental mark of Christian identity is that it is 'rooted and grounded in love' (Ephesians 3.17; see also 1 Corinthians 13). This love is to flow out to all God's children and the entire creation, thereby fulfilling the ministry of reconciliation that God has entrusted to believers (2 Corinthians 5.18–20). Jesus defines the extent of this love, a love unto death (John 15.13), and he enjoins his followers to love one another in the same way.

This identity marker of Christian love was to characterize early believers throughout the Roman Empire, even as they experienced persecution. The call to love cut across barriers of nationality and ethnicity, for the first Christian community that came into existence at Pentecost consisted of people 'from every nation under heaven' (Acts 2.5). The Council of Jerusalem (Acts 15) legitimized the identity of the Christian community as an international, intercultural mix of Jews and Gentiles. Despite this cultural diversity and various moral challenges that arose (Acts 5—6), the early Christian community attempted to live as brothers and sisters in Christ.

 ## Christian identity and ethnicity in Africa: the experience

The challenges experienced by the Church in Africa are usually traced to the manner in which the gospel was brought to us. Much has been written about the Christian landscape in Africa, its demographic characteristics and how vibrant Christianity is. Yet observers of Christianity in Africa also remark that numerical growth has not translated into personal and social transformation. For example, one major challenge to Christian and national identity is ethnicity, which threatens to tear apart not only the nation but also the Church.

Why is ethnicity such a problem within African Christianity? However well known the history, it must be underlined that the evangelization of Africa was part and parcel of the colonial enterprise that divided up the continent of Africa at the Berlin Conference in the 1880s. Certainly ethnic groups existed in Africa before the nineteenth century and they did not always live in peace. However colonialism, with its policy of divide and rule, exacerbated ethnic conflicts that remain a major feature of African states. Hence many African states today are either experiencing war or in the process of post-conflict reconstruction.

A second major factor contributing to ethnicity within African Christianity is the historical practice of establishing denominational mission stations in particular ethnic communities. Due to comity agreements that were signed to deal with denominational proliferation in countries such as Kenya, Zambia and South Africa, certain missions were allocated geographical areas that coincided with ethnic boundaries. Therefore these missions and their African churches acquired an ethnic face.

A denomination comprised largely of one ethnic group bred resentment and fear, especially in multi-ethnic contexts such as urban or mixed settlement areas. Dominant ethnic groups also tended to conduct worship services in their vernacular, even in multicultural settings such as the cities, thus making others feel excluded. When adherents from other ethnic communities joined, they were definitely a minority and they perceived themselves as marginal to the life of the church in terms of accessing leadership and church resources. Kenyan theologian Douglas Waruta affirms that leaders were often appointed on the basis of ethnicity, to the extent that more and more dioceses were created along ethnic boundaries with each group clamouring for its own bishop. As a result of long-standing ethnic loyalty and ethnic tensions, Waruta concludes about the Church today: 'Most re-ligious groups and denominations closely scrutinized are [ethnic] in their composition and leadership. Those that happen to be multi-ethnic with a national outlook are plagued with internal inter-ethnic conflicts' (Waruta, 1992: 127).

Likewise Aylward Shorter acknowledges the following:

> It would be surprising if the Church were not both a victim and an accomplice of ethnocentrism. Up till now, Catholics have been reticent about the ways in which they have been affected by the 'ethnic disease'. Church authorities approached the ethnic problem with extreme caution, creating ethnically encapsulated dioceses, and aligning with ethnically oriented governments. Even so it was always possible to avoid appointing bishops who were ethnic outsiders, or who belonged to unpopular minority ethnic groups.   (Shorter, 1999: 28–9)

It is especially surprising that in the Synod of Bishops' *Lineamenta* (2006: 17) of the Second Special Assembly for Africa, there is little engagement with ethnicity in the Church in Africa. Although the bishops acknowledge it as a problem in the African states, they mention only briefly that Christians entrusted with organizing the political and economic destinies of their na-tions are sometimes the sources of inter-ethnic wars, corruption and other evils. When the evil of ethnicity is confined to a few sinful individuals and not perceived as a cancer that plagues the whole nation and Christian com-munity that is part of it, it can never be adequately tackled. In that case, the cost and the consequences are perilous, as a few recent examples make pain-fully clear.

The tragedy of the 1994 genocide in Rwanda shook the Christian Church to its foundations. The role of the Church in this crisis illustrates the mag-nitude of ethnic animosity that characterizes the Church in some parts of Africa. Anne Kubai writes, 'Not only were members from every denomination in Rwanda responsible for the most appalling of atrocities, but most signifi-cantly, many of these massacres took place in the buildings where many of the targets of the genocide sought sanctuary' (Kubai, 2005: 9). Kubai further adds that the Church was pathologically overwhelmed by a message of hat-red and death, thus facilitating ethnic genocide. Mahmood Mamdani also asserts, 'But for the army and the church, the two prime movers, the two organizing and leading forces, one located in the state and the other in the society, there would have been no Genocide' (Mamdani, 2001: 232–3). This same Church that failed in its prophetic and pastoral role, and stands ac-cused of complicity in the tragedy, continues to face the challenge of foster-ing forgiveness and reconciliation.

In Kenya, too, the Church faces the challenge of credibility after failing to provide moral leadership during the last few years. The country faced two major votes in the political arena: a referendum on the draft constitu-tion in 2005 and the general elections in December 2007. Throughout this period, church leadership in Kenya was deeply polarized along party and ethnic lines. Few clergy stood out as neutral and in any case, adherents did not entertain neutrality. Although the widespread post-election violence in early 2008 was linked to the disputed presidential election, it formed the culmination and the last straw of deep ethnic hatred fanned by many factors over time: political interests and manipulations; unaddressed historical injustices; economic injustices, unemployment, and poverty; social exclusion, especially of the youth; and ineffective leadership. Consequently, violence erupted in certain parts of the country, against perceived enemies or outsiders, and multi-ethnic congregations in urban areas splintered along ethnic lines.

According to the Kenya Human Rights Report (2008), even clergy participated in the ethnic violence and mobilized their followers to do the same. Henry Makori (2008: 9), a *Daily Nation* columnist, wrote,

> As professed followers of the Prince of Peace, whose law is love, Christians turned on their neighbours with demonic barbarity. They killed, maimed, looted, and raped, torched and evicted. They fueled hate through telephone and email messages and laughed at their ethnicity. They became agents of evil.

Just as in Rwanda, church buildings and those who sought refuge there did not escape the violence and wanton destruction. A *Report of the Commission of Inquiry into Post-Election Violence* (Government of Kenya, 2008: 44–52) affirms that Kenyans sought refuge in church buildings, imagining them to be safe havens. To their surprise, however, they found their lives threatened by those who considered them aliens in that part of the country. For example, 30 people were set ablaze in the Kiambaa Kenya Assemblies of God Church in Eldoret, in the Rift Valley Province (Government of Kenya, 2008: 49).

In his critique of Kenyan Christianity, Makori observes that the Christian faith does not seem to touch the social justice dimension of faith. Believers have not been adequately taught that salvation includes liberation from every form of oppression, and that authentic Christian living includes not only going to church but demanding accountability from the leaders, both clergy and secular. A holistic Christian identity requires us to love and respect the other, 'to do justice, and to love kindness, and to walk humbly with your God' (Micah 6.8). The reaction of Kenyan Christians to the 2007 December elections cannot therefore be treated as a lapse in judgement that can be glossed over or casually forgiven. Unfortunately, many in the Church, society and government would want to treat it as such. There have been calls for a blanket amnesty for the perpetrators of violence without even requiring them to own up to their guilt, repent and seek forgiveness from the victims. Yet the issue is much deeper than this. It exposes a deep malaise in the spiritual, social, moral and political fabric of society. Any attempt at reconciliation has to first address the root causes.

It must also be noted that there were genuine Christian responses to the crises in Rwanda and Kenya. Many heroic Christians suffered loss of property, injury or death while protecting the victims, regardless of their ethnic identity. Nonetheless, the identity, nature and integrity of the Church in Africa have undoubtedly been brought into question. This calls for a re-evaluation of her role as a participant in God's mission. The Church faces the challenge of constructing a new community with new social relationships based on gospel values. Yet it seems the Church has failed, in some respects, to promote an authentic Christian identity that transcends barriers of ethnicity. The Rwandan and Kenyan crises revealed that many people, even the youth who have been born and raised in urban areas, place ethnic identity above national and Christian identity. The Church has also failed to contribute to forging a sense of nationhood that empowers communities. This failure has been attributed to the lack of proper formation of Christians and sincere, spiritual and prophetic leadership. Her ecclesiology and mission also need thorough evaluation for the model of Church determines how Christians understand themselves and their roles in it.

Christian identity and ethnicity in Africa: the call to gospel reconciliation

What, therefore, is the way forward in forging a Christian identity amidst diverse and conflicting ethnic identities within the Church in Africa? Certainly the experience of ethnicity in Africa reminds us that all Christians must seriously consider the relevance of their Christian faith to everyday life. So far the Church has done little to link its mission with social questions. Mission theology should include promoting integral human development, which includes awareness in social justice, human rights, the common good and social responsibility. There is also need for organizing Christians at the grass-roots level to be part of the vision of the Church. Many times Christians are truly treated as 'sheep' with no self-determination other than to follow their leaders unquestioningly. Bishops' pastoral letters have not entirely succeeded in eliciting accountability, forming people's consciences, or transforming communities. Therefore we need to create new approaches as avenues of leadership.

One avenue is to seek a deeper understanding of ethnicity that will open up new horizons for addressing ethnic tensions more effectively. The problem of ethnicity is related to the capacity of African governments to integrate ethnic identities into political society. The real question is not how to eradicate ethnicity but how to integrate it into social relationships. Ethnic diversity is a blessing that should be understood as a fruitful resource to enrich the concept of nationhood. Some studies of ethnicity have concentrated on justifying the idea that socio-political organization based on ethnicity is a primitive model. Such studies suggest that if Africa wants to make progress, she must first of all eradicate ethnicity. This approach has influenced many leaders to think that ethnicity will disappear as the process of modernity gains momentum. Ethnicity is also perceived as a barrier to political integration and an impediment to attaining the essence of nationhood. Experience has shown, however, that people in urban areas or foreign countries maintain their ethnic identities and links. These feelings are even stronger in these contexts than in rural areas, as the experience of increased cultural diversity reinforces ethnicity.

To address the challenges of ethnocentrism we must first acknowledge that it exists, and not deny it. The Church must recognize it as a structural evil, not simply a personal sin, and even accept her complicity in the problem that it has generated. For example, in February 2008 the member churches of the National Christian Council of Kenya (NCCK) publicly confessed their complicity in fuelling ethnic hatred and sought forgiveness. This is a commendable act and the NCCK has continued to reclaim her prophetic role by speaking out against injustice and proposing a way forward in healing and reconciliation.

The Church in Kenya and non-governmental organizations (NGOs) have been actively involved in post-violence healing and reconstruction initiatives, despite reports that suspicion and fear define relationships among clergy and adherents from different ethnic communities. Practical ways of creating cohesion are imperative and the Church should be part of these initiatives. First, there is need to develop and promote a theology of life. Second, we must foster educational and cultural programmes at the grassroots level, through which ethnic and cultural diversities can be appreciated and integrated into national unity. Third, there is need to recognize that in a context of cultural, religious and ethnic diversities, Christians can fulfil their mission mandate only in collaboration. Dialogue has not been a common practice in the Church, yet we need to listen to one another in order to effectively proclaim the good news. In the process of mutual listening, there is mutual learning and our common experience of God is deepened. This also facilitates common living, while respecting the dignity and difference of others.

The ministry of reconciliation is an imperative in diverse contexts. Its importance in the Church in Africa is underscored by the Catholic Church's choice of theme for the Second Special Assembly for Africa: 'The Church in Africa in Service to Reconciliation, Justice and Peace: You are the Salt of the Earth; You are the Light of the World'. The Synod of Bishops' *Lineamenta* affirms the need for a renewed vision for mission in Africa. This vision must change Africa's destiny so that reconciliation will come in the midst of much hatred and division, and that peace and justice will finally reign. But how can the different identities be negotiated and reconciled? What shape does a ministry of reconciliation take in such a situation? What theology and missiology would inform such an enterprise?

Certainly the theology that speaks aptly to this situation is that of Paul's teaching on the ministry of reconciliation. He clearly sees reconciliation as the key to the problem of 'the other' in the Corinthian community (2 Corinthians 5.18–19). The problems of divisions he addressed in the Corinthian community are no different from ours. Paul felt he had a duty to proclaim God's gospel within this complex life situation, a gospel of reconciliation. Reconciliation is essentially the restoration and renewal of a broken relationship. In 2 Corinthians this applies primarily to the relationship between Paul and the Corinthians (6.1–13); between the Corinthians and the wrongdoer in the community (2.5–11); and ultimately between God and the whole of creation (5.14–21). This ministry is essentially God's own ministry, and its scope is universal and inclusive. This divine ministry takes place first in Christ and then it is entrusted to believers. The universality of God's ministry of reconciliation manifested in and through Christ is rooted in God's love for all people. This love therefore rules out any exclusion of the other. When people see and trust in the value of Christ's atoning death, they become reconciled to God and to others as hostility is removed and fellowship is restored.

Applied to the African context, this means that the deeply painful experiences of conflict invite the Church as the people of God to mediate healing, peace and reconciliation. This ministry of reconciliation calls for an ecumenical mission and vision to accompany our members who are suffering discrimination on the basis of race, ethnicity, religion, gender, disease or disability. Treating people as 'other' indicates they are less worthy or less human, so there is need to develop theological categories that can deal with exclusion. The 'theology of embrace' proposed by Miraslov Volf (1996) speaks well to this situation. Through such a theology, the Church in Africa can find a theological basis for re-humanizing the relations that should exist between people who must live as citizens of one country and members of the Church, with obligations and duties towards one another in a just, safe and peaceful society. The Church must relate the core theological beliefs about reconciliation to her social responsibility, for the future of the whole world depends on how we deal with ethnic, national and gender otherness.

When relationships are injured, reconciliation should not be a hasty process but one that respects and restores human dignity. It is a process that leads the injured to discover the mercy of God welling up in their lives as they come to understand God's reconciliation through Christ. It is allowing the Holy Spirit to bring forgiveness and reconciliation among people who are hurting, both victims and perpetrators. Forgiving others, though difficult, should be a part of the reconciliation process. It must carry something of the boundless grace that God gives.

 # Conclusion

In conclusion, I want to suggest several markers of a Church that is well equipped to play the role of reconciliation. First, it has to be prophetic in order to promote a faith that does justice. This requires being involved in the transformation of factors that promote conflict. It should collaborate with the many Christian professionals who form an abundant resource, yet are rarely utilized. The Church needs increasingly to include professionals in the analysis of social contexts. Second, it has to be vigilant and committed to social change and human rights monitoring, in collaboration with civil society and decision-makers. The Church must always be committed to making God's presence visible in time and space. Vigilance calls for foresight in anticipating the impact of political, economic and religious policies on the population. Third, the Church must be intrusive by seeking to intervene against societal and governmental practices that violate human dignity. It needs to be part of the decision-making processes through lobbying and advocacy, together with other people of good will especially in the civil society.

Finally, the Church has to be in solidarity with its people as an agent of forgiveness and reconciliation. It must seek to mediate healing to those wounded by conflict. Just as Christ did, the Church needs to counter the sins of domination, discrimination and divisiveness with the gospel of love. This is because a 'just society cannot be achieved without the component of love' (Synod of Bishops, *Lineamenta*, 2006: #39). Justice and peace are intertwined, for justice is a prerequisite to peace. They should also be administered in the framework of forgiveness and reconciliation. The fundamental aim is to foster a Christian identity that does not eliminate difference and diversity, but that eliminates the sin of marginalizing 'the other' on racial, social, religious, ethnic or national grounds. The future of the African Church depends on how it negotiates difference and reunites divided people into one family, a people of God who stand up for justice and promote and live the gospel value of love of neighbour. In this way, the Church may contribute to making Christian identity the basic identity in relation to all other human identities.

? STUDY QUESTIONS

1 What is human identity? How can identity function both positively and negatively?

2 What does the New Testament teach about Christian identity? Discuss the specific markers of Christian identity outlined in this chapter. Give examples from your own experience of where you have seen these qualities manifested in Christians.

3 Explain why the issue of Christian identity and ethnicity has been such a challenge in Africa, drawing upon the examples cited above. How does this challenge in African Christianity relate to the experience of Christian identity and ethnicity in your own context?

4 Discuss how the ministry of reconciliation, according to Paul, applies to the problem of Christian identity and ethnicity in Africa. Of the various recommendations made for fostering Christian identity amidst cultural diversity, which ones are most relevant to your own context?

14

Theology of reconstruction

Jesse N. K. Mugambi

 Abstract

Jesse N. K. Mugambi proposes the theology of reconstruction as a leading paradigm for African Christian theology in the twenty-first century. He introduces the topic by sketching the profound political changes in the world throughout the twentieth century, with particular reference to Africa. He then sets the historical context for the theology of reconstruction by outlining key events in Africa during the latter half of the twentieth century: from the optimism of newly independent nations, through the ideological and economic conflicts produced by the Cold War, to the emergence of the new global regime of the capitalist market economy. These historical circumstances have shaped the emergence and development of liberation and reconstruction theologies. Following a brief but important consideration of theological method, Mugambi provides an overview and critique of liberation theologies. Finally, the author advocates a theology of reconstruction, based on the process of social reconstruction, which invites every member of society to participate in establishing a new social order more aligned with God's intention for humanity.

 Introduction

The year 2010 marks the first centenary of the World Missionary Conference convened at Edinburgh, Scotland, in 1910. That conference is the formative event for the modern ecumenical movement. The conference brought together 1,400 European and North American Christian missionaries, who were based in all six continents, to discuss the theme of evangelizing the whole world in their generation. They were as optimistic in their time as the contemporary peddlers of 'globalization' in the first decade of the twenty-first century. Their optimism was short-lived. The First World War broke out in 1914 and shattered the false confidence technology had instilled in the upper classes of European and North American society. The

Edinburgh Conference had been inspired by the technological achievements of nineteenth-century Europe. Yet paradoxically, the same technological optimism led to the excesses in militarism, fascism, racism and imperialism tragically manifested in the two World Wars (1914–18 and 1939–45).

History has the tendency to repeat itself, both within and between cultures. The optimism heralded in the North Atlantic by the end of Soviet Communism – with the fall of the Berlin Wall in November 1989 – was shattered by the fall of the World Trade Center in New York on September 11, 2001, followed by the subsequent 'war on terror' led by the USA and the UK. The world in general, and Africa in particular, has undergone profound political change since 1990. What has been the impact of this change on the development of African Christian theology?

This chapter explores the theology of reconstruction as a 'paradigm' for theological innovation in Africa in the twenty-first century. The term 'paradigm' refers here to the main framework for theory and practice within a cultural context. The paradigm presupposed by the modern Christian missionary enterprise was essentially entangled with the imperial expansion of Christian denominations from Europe and North America to colonies in Africa, the Caribbean, Asia and the Pacific. Missionary societies operated mainly in the colonies held by, and with the protection of, their home governments. Immediately after the decolonization of most territories in tropical Africa during the 1960s and 1970s, power relations changed significantly between the Christian missions and their 'daughter' churches.

The transfer of leadership from North Atlantic missions to African churches was a difficult process in most denominations. From the perspective of most missionaries, it meant a loss of power, while from the perspective of most African church leaders it meant 'liberation'. When many missionaries handed over and returned to their sending countries, they expected their successors to maintain the 'daughter' churches unchanged. The mission boards in the North Atlantic continued to exercise influence by setting conditions for sending their grants and personnel to the younger churches. The climax of this tension was during the mid-1970s, when the 'Moratorium Debate' dominated the discussions in ecumenical and missionary circles. In order for the African churches to truly establish their own identity, several prominent African church leaders called for a 'moratorium', or a withdrawal of missionary personnel and funds for several years. After much debate, this proposal was approved by the AACC Third Assembly in 1974. Thus, as the younger churches in the former colonies took over the reins of leadership, they often found themselves in crisis, having to manage institutions they had not created. At the same time they had to relate constructively with African governments that were also struggling to sustain national sovereignty in the context of competing imperial ideologies.

The magnitude of political change experienced in tropical Africa after 1990 is comparable to that in the 1960s and 1970s. Namibia achieved national sovereignty in 1990, and apartheid was finally abolished in 1994. The following section is a brief historical sketch of this change, in the context of which African Christian theology has evolved.

 # Historical context

There was much jubilation when most African nations attained their sovereignty in the 1960s. The younger generation, in particular, looked forward to a new era of freedom and prosperity. That optimism soon faded into disillusionment during the 1970s when the new sovereign nations became embroiled in civil strife. During the Cold War the newly independent African states suffered economic exploitation and ideological manipulation by the former imperial powers. The 1980s were characterized by political and economic decline all over the continent, as commodity prices tumbled and costs of imports escalated. The Cold War tore Africa to pieces as nations were tossed between the superpowers and their respective allies. Superpower patronage and intimidation made it difficult for African nations to exercise their sovereignty. Every African nation had to comply with the demands of its respective 'bloc masters' in return for their protection and support. Failure to comply would lead to punishments, including isolation, overthrow and sanctions. Few African leaders of the time dared to risk defiance or noncompliance. Although most African governments officially belonged to the Non-Aligned Movement, in practice they leaned ideologically towards either the East or the West. The superpowers viewed each African nation as either a supporter or an opponent. Those were difficult times, during which young Africans had to sense which ideological slogans to cheer and which to jeer, depending on the wishes of the leaders in power. Liberation was an important theme for the African elite, understood in terms of release from colonial domination, racial oppression, economic exploitation, cultural imperialism and Cold War manipulations.

The end of the Cold War in 1990 brought a new global regime with which the African elite had to deal. After the demise of communism there remained one reigning ideology, capitalism, which operated in a global market economy controlled by a few transnational corporations with the backing of the Organization of Economic Cooperation and Development (OECD). The Bretton Woods institutions – the International Monetary Fund (IMF), the International Bank for Reconstruction and Development, and the World Trade Organization – demanded 'structural adjustment'. By this phrase they meant adjusting to the 'new world order' controlled by global capitalism.

Loans from the World Bank and IMF would henceforth be provided only on the condition that borrowers committed themselves to organizing their national economic and political structures according to the dictates of the so-called 'global market'. The conditions included multiparty democracy; privatization of public services; trimming the civil service; devaluation of local currencies; opening up of national markets to international competition;

and removal of subsidies on strategic industries including agriculture, transport, water, energy and health. The African nations found themselves poorer than they had ever been. Their devalued national currencies reflected the devaluation of their citizens' labour. Thus Africans became, in essence, enslaved at home, as they tried to repay debts whose value they could not determine, and whose investment in real terms was negative.

Only after the Cold War did the countries within the OECD express interest in the 'democratization' of Africa. Their interest, however, was much more tied to economics than to politics. They wanted to ensure their own continuing access to the raw materials and markets in African countries. Their interest in the 'democratization' of Africa was only as a means towards the promotion of capitalism. Democracy is not an end in itself. It is a means to an end. For this reason they tolerated regimes which were not democratic, as long as their own economic interests were guaranteed. There has been a great deal of inconsistency in the way the OECD countries have dealt with Africa, especially with regard to economic and political reform. African countries are in a position to plead for aid only because they do not have the political clout to demand or negotiate fair trading terms. The so-called Economic Partnership Agreement between the European Union and the African, Caribbean and Pacific illustrates the problem. Since African countries do not have the power to challenge the European Union, they can only obey what they are commanded to do on a 'take it or leave it' basis.

The world's rulers have truncated Africa into North Africa, Saharan Africa, sub-Saharan Africa and Southern Africa. This is a strange demarcation of Africa, with neither roots nor justification in Africa's self-understanding. Rich foreign nations tend to describe poor African nations according to stereotypes that reflect condescension and paternalism. Ironically, democracy seems to be demanded only in tropical Africa, which is derogatorily called 'sub-Saharan' Africa. Far from promoting democracy, the wealthy nations have allowed a military 're-autocratization' of the continent, in which soldiers have left the barracks and made themselves rulers on civilian thrones. By the year 2000 only six African countries – out of 54! – had civilian leaders without military background as their heads of state: Botswana, Kenya, Malawi, Senegal, Swaziland and Tanzania. All the other countries were governed by rulers who were either military officers or former leaders in liberation movements. Under these circumstances, how can one talk about democratization? How can an electorate vote in 'free and fair' elections to choose between military and civilian candidates? The tendency is to vote for the soldiers, fearing the consequences of doing otherwise. During the Cold War the superpowers and their allies sponsored coups and counter coups. Since then, the situation has not changed significantly, except that now only one ideology is dominant. After 1990, new vocabulary became normative – 'regime change'.

Why would OECD member countries not be interested in the democratization of Africa prior to 1990? The answer can be found in the precedents.

Whatever system guarantees the West's economic interests will be supported, irrespective of its ideological worth. That is why the Arab monarchies are tolerated for the petroleum they guarantee. For the same reason, communist China enjoys favourable trade relations with the OECD, irrespective of its national ideology. The theology of reconstruction is thus articulated in the context of this global capitalist hegemony and internal civil strife in Africa. The context is determined by the historical circumstances in which churches as social institutions, and Christians as individuals, have to live and express their faith in Jesus Christ.

Reflections on theological methodology

Before tracing the emergence of liberation and reconstruction theologies, we shall briefly consider theological method – a task that is crucial for all African Christian theologians. Since the mid-twentieth century, the dominant emphasis in African Christian theology has been to highlight African responses to the gospel in specific ethnic communities from the perspective of specific denominations. Rarely has such theologizing been self-critical. The time has come for African Christian theologians to scrutinize their methodology so as to improve on it. How do we do our theology? What are our sources? What are our presuppositions? What is the content of our theologizing? Such basic questions ought to be answered before embarking on the theme at hand.

It has become fashionable in theological circles to talk of 'contextualization'. What does this word mean? What kind of process is 'contextualization'? Those who use the word presuppose that there is a given 'text' that has to be 'contextualized'. The constant is the 'text', while the variable is the 'context'. The modern Christian missionary enterprise has functioned on such a presupposition. Foreign missionaries in Africa have often assumed that their brand of Christianity is 'given', universal and constant. Conversion is viewed as acceptance of this given 'faith'. In fact, there is no 'pure' faith, unmediated through culture. All expressions of any faith are conditioned by specific cultural factors, including language.

The call for 'contextualization' is a call for relevance and applicability. How can 'contextualization' be put into effect? There are at least three possible approaches:

- **from the text to the contexts**
- **from the context to the particular texts**
- **two-way movement between the texts and the contexts.**

Any process of contextualization will yield results dependent on the approach that is chosen. If one starts from the position of the text being the constant, it will be impossible to critique the text, because the text will be presupposed to be the standard against which everything else must be judged. Questions about the authenticity of the text and the reliability of the translation will not be considered. Karl Barth is famous for this approach.

On the other hand, starting from the position of the context being the constant means the text becomes relative to variables, so that its authenticity will depend on the rendering it is given by the contextual reading. Rudolf Bultmann's project of 'demythologization' yielded a theology of this kind.

The two-way movement between text and context yields a third category of theologies, such as those of Paul Tillich and Emil Brunner. In this approach the theologian treads cautiously between the given texts and the meanings attached to them from time to time and from culture to culture.

Thus even among contemporary theologians belonging to the same culture, it is possible to produce 'contextual' theologies of different kinds, depending on the approaches that have been applied. This approach takes biblical hermeneutics seriously, discerning the meaning intended by canonical texts and relating that meaning to specific cultural contexts. The message takes precedence over the medium of its transmission.

I opt for the third approach, which allows unrestricted movement between the text and the context. On the one hand, the context provides the operational platform on which theology has to be done. On the other, the text provides the analytical stimulus for creative reflection. The theology of reconstruction is based on this two-way communication between the text and the context. The theology of liberation tended to take the text (the exodus narratives) as given, and could not critique the text for fear that it might lose authority. The next section is a critique of African theologies of liberation, out of which the paradigm of reconstruction has evolved.

❋ Theologies of liberation in Africa

It is the standard norm of all theologies of liberation to cite Moses as the role model of ideal leadership. In the book of Exodus, Moses is portrayed as a charismatic leader who dares to oppose Pharaoh on the basis of divine authority, rather than his own ability. Moses has often featured as the exemplary 'liberator', because the narrative of the exodus portrays him as the one who intercedes between Pharaoh and the people, and also between the people and God.

The first generation of African leadership during the 1960s and 1970s was invariably likened to Moses' role as a leader liberating his community from bondage. In the book of Exodus nobody dares to criticize Moses because of his charismatic authority. Only his father-in-law, Jethro the Midianite, has enough clout and courage to challenge Moses' incompetence as a leader. Jethro advises Moses to delegate his functions to improve efficiency and effectiveness (Exodus 3.1, 13–27). When Moses loses his temper in the wilderness, he leaves the people alone and retreats to the hills. On his return he finds that they have begun worshipping idols and again he loses his temper.

Leadership of this kind cannot yield constructive change. It is erratic and temperamental. Understandably, under the leadership of Moses the community wanders in the wilderness for forty years. Such has been African leadership decades since the 1960s. The exodus motif, with Moses as the exemplary leader, cannot yield effective self-actualization of a community. The initiative and creativity of individuals and communities tends to be inhibited and intimidated by the charismatic but often erratic leadership of the Moses stereotype. The first three decades (1960–1990) of national sovereignty in most African countries were a period characterized by such temperamental and inhibitive leadership. This was the contextual setting of the theology of reconstruction.

Another shortcoming of theologies of liberation is that the role of the ruling elite is overemphasized at the expense of the participation of ordinary people. The leaders claim to speak and act on behalf of the people, even when they are acting in their own personal self-interest. The common good is sometimes exploited for personal gain, and often the leadership loses contact with the followers.

Furthermore, the metaphor of the exodus is not easily transferable, especially because of its geopolitical implications. When Latin Americans, Africans and African Americans used this metaphor, it was applicable only figuratively. There was no geographical movement from the land of bondage to the 'Promised Land'. Consequently, the goal of liberation theologies has been difficult to define with any precision. While it was clear from what the liberation struggles were conducted, there was vagueness regarding where or what the struggles were leading to. In the African context, where are we now? Are we still 'in Egypt'? 'Crossing the Red Sea'? Have we yet 'crossed the River Jordan'? Disagreement about our bearings along this path of liberation leaves open the question of how useful as a social metaphor the exodus narrative really is, whenever it is extrapolated outside the biblical narrative. When a social metaphor loses its cohesive value, it also loses its efficacy as an ideological tool for social mobilization.

Despite the shortcomings outlined above, theologies of liberation have been very important in the history of Africa. They gave impetus to the struggles for liberation, and provided the ideological platform for opposition to imperial oppression. Therefore, their impact should be appreciated as initial achievements in the longer process of self-actualization of most African nations. This is the main proposition of my book, *From Liberation to Reconstruction* (1995). It is fallacious to discredit the theologies of liberation. They deserve to be appreciated as a prerequisite for the more challenging task of reconstruction after the oppressor has relinquished power, whether willingly or otherwise.

Theologies of reconstruction

During the 1960s and 1970s, as outlined above, younger nations experienced socio-political change primarily as liberation from imperial rule to national sovereignty. In contrast, during the 1990s Africans, both young and old, eagerly anticipated social reconstruction in their respective nations that had declined and become dysfunctional as a result of decades of mismanagement under superpower rivalry. Within this context, the theology of reconstruction is not just another label for the old theological discourse. It is a challenge to do theology in a new way, with new thought-forms, new presuppositions and new axioms.

Liberation is a process in which the oppressed direct their actions against the oppressors while the oppressors resist accordingly. The theology of reconstruction presupposes a different process, which is not adversarial but reciprocal. To quote from my book, *From Liberation to Reconstruction*:

> This Theology should be reconstructive rather than destructive; inclusive rather than exclusive; proactive rather than reactive; complementary rather than competitive; integrative rather than disintegrative; programme-driven rather than project-driven; people-centred rather than institution-centred; deed-oriented rather than word-oriented; participatory rather than autocratic; regenerative rather than degenerative; future-sensitive rather than past-sensitive; cooperative rather than confrontational; consultative rather than impositional. (1995: xv)

Thus, social reconstruction is a process in which all sectors of the population are invited to participate in the inauguration of a new social order. Every individual and every organization is invited to make its positive contribution for the common good of all.

If Moses is the epitome of a liberator, then Nehemiah serves as a model leader for social reconstruction. The narrative in the book of Nehemiah is a moving account of the mobilization of a desperate community under the leadership of one man, Nehemiah, through what today would be called 'participatory management'. Nehemiah is born, educated and trained in the Babylonian exile. He rises to become Chief of Protocol in the king's palace. This is a great achievement, especially considering that exiles are looked down upon by the host nation. Nehemiah is so trusted that the king grants him his request to go to Jerusalem to attend to the suffering of the people there. In Jerusalem, the people are under the rule of governors appointed by the king, but this is absentee administration in which the local rulers take advantage of the suffering people. There are three local leaders, Sanballat, Geshem and Tobiah, who have no interest in the welfare of the people. The people of Judah have been praying and hoping that Nehemiah would use his high office and come to their help, and he does.

Nehemiah surveys the whole of Jerusalem and its environs to evaluate what needs to be done to restore its past glory. He confirms that the city is in ruins but, using his management skills and knowledge, he prepares a report on the materials and the time required. On the fourth day he calls a meeting and announces that he has made all the necessary investigation. Jerusalem can be rebuilt, using local resources only. He then challenges the people:

> *'You see the trouble we are in, how Jerusalem lies in ruins with its gates burnt. Come, let us rebuild the wall of Jerusalem, so that we may no longer suffer disgrace.' I told them that the hand of my God had been gracious upon me, and also the words that the king had spoken to me. Then they said, 'Let us start building!' So they committed themselves to the common good.*
>
> (Nehemiah 2.17–18)

The method of Nehemiah is very different from that of Moses. He encourages the people and facilitates their work. He motivates them to work but does not impose himself upon them. He has confidence that they can do the work, as long as they are highly motivated.

Africa is in a similar situation to Judah in the days of Nehemiah. There are many Sanballats, Geshems and Tobiahs in the media, in politics, in diplomatic circles and in business. They are also in the World Bank and in the IMF; in embassies and universities; in churches and mission agencies; and in media houses and corporations. But there are also Nehemiahs, who are well trained and can motivate their people. There are Jeremiahs too, prophets of doom and prophets of sorrow. You can choose which profile to highlight. It seems to me that at this time in history, the figure of Nehemiah is most encouraging and most inspiring for Africa today. We can find and emulate prophets of hope, who encourage the poor and weak to keep struggling, even in the midst of great disaster. God is in charge of history, even when principalities and powers mess it up. Hope will eventually triumph over despair. This is the essence of the theology of reconstruction.

Jesus Christ serves as a model for reconstruction theology. Indeed, he was much more of a reconstruction theologian than a liberation theologian. The text often associated with liberation, Luke 4.18–19, is a citation from Isaiah 61.1–2. The rest of the fourth chapter of Luke indicates that Jesus was challenging his listeners to take responsibility for their present and future, instead of accepting their condition as a matter of unchangeable historical predicament. The gospel message is powerful because of its capacity to encourage believers to live up to their potential with God's help.

Moreover, the Sermon on the Mount is a concise outline of reconstructive theology. Jesus contrasts the teaching of Moses and his own, showing that a new social consciousness was needed in order for the Aramaic community to regain its dignity under the Roman Empire. This reconstructive theology was opposed not so much by the Romans, but by the Aramaic elite. We need to learn from that experience. At the ecclesiastical level, churches as institutions and Christians as individuals risk becoming so conformed to the norms of this world as to be like salt that has lost its taste (Matthew 5.13–16). St Paul cautions us against this risk and challenges us to become agents of social transformation rather than passive conformists (Romans 12.1–2).

The Pauline Epistles are replete with insights for theologies of reconstruction. Although St Paul began as a passionate persecutor of Christians, he underwent such a dramatic conversion on the road to Damascus that he became a refiner of Christianity rather than its persecutor. For the rest of his life he endeavoured to reconstruct Jewish religious consciousness so that it would become much more inclusive. While some Jewish Christians wanted to restrict church membership to those who had undergone circumcision, St Paul insisted that such a restriction would violate the Church of Christ (Acts 15; Galatians 2—3). In his public ministry, Jesus had viewed the Church as an entirely new community in which people of different backgrounds might together witness the love of God. People of all walks of life came to Jesus – Roman soldiers, Samaritans, tax collectors, wealthy Pharisees, poor peasants, cripples, the blind and deaf, men, women, children – everyone had something to learn and gain from interacting with Jesus. St Paul's Epistle to the Galatians is perhaps the most lucid articulation of open-minded ecclesiology.

Although St Paul did not question the institution of slavery, he challenged slave masters to treat their slaves as if they were not slaves, and the slaves to behave as if they were equals with their masters (Ephesians 6.5–9; Colossians 3.22—4.1). This was social reconstruction at its best. St Paul demonstrated that attitudes must be changed before institutions could be reformed.

Finally, the book of Revelation challenges Christians to anticipate a new heaven and a new earth, after the old heaven and the old earth have passed away (Revelation 21.1–5). This apocalyptic message challenges Christians never to lose hope, but always to work for social reconstruction wherever they are, and in whatever they do.

 Conclusion

In this chapter I have outlined the core of a theology of reconstruction, including its biblical grounding in both the Old and the New Testament. Each of us is challenged to add his or her brick towards the rebuilding of Africa, focusing particularly on rebuilding our families, societies and nations now fragmented by strife under both internal conflict and external interference and manipulation. This is not the time to apportion blame. It is the time to build. Are you and I part of the solution, or part of the problem? Are you and I builders or destroyers? This is your challenge and mine, in the theology of reconstruction. There is no time for academic rhetoric. There is time only for reconstructive reflection and action.

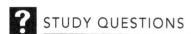

STUDY QUESTIONS

1 Outline the historical factors, both within and beyond Africa, that have contributed to the development of reconstruction theology.

2 What is 'contextualization'? Of the three approaches to contextualization that Jesse N. K. Mugambi sets forth, why does he favour the third approach? Do you agree? Why or why not?

3 According to Mugambi, what are the strengths or contributions of liberation theologies?

4 What are the weaknesses? To what extent do you agree with Mugambi's assessment? Explain your answer.

5 Define reconstruction theology and explain the biblical examples that Mugambi cites to develop his argument.

6 What insights from reconstruction theology could you apply within your own context of ministry?

15

A postcolonial South African Church: problems and promises

Tinyiko Sam Maluleke

Abstract

This chapter is based on a radio interview that Tinyiko Maluleke gave on the profile and role of the churches in post-apartheid South Africa. He acknowledges the comparatively low profile of the South African Church, following the apartheid era, yet affirms its ongoing prophetic witness at the local congregational level. He then outlines key accusations voiced by critics of the Church, including its close alliance with the new government, its alleged foreignness as a colonial religion, and its ineffectiveness in dealing with socio-economic realities such as poverty, violence, and gender inequities. Maluleke underlines the need for Christians to listen seriously to these criticisms and to take responsibility for addressing the shortcomings of the Church. He does so himself by analysing several explanations for the decline in the Church's prophetic witness. Finally, he offers concrete proposals for how the Church in South Africa can move forward to serve the people of South Africa more faithfully and effectively.

A rude awakening

During this year I have participated in a number of radio broadcasts on various topics, especially on the subject of religion in general, and Christianity in particular, in post-apartheid society. One radio show invited me in my capacity as President of the South African Council of Churches (SACC). The topic for discussion was the profile and role of the churches in post-apartheid South Africa. In my opening comments I painted a picture of a church struggling to find her feet in a changed and changing environment. I acknowledged that the ecumenical South African Church might indeed have a much lower profile, in terms of prophetic witness, than it did during the apartheid era. However, I argued that social action and prophetic activity were likely continuing at the local congregation level.

When the radio audience began calling in to the programme and entering the discussion, I was forced to stretch my point above. I further suggested that perhaps the apparent lower profile of the Church in post-apartheid South Africa was more a function of a selective media, which would rather follow other national and social concerns, than any genuine reflection of reality. Nonetheless, the barrage of hostile questions that followed was something of a rude awakening. Angry callers raised many criticisms against the Church, which can be condensed into a few key arguments.

The basic accusation was that the Church in general and the SACC in particular were both too beholden to the new government, just like the Dutch Reformed Church had been beholden to the previous government. This was one of the reasons why the Church was 'nowhere to be seen' on the social landscape of the country. As evidence, the radio callers pointed out the number of priests, theologians and church people who, as they put it, had 'jumped ship' and become politicians, civil servants and business people. In particular, they decried the volume of traffic of personnel from the Church to the state. In their view, precisely that part of the Church that was once prophetic is 'now in bed with government'.

The underlying concern is that church leadership appointments in general, and the SACC leadership appointments in particular, have now become a training ground for future civil and governmental appointments. This creates the worrying threat of church leaders spending their time waiting for that call – not the call from heaven, but the call from the government. The Church is therefore in danger of becoming not merely a training ground, but a playground of politicians. In other words, they allege, the Church is now available for politicians to use and abuse, to call and command. This is why the Church is often silent when it should be speaking; often absent where it should be present; mostly inaudible where it should be heard loud and clear; and tongue-tied when the nation is hungry for its words.

A second major argument was the age-old accusation that Christianity was a foreign and colonial religion, so that continued adherence to it is both childish and absurd. Some callers expressed intense anger against the religion that propped up and justified apartheid. Several suggested that I ought to be ashamed of myself, as an African, defending a colonial religion. '*Mu-Africa* (African), where is your pride? How can you defend a religion that has done so much harm in this country and on this continent?' Indeed, a few callers suggested very strongly that it was time for Africans to walk out of the Church back to the religion of their foremothers and forefathers.

A third cluster of arguments centred on the role of the Church – or lack thereof – in the contemporary socio-political context. Some callers cited a number of incidents of poverty and violence, asking where was the Church in these contexts and at those moments? In response, I invoked the voices of radical Black theology of South Africa, such as Alan Boesak and Itumeleng Mosala. These theologians advocate the possibility of being radically 'Black and Christian' in a way that is theologically and politically coherent. Black theology, I argued, was as potent a weapon of struggle as Black consciousness had been. While it may never have been a mass movement like Black consciousness, Black theology sought both to interpret and understand the Black religious experience in order to make it a theological, cultural and spiritual weapon of struggle for a better life. Rather than walking away from Christianity because of its collusion with apartheid oppression, I found the path of Black theology to be preferable, rational and defendable.

Nonetheless, one radio caller retorted by saying that ultimately, Black theology sounded like a massive religious false consciousness by members of an oppressed group who have been made naïve enough to believe that they can use the tools of the master to dismantle the master's house. Other callers even suggested that African development and poverty eradication were not possible as long as they are premised upon foreign religions, culture and spirituality.

Further complaints emerged concerning the profile of the Church in post-apartheid South Africa. Women contested the patriarchal nature of the Church, with many churches continuing to exclude women from positions of leadership. They pointed out that the use of language that excluded women or lowered their status, plus the tendency toward military language, could make the Church an incubator for violence against women. Others highlighted the elitist and middle-class nature of the so-called historic mission churches. They asked, 'How can such a Church deal with the real problems of poor shack dwellers and with the needs of rural communities?'

All these accusations against the Church call for careful consideration. Where are we, as a Church, in post-apartheid South Africa? And how do we respond to these allegations?

A postcolonial Church: where are we today?

It struck me that, for the majority of the callers in this and other radio discussions I have had, there is more than sheer anger, more than mere condemnation of the Church, and more than a romantic appeal for the good old days of the Church. I have sensed a genuine appeal for the Church to take her pride of place in the community of civil, labour and other faith-based organizations. It seems that the Church's prophetic absence has left a 'void' that many feel only the Church can fill. It is not that these people are romantic about the Church. It is not as if they do not know the Church's weaknesses and theological difficulties that have marred its witness in Africa. They know that, this side of eternity, the Church is not perfect and neither are its members. Yet they also know the power of the Church when it takes up its cross and follows Jesus in the path of justice and solidarity with the poor. So, more than an outright rejection of the Church and Christianity, theirs is primarily a call for the Church to stand up and be counted, or to give much-needed leadership.

I have since given up on trying to defend the Church, religion and the ecumenical movement. In my view, we Christians need a different set of strategies than the ones we have been using. To begin with, we need to listen deeply to the criticisms – even the cruellest of these. We need to hear the message, and the message behind the message. As churches, we need to take responsibility not merely for this particular phase in the history of the Church, and not only for the history of our own church denominations. Rather, as the Church of South Africa, we must acknowledge both our good and our bad legacies, and on this basis try to address our shortcomings.

These shortcomings are all too obvious, from the account above of my encounters with a hostile radio audience. Their common verdict is clear: the Church is 'nowhere to be seen'. From the lengthy discussion, several explanations emerged for the absence of the Church's prophetic witness. These explanations are neither right nor wrong; they are both right and wrong. They also do not stand in complete isolation from one another, but are interrelated. More importantly, they are informative and crucial if we are to construct a more prophetic response to the crisis. Let us review, then, some of the main explanations in circulation today.

Apartheid as a unifying force

This is an explanation that is as common as it is painful. Evidence does suggest that the end of apartheid, while welcome, has created a crisis for the Church and for many other anti-apartheid organizations at home and abroad. Without this great 'cause' and 'heresy' to fight, the prophetic Church seems to lack a potent pole around which to build its prophetic witness. Having prayed for the fall of apartheid rule, the Church appears not to know what to do next. None of the 'causes' currently available have managed to seize the imagination and energy of the Church. Yet the problem with this explanation is that it wrongly assumes that all of the Church was truly united against apartheid. The truth of the matter is that the churches' fight against apartheid was disparate and uneven.

The end of the Cold War and the waning of ecumenical solidarity

For various reasons ecumenical solidarity has waned. This is not only a South African problem, but a global one. With the demise of the Cold War, the glue that held many social movements together has dissolved. The cohesion and resources of the World Council of Churches (WCC) have suffered far more than initially expected, for various reasons: the effect of the end of Cold War ideological polarizations, the advent of Eastern Europe on the developmental scene, and the emergence of the 'war on terrorism' campaigns. Like the SACC without apartheid, the WCC without the Cold War seems to have lost her way somewhat. Likewise, without the heightened support the South African Church had come to expect from the global ecumenical family, South African ecumenism has taken a knock.

Too close to government?

The charge of being too close to government, while difficult to dismiss, probably needs to be qualified. The charge is usually made because of the many priests, former church leaders and workers now in government and 'political' positions. This situation causes a blurring of roles that is often confusing to the churches. For example, after I was elected President of the SACC, one of my first responsibilities was to attend the National Religious Leadership Forum (NRLF). This is an organization composed of members of all the major religions, which was formed at the invitation of the government. The Forum was held at the Union Buildings, where the South African Government sits and the office of the President of South Africa is located. Interestingly, I have since established that this organization meets only when government summons it, and it basically does not have a life outside of government. This organization also assists government in relativizing and 'policing' the various religions.

The sheer number of church leaders' visits to state house, compared to their visits to the country's hotspots, also strengthens perceptions of the 'closeness' of churches to government. The SACC has even established a permanent parliamentary office. Indeed, over the past few years the SACC has tended to err on the side of consulting with government at the expense of exercising its prophetic role. This partly explains the delay in the SACC speaking out against Robert Mugabe, the long-standing President of Zimbabwe. Furthermore, the fact that at least two of the former SACC General Secretaries hold prominent government positions (Director General in the Office of the President, and Ambassador to the Democratic Republic of Congo) also serves to strengthen views of a close relationship between church and government.

So here is the problem: churches know that they have to engage with government, but what is the best way to do this?

Church leadership: part of the new elite?

Post-1994 South Africa has unleashed a new elite, which now includes people who had not been members of this club previously. The problem with a postcolonial elite is that they occupy the palace of their former 'oppressors' and assume the resources previously available only to their former oppressors. In a country where the new elite has been in a hurry to amass as much power as quickly as possible, the Church has had to make some crucial choices as to what role she will play. Unfortunately, the Church has largely chosen to watch in silence. A case in point is her lack of voice in response to the ongoing saga of a certain arms deal, which is arguably the most controversial and most expensive 'deal' the new government entered. Similarly, churches may have participated in some of the major social campaigns of the democratic era, but churches have not led many of these. Where they have attempted to lead, they have often done so with much division among the churches.

Likewise, individual Christians have been highly critical of government reaction to the recent xenophobic attacks in parts of South Africa. Yet if truth were told, the churches' public silence on the plight of refugees and foreign nationals has been deafening. Even worse, the churches' absence at the moments and places where foreign nationals have been abused and killed has been sadly telling. Equally, the Church could have done far more in response to the HIV & AIDS pandemic.

✳ Outmanoeuvred by government and by politicians

The post-apartheid government has been shrewd in its dealings with religions in general and churches in particular. As indicated above, the NRLF is a clever little structure through which government can convene and control religions. Every meeting of this body is not only a government media event, but also largely an occasion for government to speak and religious leaders to listen. It appears to be government strategy to be so verbose in these meetings that there is hardly time for religious leaders to make any input. Another example is the government initiative called the Moral Regeneration Movement, an ostensibly religious and spiritual undertaking that is nevertheless led by government. So while the new government claims to be secular, it is actually driving a religious agenda of its own.

Another area in which the government constantly outmanoeuvres the churches is that of resources. One of the unspoken dreams of the NRLF is that government will make funding available to it. Such funding has not as yet materialized, but the unspoken promise has managed to keep the NRLF in anticipation and, in that way, 'under control'. Were the funding to materialize at the scale that is hoped for, the relations between government and churches would – from a prophetic point of view – become even worse. Every meeting between religious leaders and government is an opportunity for government to perform rituals that reinforce its power, its hegemony and its benevolence.

The Church is no longer hegemonic

That the Church is no longer hegemonic, or authoritative, is both true and mythical. It is true insofar as the hegemonic power once enjoyed by Christian churches, such as the Dutch Reformed Church, is past. Not only has the diversity of Christian confessions come to light, but also other religions are increasingly acknowledged. The churches now have to contend with government as well as other assertive religions and even more assertive civic organizations. Given the crowdedness of the public space in which the Church needs to operate, it is more important than ever for the Church to gain a clearer sense of its own identity and agenda. Otherwise, the Church might go chasing after every new fad as adopted and advertised by its 'alliance partners'.

On the other hand, the Church must not take its loss of hegemony too literally. The power of the Church's voice lies not in its volume, nor in the presence or absence of 'competition'. We must never forget that the Church has members across the party-political spectrum. The Church has members in parliament, in government and in the judiciary. The Church has more 'power' than we realize. In this sense the Church must continue to assume its influence for godliness in every possible sphere.

Loss of experienced and proven leaders

Like similar organizations, the Church lost a number of experienced and proven leaders after 1994. This was inevitable, since the new government needed to round up the few skilled people to lay the foundation for a new country and a new government. Churches and NGOs had to 'donate' a number of their leaders to political parties, local and national government. In addition, new opportunities opened for education and jobs in sectors of the economy previously unavailable to the majority of people. Hence it becomes clear how much the Church lost in terms of leadership.

All sorts of attempts have been made to gloss over the reality of this loss. Some suggest that these leaders are not really lost to the Church, that they have only moved workstations or changed 'parishes', as it were. However, the reality is that many leaders have retired, some have withdrawn completely from the Church, and others have died. For all intents and purposes, such leaders are no longer available. There is a natural attrition process of leaders and the Church must accept this reality. The outcome, unfortunately, is that the quality of both personnel and leadership in the Church and in church organizations may have declined.

The Church has made wrong theological choices

For a short time in the mid-1990s, sections of the South African ecumenical movement, led by a few influential theologians, flirted with the idea of 'critical solidarity with the state'. While this was never formally adopted as a resolution in any conference or assembly I can think of, it is a proposal that was made by enough influential theologians and leaders for us to worry. Indeed, some of the choices that church and ecumenical organizations have made, in terms of their engagements, only make sense when viewed against some version of critical solidarity with the state. The traffic of personnel between church organizations and government, the consult-government-first policy, the disproportionate number of trips to government sites as opposed to squatter camps, the apparent indifference to suffering, death and poverty by churches and church leaders – all these do not make sense unless we read them against the backdrop of the strategy of critical solidarity with the state.

The second illustration of a wrong theological choice is the churches' choice for silence when it might be better to speak and to act. There are different types of silence: the interested silence of the powerful and the fearful silence of the powerless; the empty silence of the hopeless and the calculated silence of the vulnerable; loud silence and soft silence; eloquent silence and incoherent silence; active silence and passive silence. There are many occasions in which the churches appear to have chosen a certain type of silence: in relation to the arms deal saga, the xenophobic violence, the worrying conduct of the ruling party, the apparent strife within the judiciary, the crisis in Zimbabwe, and the growing culture of violence in our country.

A postcolonial Church?

After considering the major allegations against the Church outlined above, we must return to the key question of where we are today as a 'postcolonial' Church. First, I should explain this term, for there are as many definitions of postcolonialism as there are postcolonialists. It has become a cliché in postcolonial studies to say that cultural and sacred texts are a central means in the imposition, legitimizing, maintenance of, and resistance against imperialism and colonialism. Postcolonial studies are therefore the study of 'texts' and 'contexts' through which colonialism is imposed, maintained, renewed and resisted.

In brief, there are three basic understandings of postcolonialism. The first is that the entire world today is postcolonial; that is, whether you live in London or in Gugulethu, colonialism is deeply embedded into your history and culture – even in ways you are not immediately aware of. If you ignore the impact of colonialism in your history, you will not understand who you are today or who you can be tomorrow. Worse still, you might not realize what you are really up against. In this sense, both the great-grandchildren of former colonialists and those of the colonized have to make sense of a world which is deeply marked, albeit differently, by colonialism.

The second understanding places the emphasis on the notion of 'post' in the term postcolonialism. It understands the 'post' to mean 'after', thus acknowledging the pastness of colonialism. The third understanding of post-colonialism interprets the term 'post' as 'since', rather than 'after'. In other words postcolonialism does not suggest an abrupt break between coloniality and postcoloniality. If anything, it acknowledges the continuing impact of colonialism years after the fact.

A few years ago, Achille Mbembe, from Witwatersrand University, spoke of a 'postcolony' and described what he saw as some of its basic characteristics. He defined postcolonies as 'societies recently emerged from the experience of colonization and the violence which the colonial relationship involves . . . The postcolony is characterized by a distinctive style of political improvisation, by a tendency to excess and a lack of proportion' (Mbembe, 2001: 102). Using his native Cameroon as a case study, Mbembe focuses on postcolonial power relations, especially the 'power' of the state in a postcolony. He rejects 'binary categories used in standard interpretations of domination, such as resistance vs. passivity, autonomy vs. subjection, state vs. civil, hegemony vs. counterhegemony, totalization vs detotalization' (Mbembe, 2001: 103).

He attempts to understand how the state, through the mode of 'commandment', deploys an overwhelming array of symbols, performances, ideas and constant reminders as a means of wielding power, both directly and indirectly. These ideas can include notions such as safety and security, moral regeneration, nation-building, and the war against poverty. He notes that the tyranny of the postcolony is intimate – it binds the powerful and the powerless together in one destiny, until they are convinced that the choice they have is one of either staying together, going up together, or going down together.

Drawing upon this explanation, I want to suggest that the Church in a postcolony is one of the first victims and vendors of the (violent) power of the state. Indeed, the Church comes to this task well equipped – with doctrine, ritual, ceremony and words. If I am correct in suggesting that fourteen years later, South Africa is proving to be a typical postcolony, then the Church may slowly but surely be sucked into the postcolony's logic and system of commandment. Could this be where the language and conduct of critical solidarity emanate from? And where do we go from here?

Conclusion: a way forward

In considering how to move forward as the Church in South Africa, the first lesson we must learn is to listen seriously to the critique from ordinary South Africans. They know our heroic struggles and our past achievements in this country, and they are now pleading for moral leadership. What they need are churches that are HIV-competent, that will speak against violence, that will defend the poor and the strangers in our midst, and that will speak truth to 'Pilate', despite the cost.

Second, in order to do these things, the Church needs to get off the 'apartheid is dead' bandwagon because no, apartheid is not dead. We need to see it in its latest guises and mutations. When 60 per cent of our population still lives in poverty, then apartheid is not dead. When our discussions and activities for human rights protection seem oblivious to the fact that some among us are more human than others, then apartheid is not dead. When certain leaders, in order to gain popularity and garner votes, appeal to ethnicity in ways that are reminiscent of grand apartheid years, then we know that apartheid is still alive and kicking. When millions in our country still die needlessly of preventable, curable and manageable diseases, then we know that apartheid is not dead. The Church must wake up to the fact that the evil system underlying apartheid is still very much alive in our midst.

Third, the time has now come for South African churches to bid farewell to critical solidarity with government, which proved to be a monstrous error. Theological miscalculations of this scale are very costly, in this case causing tremendous mayhem and death. The strategy of critical solidarity has made it possible for us to stand by and watch the abuse of power and resources. It has enabled us to let the poor die. Critical solidarity with government means that we have ceased being in solidarity with the poor. Let us confess this sin of critical solidarity, this post-apartheid heresy. Now is the time for us to renew our pledge of solidarity with the poor – the only people worth being in solidarity with.

Fourth, like Zacchaeus of old, the Church needs to climb down the tree of elitism. The Lord is calling the Church back to the ground, to be among the masses, the people. The Church must offer herself anew to South Africa and to South Africans, in ways that are not hegemonic. She need only be faithful, as far as it is humanly possible, in bearing witness to the God of justice.

Fifth, the Church must attend to the crisis of leadership, as well as the crisis of follower-ship. Frightening models and notions of leadership are circulating in our society, and there is a follower-ship that appears to support them. When our leaders choose to buy arms instead of education, and when leaders prefer the emotional language of dying and killing instead of the patience of dialogue and persuasion, then we know that we are in trouble.

We should be fearful when would-be leaders wish to gain positions by any possible means, and when our young people use their knives, machetes and guns as means of communicating with one another and with the world. The people of South Africa are looking around for leadership with integrity. Can the churches offer this leadership?

Finally, following the example of Archbishop Desmond Tutu, the Church needs to offer its own special gift to this country – the gift of eschatological faith. In common language this is the gift of imagination. In the midst of the chaos of crime, the ravages of HIV & AIDS, the despair born out of a seemingly crumbling political establishment, the Church must continue to imagine a different country, a better country. This is what Archbishop Tutu managed to do for us when, in the midst of the violence of the 1980s and the 1990s, he held out a mirror of a different country, of a better people whom he called 'the rainbow people of God'. Such is the level of imagination we as Church and as civil society are called upon to display today.

 STUDY QUESTIONS

1 What was the 'rude awakening' which Tinyiko Maluleke experienced during his radio interview?

2 Maluleke addresses eight explanations, raised in the radio discussion, for why the South African Church has lost its prophetic witness in the post-apartheid era. For each explanation, summarize the key criticism levelled against the Church and how Maluleke responds to it.

3 Discuss the specific proposals that Maluleke makes for the South African Church to revive its prophetic witness. Which proposal strikes you as the most urgent, and why?

16

African Christianity in diaspora

Afe Adogame

 Abstract

Over the last few decades, a huge number of new African religious communities have inserted and asserted themselves in the diaspora, or the spread of Africans around the world, beyond Africa. This is particularly the case with African Initiated Churches and Pentecostal/charismatic churches. It is also particularly true within Europe and North America, which are considered to be new, promising mission fields. The entrance of these churches is significant in contributing to the religious mosaic of these new geo-cultural contexts, and to their growing religious diversity. This chapter explores the tremendous growth, demographic spread and complex diversity of African Christian communities within the religious landscapes of Europe and North America. It focuses on how, and to what extent, local, contextual factors influence their emerging theologies and identities. These theologies are largely shaped by constant negotiation between resilience, transformation and change. Thus, the nature of these 'emergent' theologies needs to be understood against the backdrop of the complex variations in African Christianity vis-à-vis their interaction with the new host culture.

 Introduction

The twentieth and twenty-first centuries mark the gradual but systematic shift of Christianity's centre of gravity from the Northern to the Southern hemisphere. The significant growth of African, Asian and Latin American Christianities can no longer be ignored. They are extremely important for world Christianity in general, and for the challenges it faces. Some decry the decline of Christianity in the West, where secularization is a powerful force. However, this view overlooks a new tendency in which dynamic currents of Christianities from the global South now contribute to the religious transformation and diversification of the West, particularly Europe and North America. While Europe is viewed as the 'dark, prodigal continent', African churches engage in new forms of mission which enable them to gradually insert themselves into the religious landscapes of Europe and North America.

Today, African Christian communities continue to mushroom largely across Europe and North America. We must consider the explanations for their expansion and visibility in order to understand their emerging theologies in the new geo-cultural contexts. A brief historical outline of new African migration into Europe and North America will help us understand the particular circumstances of immigrants. These include the specific social, cultural, economic, political and religious realities of the host context that shape their current life and thought. We will then reflect on how, and to what extent, these new circumstances have enabled them to contemplate, write, sing, eat, dance and do their theologies.

A brief history of the African diasporas

The cultural exchange between Africa, Europe, the Americas and the Arab world has a long history that predates the fifteenth century and the era of the slave trade. Throughout these periods, Europeans were interested in Africa for three main reasons: commerce, politics and religion. Their imperial expansionist agenda generated new situations that brought Africans at various times to other continents such as Europe and the Americas. 'African diaspora' is one theoretical construct to describe this global dispersal of local African populations at different phases of world history. The term 'Black Atlantic' refers to the voluntary and involuntary migration of Africans to Europe, Latin America and North America since the age of discovery. African diaspora goes beyond Europe and the New World to include the Mediterranean and Arab worlds.

The emergence of African diaspora communities can be located in different waves of emigration. The first historic diaspora involved healthy, virile Africans captured in the slave trade and taken involuntarily to various cities in Europe, the Americas, the Mediterranean and Arabia. Physical contact between Africa and the West increased in frequency in the nineteenth century. Western powers sought overseas colonies for settlement areas, sources of raw materials and markets for manufactured goods. This drive preceded the colonial politics of the 1880s and the subsequent division of Africa. A second community of African diaspora is located in the wave of migrants resulting from the 1884–5 Berlin–Congo Conference. This conference partitioned the African continent into artificial geographical zones of European influence, expropriation and exploitation. The period including the two World Wars (1914–1945) also witnessed considerable demographic shifts within and beyond Africa.

A new phase in the history of African diaspora has begun, especially in recent decades, with the unprecedented rise in the number of African migrants into Western Europe, North America and elsewhere. The composition and direction of contemporary international migration show remarkable changes that make this phase different from the historical African diaspora in several respects. Previously, African migration to Europe had followed the historical and linguistic trails of colonialism with the UK and France as preferred destinations for migrants. More recently, African migration became more diffuse in nature with immigrants from several African countries flocking to countries with which they had no colonial ties, mainly in Western Europe, North America, and the Arab world. This trend brought greater diversification in both the number of countries sending and receiving the immigrants. The migrants include both highly and less-educated labourers, resulting in a loss of manpower in original home countries.

This increase in contemporary international migration, the streams of migrants criss-crossing geo-cultural boundaries, and the growing number of refugees and asylum seekers are connected with various local and global factors: from economic to political, social to religious, 'pull' to 'push' factors, voluntary to involuntary. For example, the 1990s witnessed a major increase in involuntary or forced migration. By the middle of the decade, refugees and internally displaced persons in some countries outnumbered voluntary international migrants by a ratio of more than two to one.

In the last few decades, the USA has experienced a massive immigration influx from Latin America, Asia and Africa on account of the liberalized provisions in the Immigration Reform Act of 1965, together with the prevailing economic, social and political constraints within these countries. New African immigrants have joined the flow process through chain migration, family reunion, labour drives and refugees. The establishment of the Diversity Immigrant Visa Lottery (Green Card Lottery) in the Immigration Act of 1996 provided a new twist. This initiative, which aimed to further diversify the American population, has transformed the demography of new African immigrants in the USA.

The dynamics and directions of global mobility, and African participation in international migration, particularly in Western Europe and North America, have become more pronounced, despite the imposition of stricter immigration controls by these countries. The regional policy harmonization through the North American Free Trade Agreement has partially hindered the flow of legal immigration and asylum flows. Yet it has also indirectly transformed illegal immigration.

Many Africans who undergo these complex forms of migration carry with them traits of their religious and cultural identities. As a matter of fact, staying in new geo-cultural contexts often encourages these migrants to identify, organize and reconstruct 'their religion' both for themselves and their host societies. Thus, there has been a rapid proliferation of new African Christian communities in diaspora over the last three decades.

The ongoing high rate of unemployment creates difficulties for immigrants and foreigners, particularly those migrants without proper immigration documents. They are especially vulnerable to the controversial politics

163

of unemployment, when public hostility against immigrants sometimes becomes so intense that people view them as criminals. Many immigrants confront socio-cultural and political realities daily such as enduring institutional racism in Western societies, random police checks and harassment, brutality and surveillance. There are certainly some migrants who experience relative upward social mobility and can boast of good jobs in their chosen professions. However, most migrants find less opportunity and remain perpetually in limbo. Therefore many undergo physical stress, emotional crisis and psychological trauma. These realities partly explain why most African Christian communities become havens for immigrants seeking security and communal support.

✳ Typology of African churches in diaspora

African churches in the new diaspora reveal a complex variety in terms of their historical origins, demographic spread, social composition, polity, ethics and liturgical orientation. The range of churches can be separated into two broad categories: religious communities existing solely as branches or mission posts of mother churches headquartered in Africa, and those which were established independently by Africans living in diaspora. This second category of independent churches is expanding from North America and Europe to Africa and other parts of the world.

In terms of their origins, belief systems and ritual traditions, a working typology can be outlined as follows: mission churches (Methodist, Anglican, Catholic, Coptic, Orthodox); AICs (such as the Aladura, Kimbanguism); charismatic/Pentecostal; groups existing within foreign-led churches (such as the African Christian Church, Hamburg under the *Nordelbian Kirche* in Germany); and an increasing number of African clergy within or outside mainstream churches ministering solely to African groups. Supportive or interdenominational ministries, para-churches, fellowship groups and house cells are also common. Freelance evangelists and short-term missionaries from Africa embark on frequent visits to a network of churches overseas.

One of the earliest African churches that took root in Europe in the early twentieth century was the African Churches Mission (ACM), founded in 1931 by the Nigerian-born Daniels Ekarte in Toxteth, Liverpool, UK. Liverpool's socio-political and economic milieu is important in order to understand the circumstances under which the ACM was born, grew and developed until its closure by local authorities in 1964. The 1960s was a period when many African countries attained political independence from European colonial hegemony. It also marked another significant decade in which African migrants charted new routes into the diaspora. This new stream of migrants included students furthering studies abroad, civil servants, businessmen and diplomats deployed to serve in newly established African embassies/consulates in foreign countries. Many of these migrants became involved in religious activities that either led to establishing new branches of their church, or founding new churches.

The AICs (Aladura) were the most popular of the churches established in Europe in the 1960s and 1970s. They have come to represent a very significant factor in the contemporary life situation of the new African diaspora. This brand of Christianity, which is deeply influenced by African culture, was only planted overseas from the 1960s, first in the UK and afterwards in continental Europe. These AICs have increased demographically since the establishment in London of the first branches of the Church of the Lord (Aladura) (1964), Cherubim and Seraphim (1965), and the Celestial Church of Christ (1967). Another AIC founded in London, the Aladura International Church, emerged through the charisma of its leader, Olu Abiola.

The Coptic Orthodox Church, planted by Egyptian immigrants, is another variant of African Christianity that made inroads into the diaspora. A tenth of the over 10 million Copts migrated from the mid-1950s and 1970s to North America, Europe, Canada, Australia and the Arab world as an escape from religious discrimination and persecution in Egypt during the last half of the twentieth century. They established churches, cultural centres, and monasteries that became places of worship, retreat, social gatherings and pilgrimage sites in the diaspora. Bishops and priests were consecrated by Pope Shenouda III in Cairo and assigned to govern dioceses within and outside Egypt such as in Israel, Sudan, Western Africa, Europe and the USA.

The religious geography of African churches in diaspora is most spectacular in the 1980s and 1990s with the African-led Pentecostal/charismatic movements. It is these African churches that have witnessed the most remarkable public visibility. This includes groups such as the Redeemed Christian Church of God and the Church of Pentecost International, with headquarters in Nigeria and Ghana respectively. There are also several African-led churches which started in Europe, such as the Christian Church Outreach Mission International led by Bishop Dr Abraham Bediako (Hamburg). Another notable example is the Kingsway International Christian Centre in East London, founded by the Nigerian-born Matthew Ashimolowo. It is believed to be the largest single Pentecostal congregation in London with claim to a population of 3,000 in each of three scheduled Sunday worship services. African churches have likewise expanded into Eastern Europe (the former USSR), with the example of the Embassy of the Blessed Kingdom of God for All Nations (formerly known as the Word of Faith Bible Church). Founded by Sunday Odulaja in Kiev, Ukraine, it represents an exceptional African-led church in Europe with a non-African membership majority.

This religious mosaic of the African diaspora is further characterized by African groups, clergy and laity existing within foreign churches. Examples include the African Christian Church, Hamburg under the *Nordelbian Kirche* in Germany, and African groups within the American and European churches such as the Episcopal/Anglican, Methodist, Lutheran and Catholic. There are growing numbers of Nigerian Roman Catholic and Anglican priests in the USA, as well as Tanzanian Lutheran and Ghanaian Methodist priests in Germany. African priests/ministers are employed by host churches with African congregations as their primary constituency.

This exportation of clergy and missionaries on 'reverse-mission' from Africa demonstrates the global stature of African Christianity. The 'reverse flow' initiative, which entails sending African missionaries abroad, increased as an outcome of the moratorium by the Lutheran World Foundation. The aim was to awaken peoples of the global South to their responsibility, to create new goals, and to formulate a viable evangelical strategy towards Europe. In the early 1980s, Tanzanian Lutheran pastors were sponsored to serve in various parishes in Germany. Thus, the reverse-mission agenda is becoming a very popular feature among African churches, with pastors and missionaries commissioned to head already existing branches or to establish new ones in diaspora.

 ## Socio-ethnic configuration

Individual students or people on business and official assignments initiated most of the African churches that were established in diaspora in the 1960s. These Africans generally did not intend to reside abroad permanently. Yet they met to worship together in 'house cells' or 'fellowships' which later transformed into full-fledged branches, with some obtaining official recognition or affiliation with headquarters in Africa. Since then, the arrival of migrant families and the birth of children (first and second generation) have created a major shift to long-term migrants. This shift no doubt has far-reaching implications on the status and growth of some African religious communities. The social make-up of the churches is varied and complex. The majority of members are educated elites of their countries or those who have ventured out in search of the perfect opportunity to prosper.

Most recently, the membership has been characterized by skilled and unskilled factory workers, the unemployed, asylum seekers and refugees. African churches are yet to make remarkable incursions into the white population. Many churches seem to lack a cross-cultural appeal, thus leaving their membership predominantly African. In fact, some of them are simply labelled as ethnic or national churches. A few others have transcended racial-ethnic boundaries to include non-Africans in their membership, often on account of bi-racial couples, friendship, or as a result of personal evangelism. With such a socio-ethnic structure, African churches in diaspora largely remain the locus of identity, community and security primarily for African immigrants.

Emergent theologies in the new African Christian diaspora

Describing the theologies of African Christian communities in the West is difficult due to their complex diversity, their socio-cultural identities and their membership structures. Since most are relatively new in diaspora, their evolving theologies will emerge out of ongoing struggles over resilience, transformation and change. Suffice it to isolate some outstanding ingredients that will most likely shape these emergent theologies.

AICs and the Pentecostal/charismatics describe themselves as genuine Christian churches supplanting the lukewarm religiosity of mission-related Christianity. The Bible is accorded supremacy in matters of doctrine, faith, ritual and conduct. The bedrock of their belief system is the pre-eminence of benevolent powers: God, Jesus Christ, the Holy Spirit, the legion of angels. At the same time, the stark reality of the numerous malevolent spiritual powers is not questioned. They vehemently renounce any relations with occultism and traditional religion. Basically, many African churches in the new diaspora share a similar mentality in their belief system, employing a traditional hermeneutic of spiritual power but casting it within new conceptual frames of reference. In spite of claiming to uphold the primacy of the Bible, members of these newer brands of Christianity in Africa and the diaspora have world views that are evidently suffused with features that demonstrate some affinity with traditional African world views.

One basic feature that reveals such an affinity and continuity with traditional African world views is the belief in spiritual forces – benevolent and malevolent. This belief, together with the associated practice of rituals, is observable in its resilience. However, many African Christians demonstrate a remarkable change in the constitution of this belief, as well as the agency and strategies through which they enact and authenticate rituals. For example, most African Christians abandon any recourse to divinatory methods or any ritual sacrifices. Instead, they wage 'spiritual warfare' on enigmatic forces through elaborate prayer rituals, prophecy, trance, visions and dreams. Therefore their liturgical tradition includes highly expressive action characterized by many rituals to resolve individual and collective existential problems. Members interpret each segment of the ritual worship as being full of religious symbolism and meaning.

Thus, most African Christians retain traditional views concerning the origin or causes of disease, illness and evil. Nothing is given to chance, be it childbirth, naming, marriage, infertility, academic examination, promotion, unemployment, acquiring visas, xenophobia (fear of other people groups), death, dreams, accidents, sickness, poverty, loss of property, homelessness, etc. As far as these Christians are concerned, natural problems can be resolved through natural and spiritual means, but 'spiritual' problems can be diagnosed and solved only through 'spiritual' means. Illnesses that defy medical prognosis are easily interpreted as 'spiritual attack'. Barrenness and premature death are usually not treated as natural occurrences. Those who experience a prolonged state of unemployment often read spiritual meanings into their difficulties. In virtually all circumstances, African Christians hold fervently that an afflicted person must be healed and, at the same time, that the malevolent powers responsible must be overcome.

The resilience of traditional world views and ritual practice is evident in the new African Christian diaspora. Church members seek to ensure continuity and to retain several practices, as they face the same dangers in their new locations. They generally believe that witches, wizards and sorcerers shuttle across geographical boundaries unrestrained. In other regards, many Africans find their sojourn in Europe more complicated than they had anticipated. Their previous hopes of 'survival' upon arrival in Europe are dashed. They then perceive Europe as the 'Dark Continent' in dire need of spiritual regeneration.

Life is particularly difficult for African migrants because of declining European economies, retrenched welfare systems, cultural gaps, xenophobia at individual and institutional levels, acute unemployment, police harassment and brutality, dashed hopes, stress, loneliness, extended family expectations from home, and mounting unpaid bills and mortgages. Under these conditions, many Africans find spiritual, psychological and material succour in the Church. Through elaborate rituals, members find a sense of identity, security and protection. Thus the emerging theologies are experiential in many respects, being orientated in belief and practice to both this world and other spiritual realms.

Furthermore, there is a certain link between a theology of hope and a theology of empowerment in the diaspora. For example, many African Christians hold dear to their hearts the following chorus by Bill Gaither, and adapt it as indicated to include the communal plural:

> Because He Lives, I can face tomorrow
> Because He Lives, All fear is gone
> Because I know oh, oh, He holds my future
> And life is worth the living
> Just because He Lives!
>
> Because He Lives, We can face tomorrow
> Because He Lives, All fear is gone
> Because We know oh, oh, He holds our future
> And life is worth the living
> Just because He Lives!

Thus the church vicinity becomes a space in which the theology of hope and security is embraced and articulated in song.

In some contexts, Black African youths are most vulnerable to racial injustice and its violent attacks. They seem also to be the most volatile sector of African immigrant communities. Therefore, the issue of identity among Black African youth has become a major priority within their hierarchy of needs. Since some of the African and Black Christian communities may not recognize these needs, nor adequately address them, they are consequently confronted with the risk and the reality of losing young people from their worshipping communities. These young people, who experience xenophobia and alienation in many European societies, call for a Church that is responsive to their identity crisis and social, economic, political and spiritual needs. In view of this crisis, Ronald Nathan advocates a Black church with a pan-African orientation, with philosophical assumptions that are Afrocentric, which would in turn affirm the primary African and Caribbean cultures of these young people. He explains:

> Its theology would further liberate the black churches in the United Kingdom, at least from its [sic] obsession of wishing to please and be admitted to the mainstream, which normally is understood as white and Eurocentric. Such a theology will be contextual and will respond fully to the cultural issues of African-Caribbean youth in Britain. It will see art, drama, music, dance, and history as vehicles for reinforcing cultural orientation, and utilize these tools for spiritual, social, educational, political and economic change and transformation . . . This would create a strong identification with black street culture, which is the most visible aspect of black youth in British multiculturalism.
>
> (Nathan, 2000: 351)

This tendency by some African churches in Europe, of 'wishing to please and be admitted to the mainstream', is not unconnected with what I have described elsewhere as the politics of religious networking. This development has partly resulted in the establishment, for instance in Germany, of theological training institutions and Bible schools to train African pastors and church leaders. In the face of contemporary religious, political and socio-cultural realities, African churches in Europe are increasingly engaged in charting local-global religious networks in their efforts to insert and assert themselves in the host religious landscape. Networks among several immigrant churches exert an enduring impact by creating a sense of identity and security in these communities. They also facilitate African immigrants' quest for legitimatization within Western societies.

Nathan's call for a Black church with an Afrocentric focus and pan-African theology was not intended to insulate it from the rest of UK society. He remarks,

> This pan-African and Afrocentric black church would develop long-term strategies with various black (African) communities for the leadership and development of their local communities. They can then act as buffers and mediators between governmental authorities on behalf of their members and their local communities.
>
> (Nathan, 2000: 351)

In actual fact, he links this with the missiological principle of identifying people's groups and then developing strategies for 'inculturation' and cultural saturation. He further observes,

> Missionaries have used such means of reaching other groups in the two-thirds world for decades. What is different is that it is now taking place upon European soil, and by people who are considered to be resistant to the assimilationist policies of European states.　　　　　　　　　　(Nathan, 2000: 351)

One backlash, however, is the extent to which such an African-centred institution would go to facilitate the evangelization of white Europeans for which many mission statements of African churches have been carefully carved out.

Nathan's model, coupled with the traditional African world views described above, is indeed a dominant factor in explaining why most African churches have not made significant inroads into the minds and psyches of their Western neighbours. On the one hand, some white Europeans, even though they are Christians, feel uneasy attending churches that are African-led or where Africans are in the majority, due to the long duration and loud volume of services, language barriers, and other cultural factors. The focus on witches, the devil, sorcery and evil does not seem to attract many Europeans. On the other hand, African churches have been criticized in some circles for diluting their cultural distinctiveness in order to accommodate Western converts. Most African churches in diaspora are therefore split between assimilating notions of the global, while at the same time maintaining aspects of their religious and cultural identities.

The public often perceive African churches as conservative in the sense of upholding a literal, uncritical interpretation of the Bible. In reality this may not be the case. For instance, most African churches on the continent and in diaspora have a similar resolve on the issues of gay priesthood, gay marriages, homosexuality, cross-dressing, smoking and alcohol. As far as they are concerned, these issues are non-negotiable as they claim that the Bible is very clear about them. It is against this backdrop that their posture in the current global debates on gay priesthood can be better understood.

 Conclusion

An important element of 'doing theology' is dialogue that is not confined to the seminary or the academy. African churches in diaspora offer spaces of dialogue which are empowering in themselves, both in intra-religious networking and in weekly church programmes. Through these programmes, they engage in theological reflection with grass-roots men, women and even children in Bible study groups, house-cell fellowships, seminars and workshops. Some have instituted theological training programmes through Bible schools or seminaries. Furthermore, women are becoming more and more empowered through these discussions in the new context as they name their world themselves, tell their own stories, express their anger and hurt, and grapple with their own understanding.

These developments need to be understood against the backdrop of the 'conventional' non-theological, educational background of many leaders of African churches in diaspora today, although a handful of them have studied theology in the very normative sense. Increasingly, they train one another to write and to contribute to such a theology. Thus African churches, through their numerous programmes based on the specific socio-cultural and political contexts in which they operate, are developing, writing and accessing a theology of their own.

 STUDY QUESTIONS

1 The emergence of African diaspora communities can be located within different waves of emigration. How does this trend account for the proliferation of African Christianity in diaspora?

2 Outline a typology of African Christian communities in diaspora.

3 What factors contribute to the origin and demographic spread of African Christianity in diaspora?

4 How would you assess emerging theologies within African Christians in the diaspora?

Copyright acknowledgements

Chapter 9 is adapted and reprinted, with permission, from 'What's in a Name? – Forging a Theoretical Framework for African Women's Theologies', *Journal of Constructive Theology*, vol. 12, no. 2 (December 2006), pp. 5–24.

Chapter 11 is adapted and reprinted, with permission, from 'Interfaith Relations in Africa: What It Is and What It Stands for', *PROCMURA: Occasional Papers*, vol. 1, no. 1 (January 2004), ed. Johnson A. Mbillah and John Chesworth.

Chapter 12 is adapted and reprinted, with permission, from a chapter of the author's Ph.D. dissertation, subsequently published as *Suffering and God: A Theological Reflection on War in the Sudan*. Nairobi: Paulines Publications Africa, 2002.

Chapter 13 is adapted and reprinted, with permission, from 'Human Identity and the Gospel of Reconciliation: Agenda for Mission Studies and Praxis in the 21st Century: An African Reflection', *Mission Studies*, vol. 26, no. 1 (2009), pp. 17–30.

BECAUSE HE LIVES. Words by William J. and Gloria Gaither. Music by William J. Gaither. Copyright © 1971 William J. Gaither, Inc. All rights controlled by Gaither Copyright Management. Used by permission.

References and further reading

AACC, All Africa Conference of Churches. *Drumbeats from Kampala: Report of the First Assembly of the All Africa Conference of Churches.* London: Lutterworth Press, 1963.

Abble, A. *et al. Des prêtres noirs s'interrogent.* Paris: Les Éditions du Cerf, 1956.

Adogame, A. 'African Christian Communities in Diaspora', in *African Christianity: An African Story,* ed. Ogbu Kalu (Pretoria: University of Pretoria, 2005), pp. 494–514.

Adogame, A. and Weisskoeppel, C. (eds). *Religion in the Context of African Migration.* Bayreuth African Studies Series. Bayreuth, 2005.

Anderson, A. H. *African Reformation: African Instituted Churches in the 20th Century.* Asmara: Africa World Press, 2000; Trenton, NJ: Africa World Press, 2001.

Anderson, A. H. *Introduction to Pentecostalism: Global Charismatic Christianity.* Cambridge: Cambridge University Press, 2004.

Anderson, A. H. *Zion and Pentecost.* Pretoria: University of South Africa Press, 2000.

Antonio, E. (ed.). *Inculturation and Postcolonial Discourse in African Theology.* Frankfurt: Peter Lang, 2006.

Armour, R. *Islam, Christianity, and the West: A Troubled History.* Maryknoll, NY: Orbis Books, 2003.

Armstrong, K. *A History of God: The 4,000-Year Quest of Judaism, Christianity and Islam.* New York: Ballantine Books, 1993.

Asamoah-Gyadu, J. K. *African Charismatics: Current Developments within Independent Indigenous Pentecostalism in Ghana.* Leiden: E. J. Brill, 2005.

Ayegboyin, D. and Ishola, S. A. *African Indigenous Churches.* Lagos: Greater Heights Publications, 1997.

Baëta, C. G. *Prophetism in Ghana: A Study of Some Spiritual Churches.* London: SCM Press, 1962.

Baëta, C. G. (ed.). *Christianity and African Culture.* Accra: n.p., 1955.

Barrett, D. B. *World Christian Encyclopedia: A Comparative Study of Churches and Religions in the Modern World: AD 1900–2000*. Oxford: Oxford University Press, 1982.

Bediako, K. *Christianity in Africa: The Renewal of a Non-Western Religion*. Edinburgh: Edinburgh University Press; Maryknoll, NY: Orbis Books, 1995.

Bevans, S. B. *Models of Contextual Theology*. Maryknoll, NY; Orbis Books, 1992.

Boos, E. 'Evangelization through Dialogue and Inculturation', *AFER*, vol. 40, no. 2 (1998), pp. 66–84.

Bosch, D. 'The Problem of Evil in Africa: A Survey of African Views on Witchcraft and of the Christian Church Response', in *Like a Roaring Lion*, ed. P. R. C. de Villiers (Pretoria: CB Powell Bible Centre, UNISA, 1987), pp. 38–62.

Browne, M. (ed.). *The African Synod: Documents, Reflections, Perspectives*. Maryknoll, NY: Orbis Books, 1996.

Bujo, B. *African Christian Morality at the Age of Inculturation*. Nairobi: Paulines Publications Africa, 1998.

Bujo, B. *Christmas: God Becomes Man in Black Africa*. Nairobi: Paulines Publications Africa, 1995.

Bujo, B. *The Ethical Dimensions of Community: The African Model and the Dialogue between North and South*. Nairobi: Paulines Publications Africa, 1998.

Bujo, B. *Foundations of an African Ethic: Beyond the Universal Claims of Western Morality*. Nairobi: Paulines Publications Africa; New York: Crossroads, 2001.

Chapman, C. *Cross and Crescent: Responding to the Challenge of Islam*. Leicester: Inter-Varsity Press, 1995.

Charlton, T. (ed.). *Exploring Our Christian Life – In the Light of the African Synod*. Nairobi: Paulines Publications Africa, 1994.

Chipenda, J. B. and others (eds). *The Church of Africa: Towards a Theology of Reconstruction*. Nairobi: All Africa Conference of Churches, 1991.

Corten, A. and Marshall-Fratani, R. (eds). *Between Babel and Pentecost: Transnational Pentecostalism in Africa and Latin America*. Bloomington and Indianapolis: Indiana University Press, 2001.

Cox, H. *Fire from Heaven: The Rise of Pentecostal Spirituality and the Reshaping of Religion in the Twenty-First Century*. Reading, MA: Addison-Wesley, 1995.

Cragg, K. *Christianity in World Perspective*. London: Lutterworth Press, 1968.

Dau, I. M. *Suffering and God: A Theological Reflection on War in the Sudan*. Nairobi: Paulines Publications Africa, 2002.

175

Dayton, D. W. *Theological Roots of Pentecostalism.* Metuchen, NJ: Scarecrow Press, 1987.

De Gruchy, J. W. *Christianity and Democracy.* Cape Town: David Philips, 1995.

Dedji, V. *Reconstruction and Renewal in African Christian Theology.* Nairobi: Acton Publishers, 2003.

Deng, F. M. *The Dinka of the Sudan.* Dallas: Holt, Rinehart & Winston, 1972.

Dickson, K. and Ellingworth, P. (eds). *Biblical Revelation and African Beliefs.* London: Lutterworth Press, 1969.

Draper, J. A. 'Old Scores and New Notes: Where and What is Contextual Exegesis in the New South Africa?', in *Towards an Agenda for Contextual Theology: Essays in Honour of Albert Nolan,* eds M. T. Speckman and L. T. Kaufmann (Pietermaritzburg: Cluster Publications, 2001), pp. 148–68.

Dube, M. W. 'Divining Ruth for International Relations', in *Other Ways of Reading: African Women and the Bible,* ed. M. W. Dube (Atlanta: Society of Biblical Literature; Geneva: WCC Publications, 2001), pp. 79–98.

Dube, M. W. *Postcolonial Feminist Interpretation of the Bible.* St Louis: Chalice Press, 2000.

Dube, M. W. and Kanyoro, M. (eds). *Grant Me Justice! HIV/AIDS and Gender Readings of the Bible.* Pietermaritzburg: Cluster Publications; Maryknoll, NY: Orbis Books, 2004.

Fortes, M. *Religion, Morality and the Person: Essays on Tallensi Religion.* Cambridge: Cambridge University Press, 1987.

Gambari, I. 'The Role of Religion in National Life: Reflections on Recent Experiences in Nigeria', in *Religion and National Integration in Africa: Islam, Christianity and Politics in the Sudan and Nigeria,* ed. J. O. Hunwick (Evanston, IL: Northwestern University Press, 1992), pp. 85–100.

Gibellini, R. (ed.). *Paths of African Theology.* Maryknoll, NY: Orbis Books, 1994.

Gifford, P. *African Christianity: Its Public Role.* London: Hurst & Co., 1998.

Gifford, P. *Christianity and Politics in Doe's Liberia.* Cambridge: Cambridge University Press, 1993.

Gifford, P. *Ghana's New Christianity: Pentecostalism in a Globalizing African Economy.* Bloomington: Indiana University Press, 2004.

Gilroy, P. *The Black Atlantic: Modernity and Double Consciousness.* Boston, MA: Harvard University Press, 1993.

Government of Kenya, *Report of the Commission of Inquiry into Post-Election Violence.* Nairobi: Government Printer, 2008.

Guillebaud, R. 'The Idea of God in Ruanda-Urundi (Burundi)', in *African Ideas of God*, ed. E. W. Smith (Edinburgh House Press, London, 1950), pp. 180–200.

Gyekye, K. *African Cultural Values: An Introduction*. Accra: Sankofa Publishing Co., 1996.

Hauerwas, S. *Naming the Silences: God, Medicine and the Problem of Suffering*. Grand Rapids, MI: Eerdmans, 1990.

Healey, J. and Sybertz, D. *Towards an African Narrative Theology*. Nairobi: Paulines Publications Africa, 1996.

Heijke, J. 'The African Bishops' Synod of 1994', *Exchange*, vol. 25, no. 2 (May 1996), pp. 136–62.

Hexham, I. (ed.). *The Scriptures of the Amanazeretha of Ekuphakameni*. Calgary: University of Calgary Press, 1994.

Hill, B. R., Knitter, P. and Madges, W. *Faith, Religion and Theology: A Contemporary Introduction*, rev. edn. Mystic, CT: Twenty-Third Publications, 1997.

Hillman, E. *Toward an African Christianity: Inculturation Applied*. New York and Mahwah, NJ: Paulist Press, 1993.

Hiskett, M. *The Course of Islam in Africa*. Edinburgh: Edinburgh University Press, 1994.

Hollenweger, W. J. *Pentecostalism: Origins and Developments Worldwide*. Peabody, MA: Hendrickson, 1997.

Holter, K. *Old Testament Research for Africa: A Critical Analysis and Annotated Bibliography of African Old Testament Dissertations, 1967–2000*. New York: Peter Lang, 2002.

Hulley, L. and Kretzschmar, L. (eds). *Archbishop Tutu: Prophetic Witness in South Africa*. Cape Town: Human & Rousseau, 1996.

Jenkins, P. *The New Christendom: The Coming of Global Christianity*. Oxford: Oxford University Press, 2002.

Kanyoro, M. R. A. *Introducing Feminist Cultural Hermeneutics: An African Perspective*. Cleveland: The Pilgrim Press, 2002.

Kateregga, B. D. and Shenk, D. W. *Islam and Christianity: A Muslim and a Christian in Dialogue*. Nairobi: Uzima Press, 1980.

Katongole, E. (ed.). *African Theology Today*. Scranton, PA: University of Scranton Press, 2002, 2005.

Kobia, S. *The Courage to Hope: A Challenge for Churches in Africa*. Nairobi: Acton Publishers, 2003.

Korem, A. K. and Abissath, M. K. *Traditional Wisdom in African Proverbs*. Accra: Publishing Trends, 2004.

Kubai, A. *Being Church in Post Genocide Rwanda: The Challenges of Forgiveness and Reconciliation*. Uppsala: Life and Peace Institute, 2005.

McGrath, A. E., *Suffering and God*. Grand Rapids, MI: Zondervan, 1995.

Magesa, L. *African Religion: The Moral Traditions of Abundant Life*. Maryknoll, NY: Orbis Books, 1997; Nairobi: Paulines Publications Africa, 1998.

Magesa, L. *Anatomy of Inculturation: Transforming the Church in Africa*. Maryknoll, NY: Orbis Books, 2004.

Makori, H. 'It Cannot be Business as Usual', *Daily Nation* (31 March 2008).

Maluleke, T. S. 'Postcolonial Mission: Oxymoron or New Paradigm?' *Swedish Missiological Themes*, vol. 95, no. 4 (2007), pp. 503–27.

Mamdani, M. *When Victims Become Killers*. Kampala: Fountain Press, 2001.

Manus, C. *Intercultural Hermeneutics*. Nairobi: Acton Publishers, 2005.

Martey, E. *African Theology: Inculturation and Liberation*. Maryknoll, NY: Orbis Books, 1993.

Masenya, M. (ngwana' Mphahlele), 'A *Bosadi* (Womanhood) Reading of Proverbs 31:10–31', in *Other Ways of Reading: African Women and the Bible*, ed. M. W. Dube (Atlanta: Society of Biblical Literature; Geneva: WCC Publications, 2001), pp. 145–57.

Maxwell, D. *African Gifts of the Spirit: Pentecostalism and the Rise of a Zimbabwean Transnational Religious Movement*. Oxford: James Curry; Harare: Weaver Press; Athens, OH: Ohio University Press, 2006.

Mbembe, A. *On the Postcolony: Studies on the History of Society and Culture*. Berkeley and Los Angeles: University of California Press, 2001.

Mbiti, J. S. *African Religions and Philosophy*. London and Nairobi: Heinemann Educational Books, 1969; 2nd edn, Portsmouth, NH: Heinemann, 1990.

Mbiti, J. S. *Concepts of God in Africa*. London: SPCK, 1970.

Mbiti, J. S. *The Prayers of African Religion*. London: SPCK, 1975.

Mosala, I. J. *Biblical Hermeneutics and Black Theology in South Africa*. Grand Rapids, MI: Eerdmans, 1989.

Mugambi, J. N. K. *Christian Theology and Social Reconstruction*. Nairobi: Acton Publishers, 2003.

Mugambi, J. N. K. *The Church and Reconstruction of Africa: Theological Considerations*. Nairobi: All Africa Conference of Churches, 1997.

Mugambi, J. N. K. *Democracy and Development in Africa: The Role of Churches.* Nairobi: All Africa Conference of Churches, 1997.

Mugambi, J. N. K. *From Liberation to Reconstruction.* Nairobi: East African Educational Publishers, 1995.

Mugambi, J. N. K. (ed.). *The Church and the Future in Africa: Problems and Promises.* Nairobi: All Africa Conference of Churches, 1997.

Mugambi, J. N. K. and Magesa, L. (eds). *Jesus in African Christianity: Experimentation and Diversity in African Christology.* Nairobi: Initiatives Ltd, 1989.

Mursell, G. (ed.). *The Story of Christian Spirituality: Two Thousand Years, from East to West.* Oxford: Lion Publishing, 2001.

Nadar, S. 'A South African Indian Womanist Reading of the Character of Ruth', in *Other Ways of Reading: African Women and the Bible,* ed. M. W. Dube (Atlanta: Society of Biblical Literature; Geneva: WCC Publications, 2001), pp. 159–75.

Nathan, R. 'African-Caribbean Youth Identity in the United Kingdom: A Call for a Pan-African Theology', *International Review of Mission,* vol. 89, no. 354 (2000), pp. 349–53.

Nketia, J. H. *Funeral Dirges of the Akan People.* Accra: Achimota Press, 1955.

Nzimande, M. K. 'Reconfiguring Jezebel: A Postcolonial *Imbokodo* Reading of the Story of Naboth's Vineyard (1 Kings 21:1–16)', in *African and European Readers of the Bible in Dialogue: In Quest of a Shared Meaning,* eds H. de Wit and G. O. West (Leiden: E. J. Brill, 2008), pp. 223–58.

Oduro, T. A. *Christ Holy Church International (1947–2002): The Challenges of Christian Proclamation in a Nigerian Context.* Unpublished Ph.D. dissertation, Luther Seminary, St Paul, MN, 2004.

Oduyoye, M. A. *Hearing and Knowing: Theological Reflections on Christianity in Africa.* Maryknoll, NY: Orbis Books, 1986.

Oduyoye, M. A. *Introducing African Women's Theology.* Sheffield: Sheffield Academic Press, 2001.

Oduyoye, M. A. and Kanyoro, M. R. (eds). *The Will to Arise: Women, Tradition and the Church in Africa.* Pietermaritzburg: Cluster Publications, 2006.

Okolo, C. B. *The African Synod: Hope for the Continent's Liberation.* Eldoret, Kenya: AMECEA Gaba Publications, 1994.

Okoye, J. C. 'The Special Assembly for Africa and Evangelisation', *Studia Missionalia,* vol. 44 (1995), pp. 275–85.

Okure, T. 'Christian Identity and the Challenge of Authenticity: A View from Africa', *Christian Identity II Forum Mission Year Book,* vol. 3 (2007), pp. 171–99.

Okure, T. 'Feminist Interpretation in Africa', in *Searching the Scriptures: A Feminist Introduction*, ed. E. S. Fiorenza (New York: Crossroads, 1993), pp. 76–85.

Olupona, J. K. and Gemignani, R. (eds). *African Immigrant Religions in America*. New York: New York University Press, 2007.

Otto, R. *The Idea of the Holy: An Inquiry into the Non-Rational Factor in the Idea of the Divine and Its Relation to the Rational*, 2nd edn. London: Oxford University Press, 1923, 1950.

Palkar, S. 'Feminist Literary Theory: Creating New Maps', in *Women's Writing: Text and Context*, ed. J. Jain (New Delhi: Rawat Publications, 1996).

Parratt, J. (ed.). *A Reader in African Christian Theology*. London: SPCK, 1987, 1997.

Peel, J. D. Y. *Religious Encounter and the Making of the Yoruba*. Bloomington: Indiana University Press, 2000.

Phiri, I. A. 'Contextual Theologies in Southern Africa', in *Introduction to Third World Theologies*, ed. J. Parratt (Cambridge: Cambridge University Press, 2004), pp. 137–62.

Phiri, I. A. and Nadar, S. (eds). *African Women, Religion and Health: Essays in Honour of Mercy Amba Oduyoye*. Maryknoll, NY: Orbis Books, 2006.

Phiri, I. A., Haddad, B. and Masenya, M. (eds). *African Women, HIV/AIDS and Faith Communities*. Pietermaritzburg: Cluster Publications, 2003.

Pobee, J. and Ositelu, G. *African Initiatives in Christianity*. Geneva: WCC Publications, 1998.

Pritchard, E. E. *Nuer Religion*. New York: Oxford University Press, 1956.

Quayson, A. *Postcolonialism: Theory, Practice or Process?* Cambridge: Polity, 2000.

Richardson, A. 'Evil, the Problem of', in *A New Dictionary of Theology*, eds A. Richardson and J. Bowden (London: SCM Press, 1983), pp. 193–6.

Ring, N. C., Glancy, J. A. and Glennon, F. *Introduction to the Study of Religion*. Maryknoll, NY: Orbis Books, 1998.

Ryan, P. '"Arise O God!" The Problem of God and the gods in West Africa', *Journal of Religion in Africa*, vol. 11, no. 3 (1980), pp. 161–71.

Sanneh, L. *The Crown and the Turban: Muslims and West African Pluralism*. Oxford: Westview Press, 1997.

Sanneh, L. *Piety and Power: Muslims and Christians in West Africa*. Maryknoll, NY: Orbis Books, 1996.

Sanneh, L. *Translating the Message: The Missionary Impact on Culture.* Maryknoll, NY: Orbis Books, 1989.

Sarpong, P. *Peoples Differ: An Approach to Inculturation in Evangelisation.* Accra: Sub-Saharan Publishers, 2002.

Schreiter, R. J. *Constructing Local Theologies.* Maryknoll, NY: Orbis Books, 1985.

Schreiter, R. J. (ed.). *Faces of Jesus in Africa.* Maryknoll, NY: Orbis Books, 1991.

Sedmak, C. *Doing Local Theology: A Guide for Artisans of a New Humanity.* Maryknoll, NY: Orbis Books, 1971.

Shank, D. A. *A Prophet for Modern Times: The Thoughts of William Wade Harris, West African Precursor of the Reign of Christ.* Unpublished Ph.D. thesis, University of Aberdeen, 1980.

Shorter, A. *The African Synod: A Personal Response to the Outline Document.* Nairobi: Paulines Publications Africa, 1991.

Shorter, A. *Christianity and the African Imagination. After the Synod, Resources for Inculturation.* Nairobi: Paulines Publications Africa, 1996.

Shorter, A. 'The Curse of Ethnocentrism and the African Church', *Tangaza Occasional Papers,* no. 8 (1999), Nairobi.

Shorter, A. *Toward a Theology of Inculturation.* Maryknoll, NY: Orbis Books, 1988.

Smith, E. W. 'The Whole Subject in Perspective: An Introductory Survey', in *African Ideas of God,* ed. E. W. Smith (London: Edinburgh House Press, 1950), pp. 1–35.

Speckman, M. T. *A Biblical Vision for Africa's Development.* Pietermaritzburg: Cluster Publications, 2007.

Stinton, D. B. *Jesus of Africa: Voices of Contemporary African Christology.* Maryknoll, NY: Orbis Books; Nairobi: Pauline Publications Africa, 2004.

Sugirtharajah, R. S. (ed.). *The Postcolonial Bible.* Sheffield: Sheffield Academic Press, 1998.

Sundkler, B. G. M. *Bantu Prophets in South Africa,* 2nd edn. Oxford: Oxford University Press, 1961.

Synan, V. *The Century of the Holy Spirit: 100 Years of Pentecostal and Charismatic Renewal 1901–2001.* Nashville: Thomas Nelson Publishers, 2001.

Synod of Bishops. *Lineamenta, 'The Church in Africa in Service to Reconciliation, Justice and Peace: You are the Salt of the Earth; You are the Light of the World',* 2006.

Tarimo, A. *Applied Ethics and Africa's Social Reconstruction*. Nairobi: Acton Publishers, 2005.

Ter Haar, G. *Halfway to Paradise: African Christians in Europe*. Cardiff: Cardiff Academic Press, 1998.

Ukpong, J. S. 'Developments in Biblical Interpretation in Africa: Historical and Hermeneutical Directions', in *The Bible in Africa: Transactions, Trajectories and Trends*, eds G. O. West and M. Dube (Leiden: E. J. Brill, 2000), pp. 11–28.

Ukpong, J. S. 'Rereading the Bible with African Eyes', *Journal of Theology for Southern Africa*, vol. 91 (1995), pp. 3–14.

Utuk, E. *Visions of Authenticity: The Assemblies of the All Africa Conference of Churches 1963–1992*. Nairobi: All Africa Conference of Churches, 1997.

Uzukwu, E. E. *A Listening Church: Autonomy and Communion in African Churches*. Maryknoll, NY: Orbis Books, 1996.

Van Gorder, A. C. *No God But God: A Path to Muslim–Christian Dialogue on God's Nature*. Maryknoll, NY: Orbis Books, 2003.

Volf, Miraslov. *Exclusion and Embrace: A Theological Exploration of Identity, Otherness and Reconciliation*. Nashville: Abingdon Press, 1996.

Von Holzen, W. and Fagan, S. (eds). *Africa: The Kairos of a Synod Symposium on Africa*. Rome: SEDOS, 1994.

Walls, A. 'The Translation Principle in Christian History', in *The Missionary Movement in Christian History: Studies in the Transmission of Faith* (New York: Orbis Books; Edinburgh: T. & T. Clark, 1996), pp. 26–42.

Waruta, Douglas. 'Tribalism as a Moral Problem in Contemporary Africa', in *Moral and Ethical Issues in African Christianity*, eds J. N. K. Mugambi and A. Nasimiyu-Wasike (Nairobi: Acton Publishers, 1992), pp. 119–35.

West, G. O. *Biblical Hermeneutics of Liberation: Modes of Reading the Bible in the South African Context*, 2nd edn. Maryknoll, NY: Orbis Books; Pietermaritzburg: Cluster Publications, 1995.

West, G. O. 'Shifting Perspectives on the Comparative Paradigm in (South) African Biblical Scholarship', *Religion and Theology*, vol. 12, no. 1 (2005), pp. 48–72.

West, G. O. and Zengele, B. 'Reading Job "Positively" in the Context of HIV/AIDS in South Africa', *Concilium*, vol. 4 (2004), pp. 112–24.

Zeleza, P. T. 'Contemporary African Migrations in a Global Context', *African Issues*, vol. 30, no. 1 (2002), pp. 9–14.

Index

AACC *see* All Africa Conference of
   Churches
AICs *see* Church: African Instituted
   Churches
All Africa Conference of Churches
   (AACC) xx, 37, 102-4, 140
ancestors 15-16, 18, 71-3, 76-7,
   80-1, 84-5, 119, 120
Anderson, Allan 49, 59, 61
apartheid 92, 95, 103, 140, 150-4,
   159
Ashimolowo, Pastor Matthew 57,
   165

Babalola, Joseph 59
Baëta, Christian 48, 60
baptism 130; in the Holy Spirit 57,
   58, 61
Bediako, Kwame 47
Bible 15-31, 49, 51-4, 57-9, 62,
   67, 70, 94-6, 98-9, 106, 112,
   120, 125, 144-5, 148, 167, 170;
   see also Scriptures
blessings: in African cosmology
   119; blessed water 49, 59; of
   children 51; of ethnic diversity
   134; theology of 53, 62
born again 61, 63-5
Bosch, David 121
Braide, Garrick Sokari 59
Bujo, Bénézet xix, 71

Christianity: African 11, 28, 47,
   48, 53-4, 60, 62, 102, 129,
   131, 133, 161, 165; mainline
   62; missionary 6, 11, 24, 28, 29,
   60, 102, 143, 167; Pentecostal/

neo-Pentecostal/charismatic
   56-9, 62-4, 66-7; world 48,
   161
Christology 73-6
Church: African Instituted Churches
   (AICs) 46-55, 59-60, 98, 161-7;
   Church-as-family 37, 42-3;
   Coptic 41, 164-5; mainline 47,
   62; mission 48, 63, 103, 164;
   Pentecostal/neo-Pentecostal/
   charismatic 47, 56-67, 165, 167;
   'prosperity' 61, 65; Protestant
   46-7, 53; Roman Catholic 10, 36,
   74, 135
Circle of Concerned African
   Women Theologians 91, 93,
   96-7, 99
class 24, 91, 92, 95, 98, 128, 130
Clement of Alexandria 12-13
colonialism 24-8, 31, 91, 103,
   105, 131, 141, 151, 158,
   163-4; neocolonialism 31, 88;
   postcolonialism 22, 23, 26-8,
   30, 31, 92, 95, 152, 155, 157-8
community: African indigenous xix,
   71-3, 76-7, 79-89, 97-9, 111,
   120-1, 123; Christian 3, 8-11,
   17, 38, 49, 70, 126-7, 131-2,
   134, 148; human, male and
   female 90, 97-8
corruption 41, 132
Corten, André 61, 62, 64, 65
cosmos 72, 79-82, 85, 87
creeds 57; Apostles' 57, 58
cross of Christ 65, 126
culture 4-7, 23-6, 29, 43, 54, 73-4,
   91-5, 102, 128, 143-4; African

59, 75, 88, 95–8, 165, 169; 'guilt'
70, 75 'shame' 71, 75
curses: effect of evil powers 64–5,
120; fear of 63; theology of 53

death: in African religion 82, 87,
95, 102, 119–25, 167–8; Christ's
victory over 65, 126–7, 136; in
human experience 4–5, 69
deliverance ministries: in
African spirituality 76–7; in
Pentecostalism 63–6; see also
healing
democracy 40–1, 141–2
Deng, Francis 119
dialogue 6–7, 22–3, 25, 26, 30–1,
40–2, 73–4, 88, 98, 103, 135,
170; see also methodology
dreams 51, 57, 60, 167; see also
visions
Dube, Musa W. 27–8, 30, 98–9

economics: in Africa 141–3; and
Christian engagement 38, 40, 43,
103–4, 169; and globalization
10; and hermeneutics 23–6;
impact of HIV & AIDS 9; impact
of Pentecostalism 66; and
migration 163–4; and theology 8
ecumenism 41–2, 101–6, 140,
153–4
ethics: African 79–89, 121; in
Pentecostalism 64–5; sexual 10;
and spirituality 70, 72
ethnicity 114; and identity 110,
128–38
evangelization: in the African
diaspora 164, 166, 170; in AICs
48, 52; missionary 11, 94, 131,
139; as a theme of the African
Synod 37–8, 40, 43; see also
mission, Christian
evil: in ethnic conflicts 132–3, 135;
in Pentecostal theology 62, 64,
66–7; powers and spirits 49, 59,

72; problem of 118–27, 167; see
also suffering
exegesis 12–20, 21–2, 26, 30
exodus 144–5
experience: African 74, 76, 87, 129,
152; of God 126, 135; of the
Holy Spirit 57–8, 60, 62–4, 130;
human, in constructing theology
3–9; in interpreting Scripture
15–16, 19, 23–5; women's 90–6

feminism 4, 26–30, 90–100; see also
gender; methodology; patriarchy;
womanist; women

gender 4, 8, 26, 29, 91–3, 97–100,
130, 136; see also feminism;
patriarchy; womanist; women
gifts of the Spirit 58, 64
globalization 10, 88, 139, 141, 143,
170

Harris, William Wade 15–16, 59
healing 48–50, 57–60, 63–5, 76–7,
83, 104, 121, 123, 135–7, 168;
see also medicine
hermeneutics 21–31, 92,
144; feminist 26, 94–7, 99;
inculturation 23–4; liberation
24–6; postcolonial 26–8, 99; see
also interpretation; methodology
HIV & AIDS 9, 10, 30, 44, 93, 97,
100, 104, 115, 155, 159–60
Holter, Knut 21–2
Holy Spirit 15, 19, 47, 52, 57, 58,
59, 60, 61, 62, 63, 64, 75, 111,
130, 136, 167
human rights 10, 40, 42, 44, 85–8,
95, 103, 105, 110, 114, 134, 137,
159

Idahosa, Benson 61
identity 64, 73–4, 85, 88, 94, 110,
116, 128–38, 140, 156, 166,
168–9

imperialism 24, 26–7, 91, 99, 140–1, 145–6, 157, 162
incarnation 3, 5, 8, 14, 70, 74–5, 126–7; *see also* methodology
inculturation 6–7, 22–6, 39–40, 73–5, 79, 94–5, 98, 169; *see also* methodology
interfaith 92, 99, 103, 109–17
interpretation 15, 18, 21–31, 75–6, 94–5, 98, 170; *see also* hermeneutics
Islam 28, 41, 99, 109, 113–14, 116; *see also* Muslim

justice 40–1, 44, 85, 92–4, 98, 100, 104–6, 115, 129, 133–5, 137, 153

Kanyoro, Musimbi 30, 94, 95, 97
Kimbangu, Simon 47, 59

leaders 36, 38–41, 43–5, 50, 61, 64, 66, 83, 97, 101, 109, 113–14, 117, 131–5, 140–6, 151–60, 165, 169, 171
liberation 4, 6, 7, 24–6, 28, 44, 74, 95–100, 102–4, 129, 133, 140–7; *see also* methodology; theology: liberation
liturgy 7, 40, 46, 47, 57, 59, 164, 167; *see also* worship

Magesa, Laurenti xix, 71, 76, 120, 121
Maluleke, Tinyiko 100
marriage 50–1, 72, 95, 124, 167, 170
Marshall-Fratani, Ruth 61, 62, 64, 65
Masenya, Madipoane 26, 95
Matthews, Zachariah K. 101
Mbembe, Achille 158
Mbiti, John 102, 120, 123, 124
media 38, 57, 61, 147, 151, 155
medicine 59, 77, 82-3; *see also* healing

methodology 25–6, 30, 143–4; adaptation 74; of African Synod 37–9; comparative 21–2; contextual 3–11; healing 49–50; historico-critical 25; inculturation 6–8, 74; literary 26, 30; narrative 96; sociological 25; *see also* dialogue; feminism; hermeneutics; inculturation; interpretation; liberation; postcolonial; reconstruction
miracles 48, 58, 65
mission, Christian 13–14, 56, 101, 104–6, 115–17, 128–9, 134–5, 162
morality 6, 38, 57, 63, 65, 67, 69–71, 80–2, 84–6, 120–1, 131–3, 155, 158–9
Mosala, Itumeleng 24–5, 30, 151–2
Moses 13, 15, 16, 144–7
Mugambi, Jesse N. K. 76
Muslim 19, 28, 36, 42, 109–10, 113–17; *see also* Islam

Nadar, Sarojini 26, 92
Nathan, Ronald 169–70
Nehemiah 146–7

Oduyoye, Mercy Amba 90–1, 92, 93, 94, 95, 96
Okure, Teresa 26, 29, 97, 130
oppression 4, 6, 25, 41, 65, 98, 133, 141, 145, 152; of women 44, 91, 96, 99
oral theology *see* theology: oral
Organization of African Instituted Churches 53
Otabil, Mensa 61, 66
Oyedepo, David O. 61, 66

palaver xviii, xix, 82–6
Parratt, John xx
patriarchy 26, 30, 53, 91–3, 95, 152; *see also* feminism; gender; women

Paul, St 15, 18, 58, 64, 130, 136, 148
peace 8, 40–1, 44, 77, 85, 88, 103, 110, 112–17, 129, 131, 133, 135–7
Peel, J. D. Y. 28–9
Phiri, Isabel 92–4
pluralism 39, 42, 88, 110
Pobee, John 47–8, 53, 54
politics 8, 9, 23–7, 36, 38, 40–3, 61, 66, 83, 101, 103–5, 115–16, 129, 132–5, 137, 140–2, 146–7, 151–2, 154–6, 158, 160, 162–4, 169
postcolonial *see* colonialism; hermeneutics: postcolonial; methodology
poverty 8, 42, 66, 77, 86–7, 100, 103–4, 121, 133, 151–2, 157–9, 167
power 27–8, 64, 76, 92, 104, 140–2, 152, 155–6, 158–9, 162; in African religion 18, 77, 119; in AICs 59, 167; evil/principalities and powers 59, 64–5, 67, 147, 168; of God 49, 67, 68, 70–1, 75, 77; of the Holy Spirit 59–60, 62, 63; of Jesus 76–7
prayer 48–53, 57, 59, 60, 62, 64–6, 70–3, 76–7, 121–5, 146, 153, 167
prophecy 12, 14, 47, 53, 56, 58, 60, 62, 66, 167
prophet 41, 53, 66, 77, 104–6, 125, 132, 134–5, 137, 147, 150–5; African 15, 47, 59, 62

race/racism 24, 41, 91–2, 95, 98–9, 128, 130, 136, 140, 164
reconciliation 40, 83, 101, 103, 106, 128–38
reconstruction 131, 135, 139–49; *see also* methodology
redemption 8, 60, 71, 75, 125–7
religion 25, 26, 62, 69, 97, 99, 109, 110, 113, 115, 128, 136, 150, 152, 154–6, 162; African 10–11, 16–19, 28, 40–1, 53, 59, 62–4, 67, 71–2, 74, 75, 79, 81, 99, 112, 122–3, 125, 163, 167
revelation 3, 5–8, 11, 17, 49, 60, 73, 75, 110, 148
rite/ritual 51, 59, 67, 72, 79, 81, 82, 95, 102, 158, 164, 167, 168

salvation 49, 58, 65, 71, 75, 129, 133
Sanneh, Lamin 14, 47
Scriptures 4–5, 10, 12–20, 31, 54, 59, 75, 77; *see also* translation
sexuality 10, 95, 130, 170
Shembe, Isaiah 59
Shorter, Aylward 132
signs and wonders 58
sin 44, 49, 58, 62, 64–6, 70, 71, 75, 84, 121, 125, 130, 132, 135, 137, 140, 159
spirit 18, 63, 69, 82, 85, 119; evil 49, 64, 67, 72, 119–20, 167; *see also* Holy Spirit
spiritual 15, 24, 37, 38, 48, 51, 53, 56, 60, 62, 65, 67, 68–78, 85, 96, 102, 106, 112, 119, 122–3, 133, 134, 152, 155, 167–9; churches 59, 60
suffering 49, 65, 72, 75, 77, 85, 88, 104, 105, 118–27, 136, 146, 157
Sundkler, Bengt 66–7
symbol 51–2, 59, 65, 75, 81–4, 122, 128, 158, 167
synod 35–45, 132, 135, 137

theology: AICs 49–54; Black 4, 151, 152; feminist 4, 91, 93–7; *see also* gender; hermeneutics; womanist; women; inculturation 38–9; liberation 4, 7, 98, 100, 103; narrative 96; oral 57, 67; Pentecostal 57, 61, 63–7; reconstruction 139–49
tongues, speaking in 58, 60–1

transformation 7, 10, 22–3, 63–5, 96, 99, 104, 128–9, 131, 148, 161, 167, 169
translation 12–20, 144; *see also* Scriptures
Tutu, Desmond 160

ubuntu (humanness) 95, 112
Ukpong, Justin 22–5

Vatican II 7, 10, 39, 41, 42
visions 51, 57, 58, 60, 167; *see also* dreams

Walls, Andrew 13
Waruta, Douglas 131–2
West, Gerald 26–7, 30

witchcraft 49, 53, 59, 63, 64, 65, 75, 119, 121, 168, 170
womanist 26, 91–2, 94–5; *see also* feminism; gender; women
women 5, 36–7, 42, 48, 51, 90–100, 103, 152, 170; liberation of 44; *see also* feminism; gender; liberation; oppression; patriarchy; womanist
World Council of Churches (WCC) 154
world view 6, 23, 48, 49, 54, 59, 63, 64, 74, 77, 81, 90, 119, 167–8, 170
worship 15, 19, 38, 46, 47, 48, 51–4, 56–8, 60, 63, 67, 70–3, 76, 102, 131, 165–7